When Salil Tripathi began writing a
decided to veer off the beaten track and ....
place. He looked deep into a country and its people through the prism
of history, culture and literature. *Detours: Songs of the Open Road* is in three parts--
in *War & After* he offers a riveting account of places that were shattered due to
terrible wars or had

experienced human rights violations; in *Words & Images* he visualises landscapes
through the writing or art inspired by those places; and in *Loss & Remembrance*
he takes us on a moving personal journey to places he visited with his late
wife, or which he revisited with his sons after her death. A journey through
Bogota, Berlin, Jakarta, Nigeria, South Africa, Valparaiso, Alhambra, Istanbul,
Shilaidaha, San Francisco, and many other places, *Detours* is a remarkable
account of a man's wanderings as he holds your hand and takes you through
fascinating journeys which you make your own.

Salil Tripathi was born in the city then known as Bombay, and studied at New
Era School and Sydenham College. He graduated with MBA at Tuck School at
Dartmouth College in United States. He has been a correspondent
for *India Today* and in the 1990s worked in Singapore for magazines including
Far Eastern Economic Review. He is contributing editor at *Mint* and *Caravan*, and has
won several journalism awards. Salil chairs PEN International's Writers-in-
Prison Committee.

His previous books are *Offence: The Hindu Case* (Seagull, 2009) and *The Colonel Who
Would Not Repent* (Aleph, 2014, and Yale, 2016). He now lives in London.

Detours

Songs of the Open Road

Salil Tripathi

TRANQUEBAR PRESS

An imprint of westland ltd

61, II Floor, Silverline Building, Alapakkam Main Road,
Maduravoyal, Chennai 600095

93, I Floor, Sham Lal Road, Daryaganj, New Delhi 110002

First published in TRANQUEBAR PRESS by westland ltd 2015

Copyright © Salil Tripathi 2015

Due diligence has been followed by the author while seeking
permissions from authors quoted in the book

ISBN: 978-93-85152-92-4

Typeset by PrePSol Enterprises Pvt. Ltd.

Printed at Manipal Technologies Ltd, Manipal

CONTENTS

Preface   vii

WAR & AFTER

GABRIEL AND HIS LABYRINTH   3
THE WEEK OF LIVING DANGEROUSLY   24
ICH BIN EIN BERLINER   34
A PAGODA, A PRINCESS, AND A KING   44
THE BRIDGE OVER TROUBLED WATERS   59
THE KILLING FIELDS OF CAMBODIA   72
WALK LIKE AN EGYPTIAN   95
AH, BUT YOUR LAND IS BEAUTIFUL   105
SINGING IN A CAGE   124
PRAISE THE LORD AND BUY INSURANCE   142
UNTIED AND UNITED   164

WORDS & IMAGES

BAMBAI MERI JAAN!   177
SHIMMERING CANALS, SIMMERING DISCONTENT   188
LIGHTING LITERARY LAMPS IN THE CITY OF LIGHTS   198
THE LAST GOOD COUNTRY   213
TRUE AT LAST LIGHT   223
THE MOOR'S LAST SIGH   235
THE SEA, THE SEA   242
NO PLACE TO HIDE   249
THE DELIGHT OF THE UNKNOWN   260

THE QUIET PATH OF POETS   267
CHASING A DREAM IN A PARK   277

LOSS & REMEMBRANCE

FOUR SEASONS IN VERMONT   291
THE BLUE PERIOD   301
ACROSS THE HILLS AND TOWARDS THE LAKE   309
TWO SEASONS IN STOCKHOLM   317
IF ON A SUMMER'S NIGHT A TRAVELLER….   325
AT THE EDGE OF THE CLIFF   334
THE SCREAM AT THE EDGE OF THE WORLD   345
MY TRAVELS END AT GOLDEN GATE,   353
NOW YOU CAN SLEEP, FOR IT IS LATE

SELECT BIBLIOGRAPHY   369

PREFACE

This book came about because one afternoon in early 2007 at the editorial office of a newspaper not yet launched, the editor of its weekend section decided to risk letting me write a travel column which wasn't really going to be a travel column. Priya Ramani at *Mint* liked the idea of my writing about places I would visit, reflecting on the history and politics of the place, but looking at the place through its literature and culture. I would not mention the food I ate or drinks I enjoyed there unless it was necessary; I would not name hotels, nor would I give any information about prices or other practical information, such as how to get there, was a visa necessary or not, and what sights had to be seen.

Instead, I'd write about what I felt about the place, how its culture may have influenced its people and its politics, what other writers, artists, filmmakers, or poets had said about the place, and how I had responded to the place.

Then one evening in 2008 in Delhi, I discussed the possibility of turning the pieces into a book with Nilanjana Roy, who was at that time setting up the editorial operations of Westland/ Tranquebar. She raised the stakes: reprinting the columns won't do. (She was right; anyone can go to *Mint*'s website and read all the pieces.) Instead, she encouraged me to reflect on those places deeper, and write fresh essays about each place, crafting each essay around a theme or a writer, an artist, or an idea, who gave meaning to the place for me. After Nilanjana left Westland to pursue her own writing, Renuka Chatterjee and Prita Maitra encouraged me to go on, and Sudha Sadhanand steered the project, giving it the final shape. To all of them, my grateful thanks.

As I started working on the essays, I looked back at the great travel writing I had read—Mark Twain, Eric Newby, Paul Theroux, Ian Buruma, Pico Iyer, and William Dalrymple are among the writers through whose words I began to look at the world differently. I had also read many entertaining accounts, of an American or British writer abroad—like S J Perelman or George Mikes—and enjoyed the tragicomedy that followed. But getting off the beaten track and travelling on roads not taken to reach quieter places seemed so much more enticing. I also read many accounts of the outsider looking in at India, the western gaze trying to make sense of the mysterious east. Mine was an attempt to look at the world through Indian eyes—not as if it was an empire-striking-back, for that would be too presumptuous: how can anyone born in India claim to speak on behalf of a billion people? Rather, mine would be an attempt to look at the world through a sensibility that had been shaped by India and later tinged by other cultures.

I hadn't left India until 1975 when I was still thirteen, on a tour organised by my school to Nepal. In 1979 I spent a few weeks in Scotland on a student exchange programme. In 1983 I went to the United States to study and returned home in 1986. I moved abroad in 1991, when I left for Singapore, and then in 1999, for England. Each journey affected in some way how I saw the world.

My work—as a correspondent first, and later, as a researcher/advocate for human rights organisations—has taken me to fifty-five countries (including India). I've learned something new from each visit; I've made lasting friendships in many cities and towns around the world. It is impossible to write down each experience. This book attempts to reveal the world I have seen.

The book is divided into three parts: *War & After, Words & Images,* and *Loss & Remembrance.* The first section, *War & After,* deals with places that have been deeply affected by armed conflict or have had human rights challenges—Bogotá, Jakarta, Berlin, Yangon, Mostar, Phnom Penh, Cape Town and Johannesburg, Singapore, Lagos, and Istanbul. In the next section, Words & Images, I write about places that I have understood better because certain writers or artists have made those places more vivid: Bombay (now Mumbai), Amsterdam, Paris, Madrid, Barcelona, Nairobi and Naivasha, Arusha and Kilimanjaro, Granada, Valparaiso and Isla Negra, Kyoto, Srimongol and Shilaidaha, Shanghai, and New York. The third section, Loss & Remembrance, is the most personal; it is, in a sense, about Karuna Sirkar, my wife who died in 2006. I have written about the places I had travelled with her in the two decades we were together, or where I could feel her presence on later visits; or the places where I went with my sons Udayan and Ameya after her passing, as the three of us tried to pick ourselves up to understand the meaning of our shattering loss: Ludlow and Proctersville, Collioure, Geneva, Stockholm, Venice, Beachy Head, Ålesund and Oslo, and San Francisco.

This book would not have been possible without the warmth many friends have shown to me on five continents. It is impossible to name everyone here, but many of them feature in the pages that follow. I'd also like to thank Priya Ramani and her colleagues who edited the column, Detours, at Lounge, Mint's excellent weekend section—Niloufer Venkataraman, Sumana Mukherjee, Aadisht Khanna, and Shamanth Rao, as well as Mint's editors I have worked with—Raju Narisetti, R Sukumar, and Niranjan Rajadhyaksha. At Westland, I thank Sudha Sadhanand, Prita Maitra for their support and encouragement, and Renuka Chatterjee, who has now moved on. Nilanjana Roy's belief in the book gave me the confidence to get started. At home, Udayan reminded me that I should finish the book and spend less time on Twitter and Facebook, and once I obeyed him and finished the manuscript, he was an enthusiastic reader; Ameya did a fine edit and suggested amazing references that have enriched the text, proving once again, that we learn from our children, and not the other way around. Karuna was a constant presence, even in her absence.

I dedicate this book to the two people who made me, and who were the greatest cheerleaders one could have— my parents, Harsha and Jaysukh Tripathi. Both now gone, but both of whom had heard many of these stories as they happened. As a tourist guide in Bombay, my mother told me about the foreigners she met, reminding me how little divided people across cultures. And my father who would open the Atlas and take out his magnifying glass to find where on earth I had gone. Once he located it, he'd smile and draw a circle around that place. It was my job to make that map messier and more crowded; as I keep doing it, I'm sure he is circling those towns somewhere and smiling.

WAR
&
AFTER

GABRIEL AND HIS LABYRINTH

The girl from the coast stood by my side as we waited for the bus that was to take us to a posh club in downtown Bogotá. It was early morning—not yet seven—but the road was already busy with traffic. Had I been there five years earlier, my hotel's receptionist would have thought of all sorts of ways to restrain me from waiting outside the hotel, even though the bus picking us up was owned by a travel agency the hotel had recommended, and the driver would be known to the people who had invited me. Nothing was safe in Bogotá then. If you were a foreigner, you were worth something.

But it was different now, even though the receptionist had just reminded me that not long ago, bearded rebels had attacked the club to which we were going. The rebels did not like tall and shiny buildings made of glass and steel in this city surrounded by hills; they claimed to represent the authentic people, those who toiled in the fields in the plains. Military guards had been defending the club, because in those days, as now, only fat ranchers wearing gold watches and expensive suits could afford to be club members. And those ranchers were the rebels' enemies. They fed their cattle better than what the peasants who worked on their farms could feed their children.

With the casual familiarity people display in Latin America, the girl turned to me as if she had known me all her life, and placed her palm in mine, and said, in Spanish, as she laughed: 'My hands are so cold!'

Her hands were indeed cold, and while soft, her palm was dry. She was unused to the chill—she was shivering like a palm tree on the Caribbean coast where she grew up—because where she lived, the sun almost never set, the air was always moist, and it was always warm. She was used to welcoming the breeze, which foretold relief from the heat and the arrival of rains. Bogotá was the big city; it was too cold for her. I felt like placing my arm around her shoulders, but I did not. Latin American writers celebrated the easy encounters between sexes; morality from another century had conditioned my teachers and my parents in India to teach many of my generation that you didn't hug a woman you had barely met. Bollywood heroes could sing, wink, dance, and flirt in what seemed like a long how-to manual of sexual harassment; we were supposed to be brought up better—we were to reveal our charms through restraint. So I smiled.

The sunlight was bright, but it offered no warmth, and it seemed as if the rays were gasping to reach the bottom of the valley where the people lived. The vast distance overwhelming the rays, weakening their heat by the time their light reached the ground. But the people made up for it through their warmth, like Magdalena did, the girl from the coast waiting with me for the bus.

She was different from the women I saw in Colombia's capital city. The women in the city wore smarter clothes and appeared more confident; whether they were smarter than Magdalena and should have been so confident was another matter. But Magdalena had a natural laugh.

She came from Barranquilla, which could as well be another country. In some senses, it is. The two regions—the hilly Andes and the Caribbean coast—are separated not only by their geography, but also by their history and culture. Those who live in the mountains, the *cachacos*, or highlanders, consider themselves to be aristocratic—they are lighter skinned and speak better Spanish. And so those who live in the valleys call them arrogant and opinionated. The *costeños* are ethnically mixed, loquacious, and believe in miracles. So the *cachacos* look down on them, in every sense.

Surrounded by hills, Bogotá is a bustling city with avenues that stretch for miles. It is nearly 8,000 feet above the sea level, and the weather is pleasantly cold, with clouds and mist often covering the Andes mountains enveloping the city. Bogotá is formal. The clubs serve dinner at the appointed time. The city's elite businessmen look miserable and take a pained look if you refer to their country as "developing" or "third world".

A few months earlier, I was in Candelaria, the part of Bogotá known for its quaint and quiet streets, which often rise abruptly, making it hard to breathe, and harder to talk and walk at the same time. I was with a friend called Luz Angela, who lived in Candelaria. She told me of the virtues of her neighbourhood: how cold it gets at night, but how calm she feels when she wakes up to the musical twitter of birds, sunlight resting on her floor, playing hide-and-seek, and through her stained glass windows she sees rainbow patterns on her bed, and she stretches her arms and looks out of her window, at those small houses and steep slopes, smiling and remembering her pleasant dreams. She lives in an apartment with high ceiling. Its walls are made of stone, and there is a cheerful courtyard with flowerpots that you can see from her window.

As if Candelaria did not sound musical enough, its geography alone exuded poetry. You would have thought a tormented poet had got lost in these streets, chasing love, and named the meandering lanes to commemorate his misty mood of the moment, spreading his emotions like a magic potion, as if in a Gabriel García Márquez novel. Candelaria's lanes are hilly, and the walls of the houses are painted in muted pastel shades—pink and cream and light brown and faint blue, all perched on cobblestoned streets. Luz Angela tells me the names of those streets: there, that street is Amora, she says; the other one Agonia, and over there, Fatiga. Love, agony, and fatigue—only a poet would think of such names, I say. She laughs when I go lyrical about these names. She is lying in her hammock, coffee beginning to hiss on her stove, and the moment is idyllic, an afternoon that stretches lazily ahead, the eyelids heavy, and outside it is quiet. She says: 'You foreigners have the time to think of poetry. We live with explosions,' and jumps off gracefully, expertly pouring the coffee into mugs, before her percolator, shaking on the stove like a tap dancer, can get any louder.

Later that evening as we walk to the public square, we see troubadours and jugglers, boys selling plastic toys and women selling pineapple. You needed lungs of iron to walk on those steep streets, and it was all right to pause every so often, given the thin Andean air. Some of the pastel-shaded walls were decorated with art, some of it ornate, some outrageous.

Beyond the Plaza de Bolívar is the Congress and the Palace of Justice. In 1985, a guerrilla movement called M-19 had attacked the court and taken hundreds of hostages. The siege ended with a government attack and many died, including eleven judges and almost all the guerrillas. But if that was war, it is peace now. The mayor of Bogotá was a former M-19 guerrilla.

Threats of explosions are never too far in Bogotá: the country has been riven by internal conflict for nearly six decades. Vast swathes of the country's territory are under the control of rebels—some leaning to the Left, some to the far Left, and some to the Right. They outdo each other in brutality. The labels —Left and Right—are meaningless; they have no ideology;

the turf war is often over land, to grow drugs, and over roads, to charge taxes on trucks and cars passing through. Bombs go off unexpectedly, and random shootings are not uncommon. You realise the importance of security because every building you visit requires you to present your passport and you pass through metal detectors. There are clearly understood rules of staying safe in a country still at war: which areas to avoid; how not to get abducted; where it is safe to go out at night; and there are intricate rules about taking taxis. When you call the cab company, the operator gives you a secret code. The driver gets another secret code. You exchange those codes when you meet the driver, and only if they match the driver trusts you, and you trust the driver: then the journey may begin. A senior international development expert tells me that merely because a car is yellow and there is a light on its top does not mean that it is a taxi. A few months later, a friend who works at a large mine told me she was abducted in a taxi. The driver took her to a cash machine, pointed a gun, and told her to empty her account. She returned home safe but traumatised. But it wasn't as bad as "then", or when her mother was young, who had warned her never to go out of the house after six.

The continuous violence from the period Colombians know as La Violencia, began in 1948, when a presidential candidate was assassinated. Thousands have died since. In her novel, _Delirium_ (2004), the Colombian novelist Laura Restrepo writes of a Bogotá 'where everyone's at war with everyone else' during the 1990s, when the whole country had either lost its mind, or loved insanity enough to be unwilling and unable to change. The story is about Agustina, an innocent woman from the elite world, slowly losing her mind due to the dangerous combination of drugs, sex, greed, and class resentment. She wants to feel light but the world around her is heavy, and the clash between the two collapses her will and she succumbs to delirium and madness. The "lightness" and "heaviness" are in the context Milan Kundera used in his 1984 novel,

The Unbearable Lightness of Being, which opens with the Greek philosopher Parmenides, who sees lightness of being to mean accepting a certain lack of ultimate meaning in life, and living for the beauty of the moment, not tied down to the past, to an ideology, or even to a person. For Kundera, heaviness comes from Nietzsche and the idea of eternal return—those who are "heavy" cannot accept the unbearable lightness of being, and seek to give a meaning, a sense of constancy, and weight, to what they believe matters in life. Outwardly, "light" people are happier; "heavy" people aren't; but there is sadness in the happiness that the "light" people seek, and the "heavy" people find happiness because they think their life is more meaningful.

Restrepo's ultimate point is that you have to be insane to survive in Colombia. Here, the ordinary appears bizarre, and the bizarre feels commonplace.

One late evening in May 2006 as my friend Bill and I were walking back to our hotel from the fashionable Andina shopping district, I saw a woman dressed only in a bikini, flanked by two women wearing even less. They came to us saying: 'Vote for the Rabbit,' mocking the Presidential elections scheduled the next morning. Behind them, a giant rabbit stood, with its buck-toothed grin, swinging merrily. Realising we were foreigners with no vote in their elections, they smiled and blew kisses at us, moving on to find compatriots to convince them that their carrot-munching friend was the best mascot for a bleeding nation.

The next day, Alvaro Uribe Velez was duly re-elected, winning some 62% of the vote, defeating his Left-wing rival on the strength of his commitment to preserve law and order. During Uribe's first term, drug production might have continued in Colombian farms, illegal drug exports stayed at 550 tons a year, talks with a small Left-wing group, Ejército de Liberación Nacional (ELN), might be getting nowhere, and the conflict with the larger Left-wing group, Fuerzas Armadas Revolucionarias de Colombia (FARC), might have shown no sign of abating, but Uribe had tamed violence in urban Colombia. Murders were down, abductions had fallen, people felt safe to make daytime road trips between Colombia's three cities–Bogotá, Cali, and Medellin—and they were no longer scared of gun-toting highwaymen.

I reached the Andean highlands late one night, the plane wobbling vigorously as it found its way amid the peaks on the strip near Rio Negro. An SUV was waiting for me; soon, I was on the road.

Nobody had warned me that the airport was in the middle of nowhere, and that the journey to the city would be a long one. I could see why Colombians voted for Uribe—the road was now safe to travel. But the driver seemed to be in a hurry to take me to the hotel, as furious rain lashed the windscreen; raindrops falling hard on the roof of the SUV, as though we were being pelted by little stones.

The driver tried talking to me, asking me if I had a favourite radio station, but with my non-existent Spanish, we settled for silence. It was a dark night with blustery wind. He played opera on his radio and began humming along with the soprano, their voices merging at the perfect pitch, giving a quaintly stereophonic feel to the dark night. Miles of a lonely road lay ahead of us, and it seemed a pity there was nothing for me to see outside. I could sense rows upon rows of trees, and the sharp bends we took, the depth we descended to, and the heights we ascended again made me realise that we were on a mountainous road, without lights, the only signpost being the occasional illuminated road signs.

At some point, the SUV took a sharp turn, and there, to my left, I could see outlines of the hills and the road ahead, lit up in the glow of the lights of the city lying beneath. The spiral was stomach-churning, at the end of which, in the valley, lay thousands of lights, like scattered, twinkling candles—the city of Medellín.

It is the town that wants to forget its notorious son, Pablo Escobar. A small-time thug who wanted to crash into a political party, he earned his reputation as being one of the most feared names in the world leaving behind a trail of blood. In *News of a Kidnapping*, García Márquez's quietly understated narrative of the Medellín of more than a quarter century ago, he describes the anxiety of Luis Guillermo Perez Montoya, a Kodak executive, whose mother was abducted by Escobar after negotiations to stop the extradition of the "Extraditables"—Colombian drug lords the Americans wanted to prosecute—had broken down between Escobar's gang and the Colombian government. Perez Montoya's uncle was involved with the negotiations: since Escobar couldn't get him, they took his sister, Perez Montoya's mother.

Perez Montoya flew to Medellín looking for his mother, and as he told the driver to take him to the city, without any idea where exactly he wanted to go, 'reality came out to meet him when he saw the body of a girl about 15 years old lying by the side of the road,' García Márquez wrote. She wore an expensive dress and had applied lots of make-up, as if she was going to a party. Stunned, Perez Montoya told the driver about the dead body. Rather nonchalantly, the driver said she was one of the dolls who partied with don Pablo's friends.

That was Medellín till 1993, when the law finally circled around Escobar, the noose tightening. At the Museo de Antioquia in downtown Medellín, there is an entire wing devoted to the art of Fernando Botero, Colombia's most famous figurative artist and sculptor who was born here, but who now makes his home in Italy. Botero has chronicled the Colombian century through art—and odd humour, just as García Márquez has done it with words—and vivid imagination.

Two of Botero's paintings dealing with Medellín's bloody past are at the museum. One shows a neighbourhood destroyed by a car bomb, with homes toppled and bodies mangled. The other, more dramatic painting has the familiar image of Escobar, where you see him larger than life, on the rooftops of the *barrios* of Medellín, with a gun in his hand pointing skywards, as rows of bullets head towards him, some missing him, some penetrating his body, his eyes closed. It doesn't look as though he has fired a shot. Blood doesn't gush forth from his body, it trickles from a couple of wounds; and there are several bullet marks on his torso. The buttons of his white jacket are undone. He is barefoot. The image is frozen; he looks as though he is about to fall, as he did, ending the siege in December 1993.

Medellín has moved on from that past. The next morning I went with friends by cable car to the top of the hills that surround the city, looking at the teeming city beneath, now looking utterly normal. Later that evening, I walked in the central square near the museum with a friend, as she took pictures of Botero's giant sculptures gracing the square. Colombians sold food, toys, ice cream, and newspapers; the breeze was mild. But our hosts insisted that a guard would accompany us to the car, parked thirty yards away—just in case.

Despite the excessive caution my hosts showed in Medellín, the streets in Colombia's main cities are safe now. The only people to accost me at night—other than bikini-clad campaigners—are young entrepreneurial Colombians, selling cell phone time by minutes—you pay them per minute to use their phone to make phone calls. There is considerable prosperity in Bogotá, and I wonder why people would want to use other people's phones like this. I don't notice payphones —maybe that's the reason. But then a friend who analyses the economics of conflict tells me the sinister connotation, and I no longer feel sanguine about this street enterprise. Those phones guarantee randomness and anonymity, the preferred mode of communication for drug dealers and other petty criminals, who want to leave no trace of their movements to the country's stretched anti-narcotics squad, whose officers are trying to stay at least one step behind the drug dealers, and not fall behind too far.

Bogotá's relative tranquillity was because of Uribe's ruthless campaign against crime, which included recruiting and training more police and officials, arming them adequately, and taking the battle into the rebel terrain. But as anyone familiar with tactics to bludgeon extremists by using force alone knows, such actions have consequences: evidence continued to emerge of lawmakers loyal to Uribe being implicated with paramilitary forces against whom there were serious allegations of human rights abuses. And paramilitary forces —the Autodefensas Unidas de Colombia themselves, known by their Colombian acronym, AUC—began to surrender their weapons under a controversial policy, which granted them limited immunity in exchange of their willingness to disarm, demobilise, and reintegrate. Before the policy was announced, most estimates placed AUC's strength at 15,000–20,000. By 2010, some 42,000 had disarmed. Whether they were real or phantom soldiers, who knows?

The potential removal of one lawless force was a good thing, for it would mean Luz Angela in Candelaria would wake up to the music of birds, and not bomb blasts. But it had an effect on the balance of power between the Left and Right rebel forces in Colombia. It meant the Government would have to fight its own battle against the Left-wing rebels, and could not depend on the Right-wing paramilitaries to do its job.

The militias came into being after cattle ranchers (of the type who went to that posh club the rebels tried to bomb) were exasperated by the State's failure to protect them, their families, and their land, from the raids of FARC and ELN. They funded the AUC, which claimed to be vigilante supporters of the State, but as with all stateless organs—think of Salwa Judum in India—became a law unto themselves, menacing everyone. The man who tells me the story is a dashing Colombian, at that time the head of the country's intelligence service. To illustrate his point, he drew a map on the back of the restaurant's menu, sipping guanabana juice. Rebels had killed part of his family. His cute little daughter went to primary school accompanied by armed guards.

How do I make sense of all this? I turn to the Master, Gabo, as García Márquez was known across Colombia. Many Colombians were embarrassed that he lived in Mexico City, but when he did come to Bogotá, or to Cartagena de Indias, the response was electric. A friend who is a former oil industry executive remembers having dinner at a fashionable restaurant one evening in Bogotá, when suddenly all the patrons rose and began to applaud. My friend thought it must be a diner's birthday. No, his host told him in a hushed tone: *He* is here. "He" was García Márquez, who had entered the restaurant, and as soon as other diners found out, they rose and clapped their nation's chronicler. The elite may have been busy clinking champagne glasses, discussing stock prices, and carving steak, but they paused and recognised their finest literary talent and rose to applaud.

It takes someone like García Márquez to make sense of the Colombian reality, which is so convoluted and complicated, where angels act devilishly, and devils look like angels. In his Colombia, deep-rooted fears and anxiety merge with humdrum reality, and extraordinary discoveries that appear like a fantasy intrude in a grim moral landscape, enlivening it. Imagine, voting for a rabbit because half-naked women on the streets ask you to do so on an evening with wintry chill, in a country in the midst of a civil war. I want to go to Gabo's territory—at the tip of Colombia, with the beautiful city of Cartagena and other towns like Aracataca and Riohacha, which have all blended to become the mythical Macondo.

ॐ

Magdalena, who I met at the bus stop, came from Barranquilla. Banana plantations surrounded the town. There are oilfields to the south, and to the east lies the arid landscape bordering Venezuela, where goats keep company with cacti. The flight from Bogotá to Barranquilla takes barely an hour, but it is a journey across contemporary Colombian history and political divide. García Márquez wrote his early journalism in these parts, and that experience permitted him to maintain his contact with reality.

Barranquilla is Colombia's golden gate, among the country's earliest ports and it has one of the oldest airports on the continent. Avianca, the Colombian air carrier, was founded here. It is described as the world's second oldest airline still in operation. The road from its airport towards this city of a million people runs along a swamp that connects the beach with the delta of the Magdalena River, which García Márquez has described as a river with an oceanic temperament. The town has a colonial core, an Americanised sprawl, and the appearance of unplanned industrial estates.

Barranquilla is a chaotic maze where cars jostle for space with animals pulling carts laden with fresh crop—it may not be wise to find out what crop they're carrying. Freshly-painted kiosks advertise miracle cures promising eternal life, sexual prowess, and protection from evil. Step aside from those busy streets, and you will find avenues lined with trees that shade the homes from harsh glare.

For literary insomniacs like me, the town matters because it was here, in its bars, that young García Márquez hung out with other young reporters, and traded stories and exchanged ideas. Those conversations nurtured him, as he gained fame as a columnist, writing a column called "The Giraffe," because it was thin, long and narrow, like a giraffe's neck.

They formed the Barranquilla Group, which included García Márquez, Álvaro Cepeda Samudio, Germán Vargas, and Alfonso Fuenmayor. Many years later, they would appear as the "four friends" of Macondo in *Cien Años de Soledad* (*One Hundred Years of Solitude*, 1967). Writing about this group in his 2002 memoir, *Living to Tell the Tale*, García Márquez said: 'Never did I feel, as I did in those days, so much a part of that city,' and with his friends they came to be known as the Barranquilla Group in the journalistic and intellectual circles of the country.

Their old bohemian hangout, La Cueva, exists, but it has been, as it is to be expected, gentrified, and restored. You won't find much of what inspired García Márquez there. I discovered it almost accidentally, as we drove towards our hotel. The streets had become quieter, the houses looked lived-in, with rocking chairs in the verandah and creeping vines with purple flowers spread out on the walls. A grandmother sat by a blue-washed wall on a large bed, the smell of last night's rain wafting through the air, and the grandfather slowly drank an increasingly warm beer.

The grandmother's face was rigid, except for the hint of a sly smile flickering on her lips. García Márquez had cultivated his tone by observing his grandmother, listening to her carefully, letting her tone become his, as he wrote *One Hundred Years of Solitude*. In his memoir he wrote how she told things that sounded supernatural and fantastic, but with complete naturalness.

> What was most important was the expression she had on her face. She did not change her expression at all when telling her stories and everyone was surprised. In previous attempts to write, I tried to tell the story without believing in it. I discovered that what I had to do was believe in them myself and write them with the same expression with which my grandmother told them: with a brick face.

Later that evening, in the restaurant, we sat under fans with four blades circling above us, valiantly trying to cool the temperature, while sweaty waiters, like descendants of the older waiter in Hemingway's short story, *A Clean, Well-Lighted Place*, hovered around. They were all old men, wearing airy, white bush-shirts, cheerfully replenishing our chilled bottles, respectful of our desire to kill time.

The hotel was large and built in the colonial era; it had alcoves and huge arches and a garden with palm trees and tourists lying by the pool, their near-nakedness blending with the elemental landscape. The grand staircase took you to your room which had a very noisy air-conditioner and television offering thirty-five channels in Spanish.

That night I dreamt of that house and those creeping vines completely surrounding the house, colouring it purple. I hadn't intended to have such a dream, but as García Márquez has said in interviews over the years, the trick of magic realism lies in making the outrageous appear ordinary, and the ordinary quite bizarre.

To dream, or to imagine, you need an uncluttered mind. A pencil and paper help, to jot it down as soon as you are awake. García Márquez and his friends didn't need any exceptional architectural beauty to inspire them. The fragrance of the guava would rekindle a memory, sometimes pleasant, like a grandmother telling a love story; sometimes bitter, like the 1928 massacre of workers of the United Fruit Company (which later became Chiquita).

In his memoir, García Márquez describes this terrain as 'a good place to live where everybody knew everybody else, located on the banks of a river of transparent water that raced over a bed of polished stones as huge and white as prehistoric eggs.' He remembered seeing the Sierra Nevada de Santa Marta and its white peaks and the banana plantations during wintertime, and recalled the line of Arawak Indians, 'moving like ants' carrying sacks of ginger on their backs and chewing pellets of coca to make life bearable. He dreamt of 'shaping balls of the perpetual snow and playing war on the parched, burning streets. For the heat was so implausible, in particular at siesta time, that the adults complained as if it were a daily surprise.' He remembered being told how the rail lines and camps of the United Fruit Company had been built at night because during the day 'the sun made the tools too hot to pick up.'

The town of Ciénaga, the site of the 1928 banana massacre, is close to Barranquilla. Cables exchanged between the US Government and its embassy in 1928 show close cooperation between the conservative Colombian Government of that time and the US authorities, to protect American corporate interests. The United Fruit Company wanted bananas to be picked by obedient workers. The power the United Fruit Company had in many Latin American countries gave rise to the phrase "banana republic" to describe those countries. Many years later, the phrase would become a yuppie brand in a post-modern twist without irony. The company wanted to keep the wages low, and it wanted the supply uninterrupted. The American administration at that time backed the interests of the American corporation. The Colombian government of the day wanted the investment and was willing to support the company. The workers were angry over their exploitation and wanted better wages. In 1928, in the town of Santa Marta, thousands of workers at the United Fruit Company's plantation had gone on strike, seeking better conditions and pay. On 6 December that year, the army moved in and opened fire on the group of strikers gathered in the town of Ciénaga. The strikers were assumed to be Communists.

Seven decades later, the situation had changed somewhat: the company still operated under a new name and new ethos, but it could no longer depend on the State to provide security. Notions of sovereignty—and the history of American interventions in the region—would prevent the firm from seeking help from Washington outright. And so the company turned to the rebels, but with disastrous consequences.

In a case of reality imitating fiction, in 2008 the American company Chiquita Brands admitted that it had paid 1.7 million dollars first to Left-wing rebels and later the Right-wing rebels, ostensibly for protection, and the groups had, in turn, unleashed their reign of terror upon each other and upon villagers they suspected of not being deferential enough. To avoid prosecution in the United States, Chiquita agreed to pay 25 million dollars in fines to the US Justice Department. Now, the victims of some of the massacres are planning to sue the company for being involved in the killings of 144 civilians by forces to whom the company had paid, and the Colombian Government wants the US to extradite some Chiquita officials. This is the kind of denouement García Márquez would find redemptive.

There are no reliable estimates of how many people died in Santa Marta. The military claimed it was less than fifty; union activists claimed hundreds were killed, and blamed the company for sending the troops. Conservatives lost the elections that followed, ending over four decades of Rightist rule in Colombia.

In *One Hundred Years of Solitude*, García Márquez writes about the hail of bullets, which mowed down people as the survivors ran in panic even as machine guns continued to fire. Pressed together, the people swirled in a whirlwind whose 'edges were systematically being cut off all around like an onion being peeled by the insatiable and methodical shears of the machine guns.' A woman with her arms spread knelt in an open space, but soon 'the colossal troop wiped out the empty space, the kneeling woman, the light of the high, drought-stricken sky...'

García Márquez had grown up listening to stories of this massacre from his elders, and it was inevitable that those killings would form a crucial element of *One Hundred Years of Solitude*. García Márquez later said that the death toll in the novel, of nearly three thousand, is exaggerated.

But that doesn't matter. In Salman Rushdie's *Midnight's Children*, another magic realist novel, the sequencing of India's Independence and Gandhi's fast around the Calcutta riots has been rearranged, and Rushdie has himself said that his narrator is suspect. Richard Attenborough did that in the film *Gandhi*: riots in Calcutta occur after Independence, not before. But *Gandhi* is meant to be historical; *Midnight's Children* was never meant to be history. Fiction writers have it easy while writing about history, Romesh Gunesekera once told me; they can make up things. Journalists can't, and shouldn't.

García Márquez knows the difference, because he began as a journalist, and like Ernest Hemingway, took great pains over getting his facts right. But while Hemingway honed and sharpened his writing skill to make his language leaner and more spare, García Márquez, who grew up in fecund, tropical territory, wanted none of the sparseness, and embellished his fiction with vivid imagination, luxuriant colours, and bursts of dreamlike metaphors and incredible coincidences.

For most of García Márquez's writing life, violence had torn Colombia apart, making guns and cocaine the leitmotif of Colombia—not its flowers, its coffee, its people, or its stories. García Márquez's prose tried to stitch his land, and weave it back together. That instability gives the country its edge, its sharpness, and reminds us of its fragility. Indeed, living on the precipice of violence has injected an air of existential angst in Bogotá, where you live for the moment, by the moment, and, most important, live up the moment.

To test that out, one evening, we took the long drive from Bogotá to its outskirts, to the restaurant that seems like a pit stop in a fantasy movie. Called Andres Carne de Res, the restaurant is an insanely decorated spectacle, where you will end up dancing at some point in the evening. It is Colombia in a microcosm, how it would like to live—without a care, dancing through the night, eating well, with nothing remembered the next morning. *The New York Times* has called it 'profound, spellbinding, beautiful, tumultuous, confusing and fattening all at once.'

Fattening, I understand easily. I'm sitting with my friend Catalina, who tells me to go easy on the delicious arepas and almojábanas spread out before us, saying the main course is yet to follow. She then insists I should not even try ajiaco, the potato-based soup. 'You've had ajiaco twice in the past week,' she says—she has been keeping the score. 'Try something new and different tonight,' she says. I'm touched; it seems she cares for my health. 'Lets all try the Argentine beef tonight,' she adds. Quite.

Later that night, at my friend Bill's suggestion, I try Guatemalan rum. (Very nice). The restaurant is noisy and cheerful. Nubile waitresses, masked and wearing impossibly tight T-shirts and figure-hugging jeans perform synchronised, impromptu dance on the crowded floor, with large posters of Hollywood starlets and 1950s Americana—badges, banners, license plates, trinkets—hanging all over the restaurant.

I also see a cross in this temple of hedonism. It is not as incongruent as it might seem. This is the country where churchgoing senators have changed votes after receiving gifts from the ruling party, passing crucial constitutional amendments; where you get a better deal on your dollar from a bank, and not on the street, because the country is awash with touts dealing in dollars, which are floating around because of illicit transactions of drugs and weapons, avoiding formal banking channels; and where a nice Catholic woman tells me matter-of-factly about her younger brother living with his girlfriend and their kids and how they are delighted, the notion of living in sin not even crossing her mind. Politics, like the Church, claims to be absolute; sin is a relative term. Nothing makes sense at first sight, and then everything does—the tranquill, pastel-hued homes of Candelaria and the huts with smoldering memories in the areas around the banana plantations; the church that surveys from the top of the mountain the city where nubile teenagers don't prize their virginity; the *cachacos* working hard to protect their skin from the sun so that they remain white, and the *costeños* who sweat in the fields; and where the commonplace seems miraculous, and a miracle quite quotidian.

ॐ

The following week it rained continuously. The sun was barely visible, except at the golden hour of twilight, and clouds covered the Andean peaks surrounding the city. The rain knew its place, as it fell lightly, a thin lace cascading on the city, like silken strands.

Then on Saturday, the sun came out as my friend Jose Rafael had promised it would, and it shone brightly as we made our way on winding roads, headed for a reservoir outside the city, to Guatavita. The ride to La Macarena, the home of our friend Ernesto, was long. As we got off when we reached his house on a hill, we saw flowers growing randomly in the verdant valley.

A vast reservoir filled the valley between us, and the hills across. Three boats sailed smoothly, leaving a meandering trail, the water looking like a sheet of grey steel. A few huts were scattered on the hill. There were grey clouds on the horizon to our right, but the sun was still bright.

By midday, the wind gathered strength, and the lamps in the veranda began to sway, the light through their lattice-like frames shifting from one spot to another, like in a dream sequence of an old Hindi film. Two of my friends stepped out to explore the anchor placed at the edge of the house. I sat by the wall, staring at the pristine lake, its surface trembling softly, disturbing the light and dark patches.

Then, out of nowhere, I saw that bolt of lightning. Sharp and bright, it dived like an arrow, leaving its jagged signature behind which disappeared quickly, an imprint impossible to forget. The cloudburst that followed, and the thunder that accompanied it, resounded in the valley. It was loud, as if the sky was falling apart, and its echo could be heard for miles. The sky had darkened; my friends had moved back into the house, safe behind those large glass windows, as we saw that celestial drama, of light and darkness, rain and wind, clouds and lightning, thumping and roaring, rising and dipping as if choreographed, like a Wagnerian crescendo.

A stream of yellow light filled parts of the sky, which had vainly tried to prevent the cloud from covering the entire sky with its dark shroud. When the clouds managed to hide parts of the mountain, they looked as though they were emerging from its peak, like billowing smoke. 'It looks like a volcano,' said Ted, our friend, the anthropologist.

The sailboats had disappeared: we sat at the large wooden table, ready to eat the Colombian puchero that Ernesto had been cooking slowly, with chunks of beef, pork, chicken and sausages boiled in a stew, and served when tender, with rice, cassava, cabbage, sweet potato and corn; the stock poured over the dish, or left next to the dish in a cup, and drunk slowly. It was delicious and nourishing, filling us with warmth, even as the sky outside had turned dark, and the rainstorm had lowered the temperature by a few degrees. We were 2,000 m above sea level, which made the afternoon pleasantly chilled.

As we saw the view from the large window, it seemed as if the mountain had disappeared behind the mist and rain, but if you looked closely, you could make out its bare, grainy outline. The tall glass window had kept the sound of the rain silent, but we could see the bursts of lightning, which continued to reverberate, the thunder obediently following the bolt seen moments earlier.

But this rain was not cruel, the kind Isabel saw in Macondo, which stole everything, washing away pasts, obliterating stories, leaving only a sad and desolate sunset, which would leave 'on your lips the same taste with which you awaken after having dreamed about a stranger,' as García Márquez described the torrential rain in *Monologue of Isabel Watching it Rain in Macondo*.

Here, we weren't among strangers. We had witnessed a different kind of dance all right. The clouds had tried to devour the mountain, but sunlight had squeezed through, pushing aside the clouds from every gap it could find, as if playing out an epic war between good and evil. We knew the sun would win, just as we knew the clouds would part, and the verdant valley would be bright again, and the colour of the sky would match the mood of the Chardonnay in my glass.

The stream of light that emerged from the clouds looked like pure gold. That yellow light bathed us, and we looked as though we were covered in gold dust. In the Spanish chronicle *El Carnero*, Juan Rodriguez Freyle wrote of the priest of Muisca covering himself with gold dust at the Lake Guatavita. My friend Luis Fernando told me that the lake at the summit of the mountain where Ernesto's house is located was the same Lake Guatavita, and the legend of El Dorado, which sparked the greed for gold that brought the conquistadores here, had begun there. That lagoon was the sacrificial site where people offered gold to the gods to appease them.

The elegant simplicity of that meal and the warmth of friends had given us a different kind of protection from those mythical powers. The lake below now looked serene, like the woman who didn't need gold to look beautiful. The divine landscape and the company of friends made us richer than all the gold offered to that other lake on the hill.

THE WEEK OF LIVING DANGEROUSLY

On a sultry evening in Jakarta, the only relief we had from the heat was from the small window of the crowded bus, through which breeze managed to get past the dozens of passengers. I had spent the day walking the streets of this vast city, which had suddenly abandoned its orderliness and acquired an unexpectedly menacing tone. People were rushing home with a sense of anxiety. The smiles on the faces of hotel receptionists were nervous. At night, someone slipped a note under my door, which said: in view of the situation in the city, you are encouraged not to look out of windows and leave the hotel only if necessary. The note was printed in bold, capital letters, in Bahasa Indonesia and English.

My job was not only to look outside the window, but also to walk those streets, especially if it was dangerous. And the sight below wasn't pretty. My hotel was on Jalan Thamrin, one of the arterial roads connecting Jakarta's business district with its political centre. Where the avenue ended, there was a majestic statue of a horse-led chariot going to battle.

The warrior under the canopy was the puzzled, anguished Arjuna, unsure if he should fight the battle of _Mahabharata_ against his cousins, the Kauravas; the charioteer was Krishna, guiding him, advising him that his dharma was to fight the good battle. This Hindu iconography was at the centre of the capital of the world's most populous Muslim country. Called _Krishna Wijaya_, the statue is flamboyant. There is another, less conventional statue of Krishna and Arjuna in Bali, the only Indonesian island where Hindus form the majority. But the one in Jakarta brings to life a million calendar images. Made of ceramic in an austere white, _Krishna Wijaya_ doesn't need the garish colours filmmaker B R Chopra's make-up artists would fill it with. With its energy, the statue has the martial feel strangely absent in other Krishna-Arjuna statues seen in India—in Rishikesh, near the Ganga, on the coastal highway in Karnataka, or on the road leading to Goa. Jakarta is a city of surprises.

Indonesia was an odd Muslim country, where a President with a Sanskrit-sounding name, Suharto, went on Haj to remind his people that he was indeed pious, even as he banned a fundamentalist Muslim party, and even if his younger son drove fast cars and was known for his playboy image. The President's gentle opponent, representing a Muslim movement for social development called, Nahadlatul Ulama told me how he admired two great Indians. I had expected him to say Buddha and Vivekananda, or Gandhi and Nehru; but he surprised me by citing Gandhi, who rose against the British, and Jayaprakash Narayan, who rose against Indira Gandhi. The nation's guiding philosophy was _pancasila_, another word drawn from Sanskrit, and social analysts explained the country's politics to me drawing on metaphors from the Sanskrit epics that Hindus revered—_Ramayana_ and _Mahabharata_. Muslim women here wore miniskirts and makeup, and alcohol was easily available. A Muslim man had once told me he ate no pork but liked bacon, and I'm still not sure if his command was poor over his English or his scriptures. Here, Eid, or Hari Raya, was celebrated with noisy *dangdut* music, inspired by Bollywood, and fatwa-issuing clerics got apoplectic with increasing palpitations, as they watched the vastly popular singer, Inul Daratista perform her famous "drill" dance, in which she wiggled her bottom at such a rapid pace, that the faint-hearted would get hypnotised, if they weren't already hospitalised.

We had a sense of foreboding that evening—as though something was imminent, as though this remarkably syncretic society was going to tear apart. A day earlier, troops had opened fire at a campus, and six students had died.

Indonesians took great pride in their army for being a people's army. At Jakarta's museum you would see realistic, militaristic paintings of the Indonesian army. It had fought the Dutch, who had returned to rule Indonesia after the Japanese surrendered to the British in 1945. The Dutch had ruled the archipelago since the seventeenth century, and seemed to think that their defeat at the hands of the Japanese in the Second World War had changed nothing and so they returned to rule as though they were entitled to their empire.

Indonesian army fought the Dutch for four years, after which the Dutch left, making Indonesia free. The army then helped consolidate power and over the years controlled Indonesia's politics and economy. Because of its role in the liberation war, Indonesian people considered the army as theirs. By shooting the students, the soldiers had changed the rules of the game, that delicate shadow puppetry, or *wayang kulit*, through which the society operated, and nothing would remain as it seemed anymore.

Indonesians were used to volcanoes that erupted spontaneously, as though the planet was still young. But what if the people decided to erupt? What now?

I had come to Indonesia with a bunch of foreign correspondents to write about its economic turmoil, and I was focussing on Indonesia's broke banks, which towards the end of my stay seemed like the least significant story to worry about. Near the campus where the students had been slain, we saw some people carrying a soothsayer on their shoulders. Earlier that afternoon, the soothsayer had predicted that Suharto's thirty-two-year-old rule would end within a week. A British journalist walking with me wasn't convinced. He had booked a flight to return to Bangkok. He suggested I do the same; nothing was going to change. It had been like this for thirty-two years. An American reporter who had lived in Jakarta for nearly eight years told me the same thing—this too shall pass.

The mood seemed too cheerful and festive. The soothsayer was smiling, greeting the large crowd. But this is the land of shadow puppetry, where nothing is what it seems. That morning I had seen tanks on the main thoroughfares. Police officers guarding important buildings were smiling, but you could not tell what the smiles meant. Were they indulging us? The prominent Chinese banker I was to meet spoke to me in a hurried tone. He had fuelled his helicopter, which was ready to fly him to Singapore from his rooftop when necessary. An American security officer had given me his card at a bar the previous night, saying: 'You can call me if you want to leave this town in a hurry.' Some reporters were indeed leaving.

I decided to stay.

A toppled monarchy looks very stable ten minutes before the revolution. And I wanted to see what happens the day after.

The next morning it wasn't possible to go to the top of Monas, as the 137-metre high obelisk, or the national monument, is known. Instead, I went on top of Wisma Antara, the building which housed the office of the magazine I worked for. All I could see, wherever I looked, was smoke. On a clear day, I could have seen as far as Sunda Kelapa, the wharf where *pinisi*, as the wooden sailing vessels from Bugis were known, still continued to call from Kalimantan. These boats would carry timber and spices to this old pepper port that the Dutch had established in the sixteenth century and called it Batavia. But that day, I could see no hints of those sails or masts; the sky was dark and grey, and the sun seemed to have disappeared. The city seemed ravaged. I saw a plume of smoke from what used to be the Chinese electronic market, in an area called Glodok.

The fourteen-metre flame atop Monas, encrusted with thirty-three kilos of gold, had disappeared, its hazy outline being the only evidence that it still existed and hadn't been reduced to ashes. And to the south, where skyscrapers, each spiffier and shinier than the next, standing close to one another as if trying to rise above the shoulders of the buildings next to them, looked dismal, as if they had suddenly grown old. Dozens of tanks rolled in columns on both sides of the road, moving clunkily and noisily, like drunken tortoises, even as they passed the sharply-defined contours of that statue of Krishna and Arjuna.

I had wanted to go to Indonesia ever since I had seen Peter Weir's film, *The Year of Living Dangerously* (1982), which, in hindsight, perhaps convinced me that being a foreign correspondent would be a cool career—if someone would hire me. The film is a dramatised account of the tumultuous events in Indonesia in the 1960s, when President Soekarno decided to denounce the West (as well as its neighbours, Singapore and Malaysia) and sought friendship—and weapons—from Communist China. Soekarno called that period *konfrontasi* (confrontation). An Australian radio journalist is reporting out of Jakarta at a time when Soekarno is leaving the great powers guessing whether Indonesia will side with the Communists or the West, and its teeming masses pose their faith in the populist. The reporter leaves the watering holes of foreign correspondents and gets to the heart of understanding Indonesia, as well as the meaning of his own life. Being that sort of a lone reporter, following leads, putting together stories armed only with a note pad and a tape recorder—that sounded like the greatest job in the world. I'd do it some day, I decided, when I saw the film at my campus in America in 1983.

The American writer Stan Sesser has described Southeast Asia as the land of charm and cruelty, and Indonesia clearly had both. There were few people more gentle and pleasant than the Indonesians; there were also few countries where people were mowed down with ruthless efficiency as in Indonesia. Right alongside gleaming skyscrapers were slums mired in deep poverty. Indeed, V S Naipaul had written about skyscrapers and chawls coexisting in Bombay in *India: A Wounded Civilization*, published soon after the Emergency of 1975-1977. But Jakarta's slums and poverty seemed more miserable, because the wealth surrounding it was so much more opulent.

In the 1990s, when I lived in Southeast Asia, it was easy to confuse the prosperity of Jakarta for the wealth of Indonesia. An economist had estimated that seventy per cent of the money circulating in Indonesia was to be found in Jakarta; another twenty per cent in Bali. What about the rest? He merely smiled. At some point, that hinterland would rise, he implied.

There was, in Jakarta, in fact an expatriate bubble, with its vast California-style malls and gated communities in suburbs like Tasikmalaya, the swanky buildings and the seductive rustle of new money on busy avenues like Jalan Gatot Subroto and Jalan Sudirman, the flashy cars and easy availability of exotic cuisine, like Philadelphia cheese-steaks and microbreweries churning out fresh, frothy, gourmet beers.

There was an older Indonesia—the quieter, perennial one, of which I had fonder memories. I had found it in the terraced hills of Bandung, in the greenery of Sumatra, in the temples in Jogjakarta and Bali. There I had seen dances like *barong*, where a demon with a large mask tormented a young child, chasing him (we bought a painting of one such act, which still adorns my wall); and you saw the electric energy of the dance *kecak*, where dozens of bare-chested young men, clad in sarongs with black-and-white checks, rose and fell like flames and waves, enacting tales from the *Ramayana*. In Bedugul, I saw artists at work, finishing a landscape by the afternoon, selling it by night. And Celuk, with its delightful silver jewellery, such as those earrings I liked seeing dangle from the earlobes of my late wife, Karuna, every time she nodded. Add to that the soothing lilt of gamelan music, which calmed us as we settled with a glass of sharp kalamansi juice on a warm, moist night, eating spicy *nasi goring* (fried rice) with prawn *lumpiah* (raw spring roll), as the waters kept lashing our hotel by the sea. You tried preserving that past in Bali, even as Jakarta intruded —with its loud music, discos, and a vast beach where the west discarded what the east coveted, and in return the east offered what the west craved for. Or, as Pico Iyer once memorably put it in *Video Night in Kathmandu* (1989): 'Rich enough to go native, the West came East to shed all its belongings, and the East scrambled in the dust to pick them up as they fell.'

The eastern pursuit of hedonism stunned the westerners; the easterner laughed and shook his head, seeing the westerner's desire to abandon his possessions. The imitative pursuit of material wealth was sharper in Jakarta. Totilawati Tjitrawasita, an Indonesian fiction writer who died at thirty-seven in 1982, wrote a poignant story, *Jakarta*, in which an old man from rural Indonesia comes to visit his brother, an official in the military government in Jakarta, and is shocked by the brother's lifestyle, and inability to meet him because he is always busy. A security guard shows the old man around the city, and points out a building with bright lights near the Presidential Palace.

Do you know what that place is?
The old man doesn't know.

The guard says: 'Do you know what a nightclub is?
The centre of night life is here. They're the places
where rich people go to spend their money. Inside,
you got dim lights, beautiful women, liquor, strip
tease dancing and loud music. A-one!'
But what do they do there? The old man wants to
know.

Totilawati writes:

'They dance, fondle, flirt.... All the usual stuff. This is
Jakarta,' the guard answers flippantly.
The old man mumbled, 'and does my brother go
there, too?'
'No, not there. He goes to Paprika. But it is the same
thing, only the cover charge is higher.'

The divide of two Indonesias, two lives, two universes, has
rarely been shown more sharply by an Indonesian writer. At
the end of Totilawati's story, Pak Pong, the old man, looks
vengefully at the cityscape.

Jakarta, with all its rustle and whirl; Bina Graha,
skyscrapers. Freedom Palace, nightclubs, and red
cars. All of them instruments that had separated him
from his brother.

He stared at the package his mother had sent with
him, then handed it to the guard. 'This is for you.
It's a piece of cloth, some batik my mother made.
She put into that cloth the love of a mother for her
child. Our birthplace is in that cloth. And she sent it
to strengthen the bonds of friendship.'

What could the guard say? Two small tears glistened on the old man's cheeks.

ॐ

I had been visiting Jakarta regularly since 1991, and seen the city's aspirations rise, like those skyscrapers, as it tried to become another Singapore, another Hong Kong, but looked more and more like another Bangkok. New townships sprouted, like bamboo shoots after the monsoon, desperately imitating California, and everyone you met in the golden bubble of stock markets and five star hotels and country clubs seemed to be planning their summer holiday in Europe. A stockbroker I knew well was headed for Firenze (as he put it) that summer, the summer of '98, even as the rupiah fell from 2,000 to a dollar to 16,000 a dollar in a matter of weeks. His holiday would cost him eight times more. But he lived in the dollar economy.

One morning in May, I stood in Jakarta's most exclusive neighbourhood, seeing the smoke-filled remains of a large house which had belonged to a Chinese tycoon who was close to Suharto. Precious jade vases lay crushed, portraits were slashed, cars lay smouldering, and sofas were turned upside down. Nothing was whole anymore.

That evening, I saw two young boys in my bus. They were from Bali. They had a small banjo-like instrument, and while I could not understand the words—Bahasa has many words in common with Sanskrit, but not enough for me to claim familiarity with the language—there was one word in that song that stood out. *Dasomuko*, it was—the ten-headed one, and there could only be one ten-headed one in a culture steeped in the *Ramayana*. Ravana, the demon.

And it seemed so appropriate. Jakarta had burned that day like Lanka had, after Hanuman had set it afire. Would Ravana fall? Could the spirited singing of the two Balinese boys bring down the ten-headed demon?

Exceptional cruelty inspires excessive optimism and bravery. Earlier that week I had met the writer Mochtar Lubis. He had referred to the business associates of Suharto's children as leeches, sucking blood from the economy. 'And you can quote me,' he had said (and I did). Looking at those Balinese boys, I thought of Minke, the protagonist of Pramoedya Ananta Toer's remarkable novels, known as the *Buru Quartet*. Pramoedya wrote those novels when Suharto had him jailed and sent off in internal exile on the island of Buru, Indonesia's labour camp, for being sympathetic to Communism. In *Footsteps*, Pramoedya writes of Minke looking at Jakarta for the first time:

> The tram moved on smoothly to the clanging of the brass bell. Betawi! Ah, Betawi! Here I am now in your centre. You don't know me yet, Betawi! But I know you. You have turned Ciliwung into a canal, with boats and rafts going back and forth, laden with goods from the interior. Almost like Surabaya. Your buildings are big and grand, but my spirit is bigger and grander.

The Balinese spirit was bigger and grander, and Ravana fell. At that moment this archipelago of thousands of islands looked broken and fragile, like scattered diamonds floating in the Indian Ocean. Putting it together again was not going to be easy. But those Balinese boys looked cheerful, as they sang the dirge for *Dasomuko*.

Suharto didn't collapse and crumble like Ravana. But the city was ablaze, in ruins, like Lanka. In the world's most populous Muslim country, in a city with sculptures of Hindu icons, you saw the hazy outline of his shadow, the way Monas had looked that morning, like the burnt carcass of Ravana, a large void. Those Balinese boys had got it right. The next morning Indonesia had a new president. The smoke began to dissipate. The sky was blue again.

ICH BIN EIN BERLINER

'Are we in the east or the west?' I asked my friend Canan, a German woman whose parents were Turkish immigrants, as we walked along the fashionable shops and bars at the Potsdamer Platz. Between the restaurants offering alfresco dining, the headquarters of large companies including Daimler-Benz and Sony, swanky stores selling music and chic clothes, microbreweries bubbling with frothy beer, and the air thick with the smell of smoked sausages and strong tobacco, it was difficult to tell that barely two decades ago this vast area was hauntingly barren, the no-man's-land between the superpowers.

She looked around, surveying the traffic, the buildings, the clean roads and the trendy people cheerfully making their way to the subway station in crisp autumn air, threw her hands up in mock despair, and smiled, her delightful eyes turning wide, saying: 'You know what? I can't tell anymore. But isn't that great?' And she laughed.

❧

I had been at Potsdamer Platz before—the Berlin Wall was etched sharp in the memories of people at that time. With the huge amount of construction going on, Berlin was full of pipes, painted pink and blue and yellow, erected comically all over the city, transporting sludge, as building companies laid foundations for more shopping centres and office complexes. The large pipes created the illusion of new kind of walls emerging before your eyes. There were other walls too, metaphoric, of the mind, which separated those who yearned for tomorrow and its freedoms of department stores and coffee shops, and those who disliked the past of drab Communist cafés but found the ostentatious capitalism of the new Berlin repugnant.

It had been more than a decade since the wall had come down, but the struggle of people against power is always, as Milan Kundera says, the struggle between memory and forgetting. And as if to remind visitors and citizens of the city's divided past, the authorities had left inlaid stones on the road where the wall stood, bearing the legend, "Berliner Mauer, 1961–1989". Those stones interrupted the smooth drive of the Mercedes Benz and Volkswagen automobiles along the roads, but it felt like a mild hiccup, the slight bump reminding you of the twenty-eight years when those brave enough to scale the wall to leave the east for the west faced sniper fire from the east and press coverage in the west. It had taken the Communists one night to erect that wall—its jagged outline not only reinforcing the artificial division, but also tearing asunder close neighbourhoods. But it also took only one night to tear it down, as people on both sides of the wall, armed with pickaxes and hammers, assaulted the barrier. And as it came down, Mstislav Rostropovich flew to Berlin, went to Checkpoint Charlie, sat on a chair, placed the cello near him, and began playing Bach. Today, the memory of the fall of the wall has turned into kitsch—you can buy what are purportedly pieces of the wall as souvenirs. You can also buy tiny models of the Trabant—the ugly car of East Germany, which made India's Premier Padmini look cute and elegant. Giant caricatures of a GI Joe and an anonymous Soviet guard can be found at Checkpoint Charlie, the threshold immortalised in countless espionage novels.

Today, Germany laughs at that period of history—think of the film, *Goodbye Lenin* (2003), which offers an almost affectionate, nostalgic view of that period, making it seem like a comical bad dream. Modern Germany also seeks humanity in that heartless Communist past, by inventing a Communist eavesdropper with a soul—as in the film *The Lives of Others* (2006). But that was a myth, as Anna Funder showed in her book, *Stasiland* (2003). But there is a more distant past in German history, which is too grim, too shocking, and people recoil when that period is made fun of: it is the Nazi past. To understand that frenzy, I wanted to go where it had all begun.

On a warm night in early September, after dinner at the home of my friends, Kean and Helen, we decided to go for a walk. Kean is a writer and broadcaster from Malaysia; Helen is an Australian diplomat. Helen decided to stay home with their newborn baby; Kean joined me. We walked along the strangely quiet avenue, where the only sound you could hear was the tinkling bells of bicycles. We were on Unter den Linden, the stately avenue that leads all the way to the Brandenburg Gate.

Soon after the Berlin Wall was built, President John Kennedy stood near the gate, and addressed the city, saying: *Ich bin ein Berliner*. He meant he was one of them, not realising that Berliner is a pastry, so what he actually said was that he was a German pastry—but the good people of Berlin cheered him nonetheless. Two decades later, another American President —this time Ronald Reagan—stood near the same gate, and said six words—'Mr Gorbachev, tear down this wall.' Those were simple, powerful words. They did not send an army to march, but they inspired those who lived on the other side of the wall, beyond what Churchill had called the iron curtain. The people began dismantling the dictatorships that chained them, ending the Cold War dramatically in 1989, the year that changed everything.

Our destination was Bebelplatz, an open square surrounded by imposing buildings. On one side was the sturdy faculty of justice; on the other, there was an officious building wrapped in a tromp l'oleil exterior, advertising an organic lemonade. A bank and a hotel formed the third side of the square, and behind us was Unter den Linden, across which was the university where Albert Einstein once taught, until he realised that teaching "Jewish" science wasn't a terrific idea in Germany. He left for safer climes, as the Nazis began rewriting even science.

It was nearly midnight and Bebelplatz was deserted. The official buildings surrounding the plaza were dark. But a glow of light emerged from the centre of the ground, a straight line, like a halo reaching far into the sky, like the steady flame of an eternal candle. As we got closer, the image became more granular, and what seemed like a lit cylinder revealed itself: you could see particles of dust, not following any path, roaming in the air, listening to their own internal rhythm, recreating the Brownian motion, disappearing from our sight as they left the illuminated path.

Their movement had no pattern, but as we stood near the light, we could see an intricate, mesmerising, randomness emerge—each particle moved along the path only it knew, but it never collided with another particle. There was order in that chaos. German thinkers and scientists knew how to see order amidst chaos.

Six decades earlier, on Unter den Linden, some Germans, harbingers of what was to follow, had unleashed chaos out of order. Thousands of men had marched in step, in perfect harmony and symmetry, the soles of their shoes hitting the ground hard in goose-steps, their movements precise as clockwork.

While the light from the ground was not blinding in its intensity, it was sharp and bright. When you looked through the thick glass towards the source of that light, the stark whiteness below hit you straight, forcing you to narrow your eyes. It was the visual equivalent of being deafened by eloquent silence—being blinded by luminous glow that mere mortal flames could not surpass. The glow was penetrating, trying to impose symmetry on an amorphous mass of particles.

In 1933, at the same square, Adolf Hitler's Nazi Youth ransacked libraries and brought books—by one count the total exceeded 20,000—and made a bonfire. Among the authors whose works they turned to ashes were Thomas Mann, who wrote the turn-of-the-century novel *Buddenbrooks* in 1901, Erich Maria Remarque, who mourned the death of youth in *All Quiet on the Western Front* (1929), Karl Marx, whose interpretation of capitalism transformed a century, and Heinrich Heine.

The choice of Heine was particularly poignant. In his 1821 play, *Almansor*, Heine had written: '*Das war Vorspiel nur. Dort, wo man Bücher verbrennt, verbrennt man am Ende auch Menschen.*' (That was mere foreplay. Where they have burned books, they will end in burning human beings.)

When you looked beneath that transparent square glass which was the source of the light, you saw rows of empty bookshelves, in stark white. At one level, they looked like cheap, easy-to-assemble bookshelves, the kind you can buy at Ikea, with names like Sven, Bjorn, or Ingmar. The shelves became meaningful only when they were filled. And the Nazi youth had burned the books that had given meaning to those shelves.

The Nazi bonfire was not some insane Taliban escapade, where they burned any book that was not the *Quran*. These men had burned specific books, by specific authors—if they were Jewish, socialist, or deemed Communist. Heine was prescient: five years after the book burning, in November 1938, on a single night known as Kristalnacht, Nazi youth destroyed hundreds of synagogues in Germany. The Second World War started ten months later; the Holocaust and its full horrors were revealed six years later.

Books represent ideas, and in a literary culture like Germany's, books were physical manifestation of creativity, thought, imagination, ideas, and argument. You could disagree with a book, shut it, challenge it; you could even defy it. But burn it? This was the country of Mann and Schopenhauer, of Kant and Hegel, of Nietzsche and Goethe. Ideas clashed against one another, ideas floated in the intellectual space, and readers made connections, and we developed an understanding of ourselves better. Wisdom flourished.

The Nazi youth wanted to make ideas which they considered small to kneel before the larger idea, and they wanted to force everyone to march in one specific way. If you stepped out, if you looked different, or thought differently, you were struck down. They wanted to tear down what they did not like. They wanted to hide behind the wall of conformity.

But if we are forced to burn our words and thoughts, we find other ways to remember them. The Soviet Union could not silence Solzhenitsyn; Suharto's Indonesia could not keep Pramoedya Ananta Toer quiet. Samizdat literature was born out of the principle that when you don't trust the printed word, you believe in the spoken word.

Our desire to remember vanquishes their insistence that we forget. In Ray Bradbury's 1953 novel, *Fahrenheit 451* (the temperature at which paper burns on its own), leaders of a dystopian society have succeeded in burning all the books they can find. But words survive. At the end of the film Francois Truffaut made in 1966 based on the novel, we meet men and women walking, talking to themselves, reciting words from books that have been burned, but remembering them so that they don't disappear from our collective consciousness.

One memorises *Wuthering Heights*, another *Pickwick Papers*, someone else *Republic*, there, *Through the Looking Glass*, and over here, *Waiting for Godot*. And a character calling himself *The Journal of Henri Brilard* says:

> Here, we're only 50 or so, but there are many, many more scattered around. In abandoned railway yards, wandering the roads. Tramps outwardly, but inwardly libraries. Oh, it wasn't planned. It just so happened that a man here and a man there loved some book. And rather than lose it, he learned it. And we came together. We're a minority of undesirables crying out in the wilderness. But it won't always be so. One day we shall be called on, one by one, to recite what we've learned. And then books will be printed again. And when the next age of darkness comes, those who come after us will do again as we have done.

Later that night, Kean took me to another part of Berlin, showing me another commemoration on its footpaths. These were the city's inlaid plaques. He told me about a sculptor called Gunter Demnig, who has been going around German cities, exploring its past, identifying the homes that belonged to Jewish families who had been evicted and sent to concentration camps. He then engraves their names in tiny plaques, and hammers those plaques on the surface of the sidewalks of particular streets, in front of the homes where they had once lived. The plaques name the families, fixing the date they were taken away, and if known, the date of their passing in a death camp. The plaques stand apart on the streets, but only slightly; they look like stumbling blocks, only marginally; and that's exactly Demnig's point. He calls them *stolpersteine*, German for a stumbling block. Like those cars driving over the stones inlaid on the roads of Berlin to remind the city of its division, these plaques are fixed at the precise spots from where families were uprooted because they belonged to a different faith. The *stolpersteine* project is an individual's obsession, a thoughtful tribute to those who perished in that collective madness, a memorial against the folly, giving dignity to those who died in anonymity.

Many Germans are uncomfortable with Demnig's obsession. Some residents have removed the plaques. Some people have vandalised the plaques. (He reinstates them; the sidewalks are public property, and the residents have no right to remove them. He doesn't have the right to place them either, but German mayors do not object to his mission.) Some residents have said, quite reasonably, that what happened was not their fault. Some have argued that Germany must move on from that past. Berlin has already built a Holocaust Memorial and a Jewish Museum. Both are sober and respectful. Germans have sought atonement and are consumed by guilt: their one-time leader, Willy Brandt, not only went to the memorial at the Warsaw Ghetto to apologise for what his nation had done; he fell to his knees, a gesture that spoke far more than any words could have. Is it time to move on?

Arguably, Germany has shown greater maturity in dealing with its past than has Japan: Germany understands guilt and expresses remorse; Japan is convulsed with shame, and is too embarrassed to admit its past. Ian Buruma, the Anglo-Dutch writer who combines history, culture, and memory in a masterly way, has contrasted the two responses in his moving book, *The Wages of Guilt* (1994). Till when should today's Germans bear the burden of what a previous generation did seven decades ago?

There are no easy answers. On another visit, I was walking with a German friend who is a diplomat. We walked along the Holocaust Memorial, with its dark blocks rising and falling like the ripples in the river Styx. They looked like the sepulchral bars of a haunting piano. Calmly, he tells me that his country does not have the luxury of forgetting. 'Do you see that tram arriving at the stop? It always arrives at its precise time. Have you driven our cars? Everything works exactly as it is meant to function. We are very good engineers, the best in the world. We pursue technological solutions for complex problems. We are logical, and we think everything can be fixed. We have manuals for everything. Our zeal is such that it can seem maddening to outsiders. When we get it right, we build world-class machinery. When we get it wrong, we get this...' he says, as he points out the memorial. He pauses for a long time, and continues: 'We forget our ethics, we apply the same efficiency and single-mindedness to fix problems. At that time we forget our humanity. We follow instructions and orders.' He has worked tirelessly with UN agencies, bringing peace in war-torn regions of the world. There is a lump in his throat as he speaks.

The diplomat is a good friend. He had not yet read Bernard Schlinck's 1995 novel, *The Reader*. But he succinctly expressed the central dilemma Hanna Schmitz faced: she worked in a jail and she had to protect the Jewish women she was in charge of. Even as the Allies bombed that jail and those women wanted to escape their certain death in that burning jail, she followed her instructions—she had to protect them by keeping them in that jail; she could not let them escape, even if it was burning. And she was incapable of understanding that she had done something wrong.

Getting Germans to deviate from the rulebook is not simple; it is a rule-bound society. Another evening, I was in what used to be East Berlin, looking for the home of Bertolt Brecht. The playwright who drew the mythical boundary of the *Caucasian Chalk Circle* lived in this city, and his home was now a museum. I was ten minutes late; the museum was closing. I requested them to let me have a quick look. No, the woman said sternly. I said I had come from very far. I told her I had seen Brecht's plays, and I was unlikely to return for a long time. To no avail. She closed the window. I could go to the beer garden at the back and stare at the windows of the museum. Its doors remained shut. Rules were rules.

How could one make such a mechanism flexible? How could the bureaucrats think beyond those rules? How could soldiers be made to respond to conscience? By filling those shelves with books; not by emptying them and burning them in a public plaza. At Bebelplatz in 1933, many young Germans, feeling threatened by ideas their leader did not like, burned the thoughts of their own fine thinkers. Burning people was the next step.

Today, in the same city, one man has been going around nailing metallic plaques on the sidewalks, so that its residents might stumble a little and begin to remember those who didn't live long enough to have the grandchildren who could have been their neighbours.

Those plaques give the city its permanence, its solidity, its continuity. That glow of light at Bebelplatz illuminates the mind. The inlaid stones outlining the former wall on the busy road keeps a memory alive. Canan cannot tell anymore which is east and which is west, and that is good—the parts are whole again. But the path has those plaques, and Germans are learning to walk carefully over their buried past. They will not step on the plaques on the sidewalk, because those plaques aren't stumbling blocks. They bear names; they are silent witnesses of this wounded city.

At Bebelplatz, those bookshelves are empty—the empty space reminding us of what Germany lost. By fixing those plaques, Demnig shows how Germany must recognise its past as it becomes whole again.

A PAGODA, A PRINCESS, AND A KING

From my hotel window, I see the vast Inya lake, at one end of which is a golden pagoda. Trees surround the pagoda on either side. At the other end are stately homes, looking modest in comparison with the pagoda, and in one of those homes the lady lives. The lady is of course Aung San Suu Kyi, daughter of Burma's (now Myanmar) founding father Aung San.

In May 2009, when Aung San Suu Kyi was still under house arrest, a former Vietnam War veteran, John Yettaw, managed to elude security forces and swam across the lake and reached her home. Her detention term was about to end, and according to Burmese law, the government would have had no choice but to release her. At such a time, Yettaw, or "the fool", as Suu Kyi's lawyer later described him, swam to her home and insisted on seeing her. He claimed he had information that her life was in danger and wanted to warn her. Saying that he was tired, he refused to leave immediately. His uninvited presence gave Burma's generals fresh excuse to keep Aung San Suu Kyi in jail, apparently for breaking the terms of her imprisonment.

In the generals' Burma, if your house gets broken into, it is your fault, not the thief's, even if you are under detention in your own house, and not in control of your life. It doesn't get more Orwellian than that, and George Orwell, after all, had chronicled colonial Burma.

I struggled to understand how it was her fault. Indeed, she should never have been in jail in the first place.

A foreign aid worker recounted Yettaw's story one evening when we met at the bar of my hotel. He paused and wryly added: 'The people here are so obsessed by what the government thinks and what it allows, that when Yettaw swam across the lake, the question everyone asked was not what it might mean, but how he could do that. *"Doesn't he know it is not allowed to swim in the lake?"'* He said the last sentence mocking the surprised look on the face of the local elite.

This was not a military to mess with, and it had always been that way. Months before Burma's independence in 1948, soldiers had stormed into the cabinet of Gen Aung San and shot him and his colleagues dead, in a crime which is still technically unsolved as nobody knows who gave orders to assassinate Aung San. That army was trigger-happy and untrained. A few years later, the British writer Norman Lewis travelled through Burma, the land that he said was "spread as a dark stain into the midnight sea". In his magnificent account, *Golden Earth* (1952), he wrote about those trigger-happy soldiers:

> That night we slept in a jungle-clearing on the way back. There was a remnant of a hut perched on stilts ten feet high, and into it the headman, Sneg and I climbed. Every time one of us turned over, this construction swayed a little. Beneath us, the soldiers thudded with unflagging energy at their drum, and sang a soldiering song with endless verses, and an extremely monotonous air. The end of each verse would be signalled by howls of laughter. In the

end, as the first wave of fever slowly spent itself, I relapsed into rambling, oppressive dreams. I was soon aroused by a discharge of shots. But it was only a soldier who had been tinkering with his Sten, which was loaded, and had shot off one of his toes.

❧

I saw Aung San Suu Kyi's home from University Road, where television vans were parked. She was expected to appear and speak to the crowd that had gathered there, to celebrate her party's sweeping victory in parliamentary by-elections in 2012. She looked as she did in photographs I had seen. Nearly two decades of incarceration hadn't dimmed her radiance. She smiled as she stepped out and spoke to everyone. Seeing her spontaneous responses to the people around her, I realised why the taxi driver who took me to my hotel, and the woman cleaning the hotel's rooms, and even the elderly man I saw dance in Bahan near her party office the night of the elections, had instinctively bowed their heads and had tears in their eyes when they spoke of her in reverential terms. I then remembered what Amitav Ghosh wrote in 1995, in his book, *Dancing in Cambodia, At Large in Burma,* when he saw her the first time. (She also makes another appearance in his writing, in a fictional account in the novel, *The Glass Palace*):

> Her gateside meetings, I'd noticed, were attended by dozens of foreigners. Only a few were reporters and journalists; most were tourists and travellers. They were people like me, members of the world's vast, newspaper-reading middle class, people who took it for granted that there are no heroes among us. But Suu Kyi had proved us wrong. She lived the same kind of life, attended the same classes, read the same books and magazines, got into the same arguments.

And she had shown us that the apparently soft and yielding world of books and words could sometimes forge a very fine kind of steel.

While many know of the nerves of steel she possesses, what I found inspiring was how that fine steel formed the backbone of so many people in the country. In Burma, there were pagodas to see, lakes to gaze at, and monks to admire as they filed past in their maroon robes, but beneath that photographic calm, there was subterranean subversion.

When I flew in to Rangoon, I was worried that if I carried books about Burma, such as the pseudonymous American author Emma Larkin's *Finding George Orwell in Burma* and *Everything is Broken,* Thant Myint U's *The River of Lost Footsteps,* or the biographies of Aung San Suu Kyi by Bertil Lintner, Peter Popham, or Justin Wintle, the customs officials would promptly confiscate them, and immigration officials might put me on the next plane out of the country. After all, many books about Burma have Suu Kyi's photograph on the cover. It was wise not to bring books with her face on the cover, I assumed.

But the moment I stepped into a cab outside the terminal, I realised how unnecessary my timidity had been. I saw a photograph of Suu Kyi and her father Aung San stuck on the cab's dashboard. On the way to the hotel, the driver showed me the flag of her political party—the National League for Democracy (NLD)—and then, as I looked around, I saw the flag, or her face, or her father's face, on other cabs, on cars, trucks, and even on public buses. Near Scott's Market in downtown Rangoon, I saw hawkers selling hats and T-shirts with her face smiling back. It felt like the emergence of a personality cult, except that she had no political power to require citizens to do any of this. She had been released from house arrest four months earlier and she was standing as a candidate in a by-election, but she was not yet an opposition member of the parliament. But for the people, she was already their leader.

Three days later, I saw young novice monks, in their robes, their faces painted with the NLD flag, smiling at foreign journalists busy photographing them. Aung San Suu Kyi had asked her citizens to shed fear; the citizens were doing just that. Explaining Suu Kyi's mystique, Larkin wrote in an essay:

> On 26 August [1988], she delivered an address to a crowd of nearly half a million people at the Shwedagon Pagoda in Rangoon, the country's holiest Buddhist shrine. Speaking beneath a portrait of her father, she declared: "I could not, as my father's daughter, remain indifferent to all that was going on. This national crisis could in fact be called the second struggle for national independence"... Burmese history and folklore is punctuated by millennial leaders and would-be kings who emerge at times of crisis to lead the people to safety. Here, in this modern era, a female version had appeared, seemingly by pure chance, during a catastrophic upheaval... the crowd was instantly smitten.

I wondered what inspired civilian courage, and looked for answers in Buddhism. The faith matters to many in Burma, and Suu Kyi herself has explained her understanding of what makes a good ruler from Buddhist precepts and principles. In an essay in her book, *Freedom from Fear,* she invokes ten duties of a king—*dana* (liberality), *sila* (morality), *paricagga* (generosity), *ajjava* (integrity), *maddava* (kindness), *tapa* (austerity), *akkodha* (non-anger), *avihamsa* (non-violence), *khanti* (forbearance), and *avirodha* (not opposing the will of the people). She further writes:

> The quest for democracy in Burma is the struggle of a people to live whole, meaningful lives to live as free and equal members of the world community. It is part of the unceasing human endeavour to prove

that the spirit of man can transcend the flaws of his own nature.

The problem is, the generals too claim to be Buddhist, and claim they are following the eight-fold Noble Path—but you judge people by their actions, not words. And in some cases, the words of Buddhists too can hurt—more recently, a Buddhist monk, Wirathu, has used exceptionally crass language to describe Muslims, and termed a senior UN human rights official a whore. In a Burma that an Orwell would recognise and despair over, dictators speak in a pious language and men in saffron robes use vile language. And the Princess herself has stayed remarkably silent, saying not a word to condemn the monks or the military, as the persecution of Rohingyas goes on....

Downtown Rangoon is bustling with shopping centres reminiscent of Calcutta (now Kolkata) or Bombay of the 1970s, with unrecognisable brands on display, and dangerous and exposed electric cables entangled around the pillars, extending their reach to other pillars, connecting various buildings—and more—with the city's power grid. That is assuming that the power grid works properly. It wasn't always like that. At the time of Burma's independence in 1948, economists and development experts thought Rangoon would become Asia's most prosperous city and Burma would feed the region. But today, cities in its neighbourhood, like Bangkok, have left Rangoon far behind. After her victory in the by-elections of 2012, Aung San Suu Kyi's first trip abroad was to Bangkok. And she recalled later that what struck her the most as the plane began its descent was how bright and glittering Bangkok looked. Burma stayed in the dark.

But there is a charming and quaint aspect to the city, with its tree-lined avenues curiously devoid of pedestrians, except, occasionally, monks in their maroon robes walking in a disciplined file. The downtown bazaars are busy, and at night, the hawker stalls come alive with families dressed in shorts and singlets sitting on aluminium stools and plastic-topped tables, slurping down warm noodles in fish soup, couples walking hand-in-hand, their eyes only for each other.

Burma and India are neighbours but far apart in many ways. Indians like to take pride in their democratic structure which has been denied to Burma, but Burma has certain features of equality—particularly between sexes—where it leaves India behind. Women are visible in public; you look at them and they stare back, smiling almost immediately. Kipling noted this in his essay on Rangoon in *From Sea to Sea* (1887). So impressed he was by what he saw of the country and its riches, he wrote:

> When I die I will be a Burman, with twenty yards of real King's Silk, that has been made in Mandalay... I will always walk about with a pretty almond-coloured girl who shall laugh and jest... as a young maiden ought. She shall not pull a sari over her head when a man looks at her and glare suggestively from behind it, nor...tramp behind me when I walk, for these are the customs of India.

Nearly fifty years later, when Orwell described Flory and his mistress in *Burmese Days* (1934), the effect of the confident Burmese woman on the Englishman was similar.

Indian intellectuals make much of the ties that bind India and Burma. Suu Kyi herself has written movingly about the links in an essay comparing the Indian colonial experience with the Burmese. She notes the diversity within Hinduism and the spirit of questioning, and admires the Bengal Renaissance, which revealed the flexible Hindu mind which was able to discard taboos and absorb the positive influences of British rule. That led Indian thinkers to meet the British challenge as equals, on intellectual and philosophical terms, she notes. In

Burma, a more classless, Buddhist society disregarded colonial rule altogether, connecting with the British only when it was necessary. She rues that gap and notes:

> There were in Burma no Rammohun Roys, no Tagores, ... people with wealth and leisure to pursue knowledge for the sake of knowledge.... [Tagore had his] quest for knowledge, freedom, universalism, truth, reason, thought joined with action within a spiritual framework.

Burmese generals had no time for Tagore or Roy. When Ne Win took over all power in 1962, he expelled Indians, and many left. There are of course Indians in Burma, and while those Indians retain some Indian characteristics—such as men wearing white lungis that they roll up above the knee, and some women apply bindi, or the dot at the centre of their forehead, they don't have a single Indian word in their vocabulary. At one point, when my driver and I could not find an address, I turned to one man who looked Indian and asked him if he spoke any Hindi—he shook his head vigorously and moved away from me.

But everyone knew the way to the pagoda.

Shwedagon Pagoda is the site of Suu Kyi's famous speech a quarter century ago. It is imposing and spectacular. When Kipling saw it for the first time, he exclaimed: 'Then, a golden mystery upheaved itself on the horizon... a shape that was neither Muslim dome nor Hindu temple spire... the golden dome said: "This is Burma, and it will be quite unlike any land you know about."'

You can see the pagoda from many parts of Rangoon, as it is set on a hill, and with its massive white sculptures encased in gold it draws your attention from afar. Rangoon does not yet have many high-rise buildings, which makes Shwedagon's imposing grandeur all the more alluring. As the sun sets, with its rays resting on the golden stupas, the light can momentarily blind you, but that twilight hour is the best time to visit. Being a tropical country, Burma is hot most times of the year, and walking barefoot on that stone and marble surface, bright and hot, is not easy. And yet, you see young boys and girls, being initiated as novice monks, wearing resplendent ornaments over their white clothes, walking dutifully towards the *bhikkhus* who will now take charge of their lives for some time, and you marvel at the devotion.

However what is most jarring is the amount of gold visible everywhere. It doesn't go with the image of Buddhism as an austere faith. I remember visiting Thai *wats* in the 1990s with my late wife Karuna, who was Buddhist. She couldn't reconcile her faith with the ostentation she saw, just as she couldn't understand why a Buddhist temple would sacrifice birds at the temple in Bangkok. I shared her sense of surprise even though I wasn't Buddhist, as I walked along the periphery of various stupas. Shwedagon, incidentally, means three golden hills, and invites devotees with material concerns. At the idol of fertility, a young woman offered flowers and bowed repeatedly; a young Thai woman travelling with us kept kneeling, praying for a promotion at work. In the alcoves I saw elderly monks, wearing dark glasses, sitting away from the sun, looking not unlike the Buddha images behind them.

And then I saw a cheerful boy, his head bald, his face grinning, sitting atop a stone lion as if it were his rocking horse, with his father keeping his hand on his back in case he were to topple, while his mother was inside the temple, praying. I took pictures of the child, who made threatening and cheerful faces at me. I laughed; the father laughed. We had no words in common, but we had found a bond.

Nearly 125 years ago, Kipling had a similar experience:

A brown baby came by in its mother's arms and laughed, wherefore I much desired to shake hands with it, and grinned... The mother held out the tiny soft pud and laughed, and the baby laughed, and we all laughed together...the lamps of the stall-keepers were twinkling and... people were helping us to laugh... I had not actually entered the Shway Dagon, but I felt just as happy as though I had.

Shwedagon guards Rangoon, and by implication, Burma. During the Second World War, the British Army decided to station its troops in the complex, ostensibly claiming it would help them survey the countryside. But there was another reason too; to remind the Burmese who was in charge.

I had one more place to visit—the final resting place of Bahadur Shah Zafar, the last Mughal emperor of India, who died as a British prisoner in Rangoon in 1862. Finding his tomb was not going to be easy, but I was determined to succeed.

How was I to find Zafar's resting place? When I asked my hotel concierge where I might find the tomb, he looked at me as if I was in the wrong country. Bahadur Shah's remains certainly were in the wrong country. Sha-Za-Fa, as many Burmese knew him, seemed elusive.

In India too, his name often appears as a footnote, an afterthought after the long line of illustrious predecessors who had spread their empire from Afghanistan to Bengal. By the time Bahadur Shah came to power, he was tired and old, with a dwindling treasury, no army, and his writ did not run much beyond the Red Fort. And yet, in the two decades he ruled, Delhi experienced what William Dalrymple, in *The Last Mughal: The Fall of a Dynasty*, called "the last great flickering of the Mughal lamp before it is extinguished."

Finally an Indian resident in the city suggested I go to Ziwaka Road, north of downtown, on the way to the university and the airport. Ziwaka Road is quiet and unpretentious, and we drove some distance, without seeing any sign of a monument. Then I saw a few soldiers, returning from their drill, walking in a relaxed manner, smiling as they talked to one another. As our car slowed down near them, they became curious, perhaps even suspicious, and their smiles disappeared. As I asked one of them where I might find Sha-Za-Fa's tomb, they shook their head, and I could see that I wasn't doing a good job explaining what I was looking for. Then, out of exasperation, I said, 'India King,' and raised my arms above my head, as if showing a crown. Immediately one of the soldiers smiled, and pointed me to the spot where we had turned off the main road.

The building where Bahadur Shah Zafar's remains are kept is in a quiet lane off the main road, away from the city, and far away from India. At the entrance I saw an arch made of metal, with golden paint, where it was written: Dargah of Bahadur Shah Zafar, Emperor of India (1837–1857).

I saw no sign of activity at the dargah. There was a poster of the emperor, looking dour and bearded, on one wall of a small café.

I walked up the stairs to the main hall, which was empty, except for two men who sat in a corner, fanning themselves. I stepped inside, and saw three graves, with sheets covering them. On one side, four men wearing caps sat across one another, continuously reciting prayers. They ignored me as I walked around them and took their pictures.

On the walls there were framed prints of engraved images of monuments from India. The walls had fading portraits of Bahadur Shah and his wife Zeenat Mahal. There was one frame with the last known photograph of Zafar, a lonely, tired man, lying on bed, waiting for death. The sense of desolation was overwhelming.

The guard pointed to the stairs outside the building, which led me to Bahadur Shah Zafar's actual burial place. The single large tomb there had a green sheet on it, with a bright yellow border. Fresh flowers were laid on the sheet. I saw an elderly couple, swaying gently while seated, their eyes shut, their open palms pointing skywards in a sign of submission, as they too recited prayers. The woman had placed a handkerchief on her head.

Again, the couple ignored me while I walked around, taking pictures. But as I turned to leave, the man rose after his prayers and asked me: 'India?' When I nodded, he smiled and told me to wait. He opened his lunch box, and gave me a piece of home-made banana cake.

The place had neither pomp nor glory. Humayun's tomb dominates the landscape in Delhi. While Akbar's capital Fatehpur Sikri was rendered uninhabitable, it survives, recalling the monumental folly of trying to transfer a city to a new location. Aurangzeb's tomb looks like a poor imitation of the Taj Mahal, which Shah Jehan built for his beloved wife, Mumtaz Mahal. Bahadur Shah was a modest man, and his tomb is similarly modest. In one of his poems he is eerily prescient about his insignificance:

Na kisi ki aankh ka noor hoon, na kisi ke dil ka qaraar hoon

Jo kisi ke kaam na aa sake, main woh ek musht-e-gubbaar hoon

(I am not the light of anyone's eye, nor am I comfort for any heart I am of no use to anyone, I am that handful of dust)

A handful of dust—Evelyn Waugh would write a novel with that title many years later, drawn from T S Eliot's *The Waste Land*. Eliot drew allusions from many cultures and languages, and in *The Waste Land* he wrote:

What are the roots that clutch, what branches grow

Out of this stony rubbish? Son of man,

You cannot say, or guess, for you know only
A heap of broken images, where the sun beats,

And the dead tree gives no shelter, the cricket no relief,
And the dry stone no sound of water. Only

There is shadow under this red rock,

(Come in under the shadow of this red rock),

And I will show you something different from either

Your shadow at morning striding behind you

Or your shadow at evening rising to meet you;

I will show you fear in a handful of dust.

A handful of dust: what remains; what is feared; what will be forgotten; what foretells.

Bahadur Shah Zafar was born when the East India Company had coastal presence in India; by the time he died, the Company ruled vast parts of India, and his empire had shrunk. But his name resonated and when the sepoys of the East India Company mutinied in 1857, they came to Delhi, and asked Bahadur Shah to take over their leadership. The king who couldn't control his wives, concubines, or sons, who had accepted with dignity British insults, now accepted with humility the symbolic honour the rebels accorded him. But the Company troops regrouped, counter-attacked, and won. They stripped him of his power, killed his adult sons, tried him, and exiled him to Rangoon. He knew the inevitability of how it would all end. One of his poems reads:

Kitna hai bad-naseeb Zafar, dafan ke liye

Do gaz zameen bhi na mili ku-e-yaar mein.

(How ill-fated is Zafar! For his own burial
He couldn't get even two yards of earth in the land that he loved.)

The British, who ruled Burma too, denied him access to pen, ink, or paper, which was particularly cruel, as he was a mystical poet, a contemporary of Mirza Ghalib. When he died in 1862, his last rites were performed in haste, to prevent another revolt. The British officials who had supervised his burial had noted triumphantly: 'A bamboo fence surrounds the grave, and by the time the fence is worn out, the grass will again have properly covered the spot, and no vestige will remain to distinguish where the last of the Great Mughals rests.' Dalrymple noted that even the turf on the grave was replaced carefully so that within a month or two no mark remained to indicate the precise burial spot. The local Muslim community remembered him as a saint and built a shrine where they thought he was buried.

But you can't bury history. In 1991, workers repairing a drain behind a shrine found the original brick-lined grave. Over the years, support from private trusts and the Indian Government have maintained the shrine. Dalrymple told me: 'At the dargah he is portrayed as a king and a Sufi saint, and that's perfectly appropriate; he'd be pleased.'

There is an old Gujarati poem about the fall of mighty empires. I couldn't recall it exactly, so I got in touch with Ramesh Joshi, who taught me Gujarati literature at school. He remembered it immediately. Behram Malbari's poem read:

Chakravarti Maharaj chalya kaal-chakrani ferie

Sagaan ditha men Shah Alam na, bhikh mangta sherie.

(Great kings must walk to the beat of the time

I saw Shah Alam's relatives begging on the streets.)

Shah Alam was Bahadur Shah's ancestor. Bahadur Shah wanted to be buried near his ancestors, but that did not happen. The emperor had lost his throne, but the poet was at peace. Outside the shrine, across the road, there is a lake surrounded by trees. Young lovers sat beneath its shade. And lotuses bloomed.

THE BRIDGE OVER TROUBLED WATERS

On one side was the mountain, on which they had painted a giant cross in white, protecting one half of the town; on the other was a minaret, offering an alternate path to salvation: two ancient faiths, coexisting on the same landscape. It was evening, and the sun rested on the gleaming cross, while a muezzin's call pierced the sky, now darkening over the town of Mostar: the minaret too shone in the gentle glow of lights. The light the heavens cast on the town was the same, distributed evenly; but the people on the ground quarrelled over what burned brighter—the cross or the minaret.

We were sitting in a restaurant by the river Neretva, watching engineers who were deftly sliding the last white stones in their slots, to complete the delicate arch which would hold up the rebuilt bridge of Mostar, called Stari Most (Old Bridge). There were about thirty people standing on a suspension bridge nearby, intently observing the engineers. When one of the men wearing a hard hat smiled, raising his thumb, all of us burst into a spontaneous applause. Fixing the bridge was hardly an architectural achievement, but the wounds this land had suffered required gentle healing. There is beauty even in Band-Aid.

The bridge in Mostar was not spectacular—it did not rise high, like the Lakshman Jhoola in Rishikesh, nor did it hang authoritatively over the river like the Howrah Bridge in Calcutta. It did not have the symmetry of the Sydney Harbour Bridge, the apparent endlessness of the Firth of Forth, or the awe-inspiring height of the Golden Gate Bridge. It was small, but it had a fond following, because it was a metaphor—it was symbolic and vulnerable.

The bridge in Mostar owed its origins to the expanding Ottoman Empire, which once commanded territory from Turkey to Hungary. The empire extended its reach by bringing more land under its control, building bridges over newly-conquered rivers. In 1453, Constantinople had become Istanbul, and by 1467, the Ottoman Empire had reached Mostar. Ninety years later, during the reign of Suleiman the Magnificent, an engineer called Mimar Hajrudin was given the task of building a bridge over the Neretva.

When completed, it was believed to be the widest man-made arch in the world at that time. It is still not known how scaffoldings were erected, how stone was transported, and how the construction was carried out. It took them nine years to build the bridge. It withstood the Austro-Hungarian Empire and survived the two world wars.

And it took one mad commander to bring it down.

The war between Croats and Bosniaks began in 1993, when a paramilitary army of hard-line volunteers came from Montenegro and Serbia, helped by the Yugoslav army, causing fear and havoc. Many Serbs fled, as did Bosniaks. The city of Mostar had people from all religious groups— Serbs with their Slavic, orthodox tradition, Bosniaks and their Islamic faith, and Croats, of whom many were Catholic. The bridge's fragile vulnerability became more visible. For centuries, the people of Mostar saw the bridge as a symbol of unity; invading armies came and went, but the bridge stood firm. Some Croats, unhappy with the presence of Bosniaks in their city, and sensing an opportunity to carve an ethnically-pure State, saw the bridge as an affront, chaining them to a past they wanted to tear apart. Croatia was an independent nation; Croats in Bosnia wanted to make off with as much territory as they could, just as Serbs in the north wanted to take away as much land as they could, and ideally reach all the way to the Adriatic, but they lacked the military means to do so. The people of Bosnia-Herzegovina were squeezed from all sides. The bridge was their link to the past when the country was united. The Bosniaks tried protecting the bridge—they hung tyres and plastic sheeting along the main span to protect it from snipers. But that November, a Croat commander, Slobodan Praljak, ordered his tanks to destroy it. The white stones came crumbling down into the river. The town was stunned.

A few years and many deaths later, once the guns had gone quiet, several divers, including some from Hungary and others from Mostar, recovered fragments of the bridge from the river, to explore if it could be put together again. But the remnants were now relics. When the international community took over administering Bosnia-Herzegovina after the Dayton Accord of 1995, rebuilding the bridge seemed a symbolic act, and so it became a priority. Appropriately, the contract went to a Turkish firm. As Michael Ignatieff points out in his moving account of the Bosnian war, *Empire Lite* (2003):

> It has become a metaphor, a bridge from the past to the future, a bridge between Croats and Bosniaks ... and a bridge between the Muslim world and Europe. The problem with all this metaphorical weight is that the promised reconciliation hasn't occurred. Instead of symbolising reconciliation, the restored bridge will be there to provide a substitute.

Substitute or not, on that night, the bridge looked beautiful, bathed by moonlight. I was with my family, joining my friends Kevin and Marija who have made Bosnia their home, and as we drank *sok od jagode*, or strawberry juice, and ate burek, a meat pie, and a flaky pastry made of cheese and spinach, called zeljanica, the evening felt sweet, warm with promise. The bridge was coming together again, and perhaps people would follow.

Bridges are important in these parts. With rivers gurgling down rolling hills and towns settling on either side, bridges connect separated halves; and in a country as culturally diverse as this, bridges have a special meaning.

The seminal novel about Bosnia-Herzegovina is *The Bridge over the Drina* (1945), whose author Ivo Andric won the Nobel Prize in 1961. The Ottomans had built the bridge over the Drina, and retreating Austrians had destroyed it during the First World War. The novel offers a moving portrait of a time when bridges united people, and Andric writes, recalling the bridge's significance:

> Here, where the Drina flows with the whole force of its green and foaming waters from the apparently closed mass of the dark deep mountains, stands a great clean-cut stone bridge with 11 wide sweeping arches. From this bridge spreads fanlike the whole rolling valley with the little Oriental town of Visegrad and all its surroundings, with hamlets nestling in the folds of the hills, covered with meadows, pastures and plum orchards, and criss-crossed with walls and fences and dotted with shaws and occasional clumps of evergreens. Looked at from a distance through the broad arches of the white bridge it

seems as if one can see not only the green Drina,
but all that fertile and cultivated countryside and
the southern sky above.... This great stone bridge,
a rare structure of unique beauty .... [that] was the
one real and permanent crossing in the whole middle
and upper course of the Drina and an indispensable
link between Bosnia and Serbia and further beyond.

Andric's description of the bridge, and how it was
destroyed, could be seen as a poet foreseeing the darkness
that lay ahead for Bosnia in the 1990s. And what followed
was indeed dark—the bridge was the place where Serb
paramilitaries committed dreadful atrocities against Bosniak
men.

Andric's bridge over the Drina, like the bridge over the
Neretva in Mostar, unites lives, linking communities and
traders. It told many stories, and it depended on what you
wanted to hear. There were happy stories connected with
bridges in this country: teenagers, in a rite of passage, jumping
off into the icy rivers below. Lovers strolling along the bridges,
admiring the sunset. Business sprouting around the bridges.

But bridges also divide people, and there were unhappy
stories too. During the Bosnian war, bodies were dumped off
the bridges to sink evidence of massacres. The week before
we were in Mostar, we were in Sarajevo, the capital, where we
had walked passed the Latin Bridge on Miljacka River.

There is nothing distinctive about the Latin Bridge. Built in
the sixteenth century during the Ottoman Empire, the stone
bridge has four arches with three pillars. It is sturdy, and was
built more for its functionality than for any artistic value. The
river isn't wide or deep; the bridge isn't high either. Nor is the
view from atop the bridge particularly noteworthy.

Today, a plaque stands there, saying that at this bridge,
on 28 June 1914, Gavrilo Princip assassinated the heir to the
Austro-Hungarian throne, Franz Ferdinand, and his wife Sofia.

During the Yugoslav era which ended in 1992, on one side of the bridge on the footpath, you could see two footsteps outlined in the concrete. Behind that you could see a sign in Cyrillic script that described what had happened there in more heroic terms. The footsteps have now been removed and a more neutral description is in place.

The feet whose impressions were planted there belonged to Gavrilo Princip, a Serbian who was a shade under twenty when he stood there and pulled the trigger that changed history.

That June morning Archduke Franz Ferdinand, who was the heir to the throne of the Austro-Hungarian empire, had gone to Sarajevo with his wife, Sofia. The royal family wasn't happy with the wedding—she was not born of royalty, nor was she from the aristocratic class, so she was not allowed to stand beside her husband at royal events in the imperial capital Vienna. In Sarajevo, the heir was away from meddlesome elders, and he could proudly sit by her side in an open car.

It was a sunny day, and the archduke had looked forward to his triumphal visit. He wore his military colours. The date had historic significance. On that day in 1389 the Serb kingdom was defeated by Turks, an incident that was a prelude to the eventual fall of Constantinople sixty-four years later, which forced European traders to look for new trading routes to Asia. Bosnia-Herzegovina would remain under Ottoman control until the Austro-Hungarian victory in 1878, and the province was eventually annexed into the Habsburg monarchy in 1908.

Serb nationalists resented Austro-Hungarian control of Bosnia-Herzegovina. For them, Franz Ferdinand represented a stumbling block, a monarchy that stood in the way of the unification of Greater Serbia.

Some local politicians had warned the archduke not to visit Sarajevo, but he was determined to go. He wanted to travel from the railway station along a long route by the river to the city hall, waving at the people. The city's Muslim mayor had urged people to celebrate his arrival by placing buntings and flags in their windows. They would travel at a leisurely pace in the open carriage. A local newspaper published details of the planned route, which seven young men were to find extremely useful.

Two assassins waited for the convoy at the Mostar Café, near the first bridge, the Cumurja. The assassins were inept; they hadn't known that the grenade they tossed would take ten seconds to detonate. It missed; another car was hit.

Princip was at the Latin Bridge. He was confused by the commotion that followed, the archduke's motorcade sped past, and he missed it. After he found out about the blast, the archduke decided to go to the hospital to see the officials who were hurt. To get there, he needed to return to the riverside and drive west. A disheartened Princip was walking near a pâtisserie when he saw two cars turn on the Latin Bridge—they weren't expected. He could see the archduke and his wife in the second car. The driver of the escort car had mistakenly turned to take the original route to the museum. A general asked the driver to reverse, saying they were going in the wrong direction. The car reversed slowly. Princip seized his chance, aimed straight at Franz Ferdinand, and shot him and Sofia. She died instantly; he died within moments of being taken to hospital. Those shots altered the course of history.

In 1914, European states had entered into a mind-boggling number of treaties to defend each other against their potential enemies. As soon as the Austro-Hungarian empire found that Serbia had supplied weapons to Princip and the other killers, it declared war on Serbia. Russia promptly mobilised its army to defend Serbia. Germany marched through Belgium and Luxembourg, threatening France, and Britain declared war on Germany. While Russia halted the Austro-Hungarians, the Germans stopped the Russian march westward. By November, the Ottoman Empire had joined the war. By 1918, millions of people had died. The conditions imposed on a defeated Germany after the war sowed the seeds of the Second World War. That hastened decolonisation, creating dozens of independent nations.

When I walked alongside the quay, I realised how distant those events seemed. The brave people of Sarajevo had suffered much worse more recently in the Bosnian war. They knew of the massacres in Srebrenica and the death camps of Manjaca. They probably wanted to turn the clock back. How far, though, was a different question—the answer to it flowed through the river between those two bridges.

There is another bridge in Sarajevo a sad memory hanging over it. At Vrbanja Bridge, two women, Olga Sucic, a Croat, and Suada Dilberovic, a Bosniak, were marching for peace along with tens of thousands of people in 1992 when they were shot at by a sniper. They are regarded as the first civilian casualties in the war that started in Bosnia that year. There is a plaque on that bridge commemorating the two young women who were innocently attempting to reclaim some of their tangled history from those who wanted to separate the strands.

Too much tragic history has traversed through these parts; the Holy Roman Empire, the Ottoman Empire, the Austro-Hungarian Empire have all left their marks, deeply embedding myths, stories, legends, and beliefs in the minds of its people, giving them long memories, so much so, that Slobodan Milosevic could nudge the region into bloody conflict by telling Serbs in a disputed speech, 'Nobody should beat you,' which many analysts regarded as coded words that stoked Serb resentment against Muslims over a six-hundred-year-old battle, igniting the Balkan war that followed in the 1990s.

And how interwoven those lives were! On another evening in Sarajevo, we walked on the pedestrian pathway that reminded us of the seamless whole this country had been before bouts of madness gripped some of its people periodically. We walked from the plaza near the opera house. The street was like a walk through Balkan history, as we began in the stately Austro-Hungarian part of the old town, with their flower-bedecked windows and bakeries and pharmacies, and then we watched the symmetry dissolve into the amorphous Ottoman part of the town, with its tea shops and minarets and a bath house and men wearing beards and some women wearing darker veils, reminding you that this town is an integrated whole, a city without borders, without any identifiable marker, where bells toll in churches and muezzins call from their minarets, and nobody seems to mind.

Indeed, Sarajevo hummed with life. There were musicians on the streets and children played in parks. Aleksandar Hemon, who now lives in the United States, writes of the "gigantic hum" of Sarajevo, "muffled by the dusk," when you could hear:

the clattering of dishwashers and buses; the music from bars and radios; the bawling of spoiled children; doors slamming; engines running; people fucking... They looked up and there were disinterested stars in the sky. Some of those stars didn't exist any longer, they had become black holes....

Meanwhile, lights would come on in homes on the green hills, and at that time, with the sky still blue, Sarajevo looked beautiful, as it did in the 1970s when it hosted the world table tennis championship; as it did in 1984, when it hosted the winter Olympics. But those sublime memories had a sinister undertone: within a decade, that failed poet, Radovan Karadzic had taken to the hills, making his nightmarish, dark visions real, as from the heights of what used to be ski slopes his men destroyed the minarets, burned a library, and shot people who followed a different faith.

Near that pedestrian plaza was the bakery—here, one morning, a shell was fired, killing twenty-two people who had queued up to buy bread. A cellist called Vedran Smailovic saw that, and then he sat in the hollow left by the shell, playing Albinoni's *Adagio* in memory of the victims. The war inspired exceptional love for the city among its writers. Hemon becomes almost poetic when he celebrates Sarajevo of the time when he was young:

> I remember linden trees blooming as if they were never to bloom again, producing a smell I can feel in my nostrils now. The boys were handsome, the girls beautiful, the sports teams successful, the bands good, the streets felt as soft as a Persian carpet, and the Winter Olympics made everyone feel that we were at the centre of the world. I remember the smell of apartment-building basements where I was making out with my date, the eye of the light switch glaring at us in the darkness. Then the light switch would go on—a neighbour coming down the stairs—and we would pull apart.
>
> It was that innocent time when he realised that there was a fundamental difference between 'girls who didn't have to wear a swimsuit top and … girls who did.… so much so that he got a slap on the back of his head for staring at a girl in a pink swimsuit, her nipples swollen.'

The war intruded, without any warning—unlike the neighbour turning on the switch giving young lovers time to pull apart, but like that resounding thud on the back of the head—bringing that halcyon age crashing down, like the bridge in Mostar. Hemon's fictional alter ego is a man called Josef Pronek. A girl Pronek fancied had lost her legs in a landmine explosion; another woman was killed by another shell, and Pronek recognised her when he saw her neck, which had a birthmark shaped like a crescent moon, and he remembered the birthmark after an intimate encounter with her in another time. Hemon reminded himself of that love, even as he was splashing us, his readers, with the warm blood, as heads exploded like watermelons.

And yet, it was necessary to build bridges there and yet it was so hard to do so. On a visit to Banja Luka, in the Serb-administered part of Bosnia-Herzegovina, I met a woman who translated for a Western broadcaster. She told me how difficult it had been for her to rent an apartment, because her lover was a Muslim. They had a child, but they hadn't had the time to get married, and she had found they were being ostracised by her neighbours, and ignored by the city council. The long-suppressed identity of faith had emerged, dwarfing the national identity Josip Broz Tito had tried to impose on this land. Churchill was wrong about calling India 'a geographic expression'—that honour belonged to Yugoslavia, where its boundaries tried to contain Croats who saw Bosniaks as their enemies, Bosniaks who fought Serbs, and Serbs who battled Croats. It was where some boundaries blurred—lovers could be necking and a neighbour would respect their privacy; but at another moment, neighbours would be at one another's throats. But to what end? In Hemon's imagination, the throat became the elegant neck of a loved one, to be pampered and caressed; in the poisoned, feverish imagination of Karadzic, it was the part of the body to be slashed.

Old epithets, which Tito had banished, had begun to recur: Croats were referred to as Ustasha, after the term by which those Croats who collaborated with the Nazis during the Second World War were known. A UN official told me that at that time they were so cruel that even the Nazis winced when they saw how they treated their prisoners. Then there were the Serbs, called Cetniks, as the graffiti had begun calling them again. And the Muslims were called balija, a rude reference to circumcised males.

Dividing people neatly, in three different piles, seemed like the natural way of doing business. In Mostar, executives of a company proudly showed me the files of their past employees —Muslim employees' records were in green folders, Croats in blue, and Serbs in white folders. Everything was separate. Had they been South African bureaucrats in the 1970s, they'd have won certificates for meritorious performance.

Mostar personified those divisions, with its parallel structures. Garbage disposal companies, schools, government departments, cultural centres, universities, hospitals: one for Croats, one for Bosniaks; one in the west, the other in the east. Many Croats still defiantly flew the Croatian flag, just as some Serbs flew the Serbian flag. At a café in western Mostar, the waitress gave me a bill that seemed too large for a cup of coffee until I realised that she had written the bill in kuna, the Croatian currency, even though Bosnia-Herzegovina's convertible mark is more stable, being pegged to the defunct German mark. 'I can't count in the other thing,' she told me somewhat contemptuously, not dignifying Bosnian currency by giving it a name. (Some Serbs would still quote prices in dinar, the Yugoslav currency.) Before the war, Bosniaks and Croats accounted for about one-third each of the city's 1,20,000, with Serbs, Jews, and the Roma making up the rest. Today, with the population down to 1,10,000, nearly 70 per cent of the people are Croats. Worried about being swamped, the Bosniaks won't unify the city's parallel structures. The physical bridge is ready; the metaphorical bridge still needs to be built.

Maintaining parallel structures is not cheap. The Croat part of the town is more prosperous, but the east has the tourist draw—the bridge. The few tourists who come dine in the east, admiring the bridge, but retire to smart hotels in the west, beyond the haunting boulevard called Bulevar, which was at one time the front-line of the war, where pock-marked shells of buildings remain unrepaired since the war. Many buildings are unrecognisable, with shattered windows, as if their eyes have been gouged.

'There is really no way back to the old bridge,' Ignatieff writes, 'just as there is no way back to the way Mostar was before the madness came. How do you build bridges between people? How do you help people to heal?' In Berlin, the people tore down a wall, but many residents said the wall in the mind remained. In Mostar, the people have rebuilt the bridge now, but the chasm remains.

On our last night in Mostar, as the sky darkened and the starlit night glowed, we saw its silhouette. The scaffolding no longer dominated the image, and it was still possible to see the fragile beauty of what Bosnia-Herzegovina used to be like. Once wounded, and heavily bandaged, the bridge was together again.

THE KILLING FIELDS OF CAMBODIA

'Angkor is at the heart of Cambodian people's identity,' Roland Paringaux had told me once at his apartment in Paris, as we sat drinking wine, surrounded by Southeast Asian art. Roland's wife is a senior official at the UN Educational, Scientific and Cultural Organisation (UNESCO). Roland is a distinguished foreign correspondent who has extensively written about Cambodia and Vietnam for *Le Monde Diplomatique*. He has also written the seminal book about the theft of art, *Razzia sur l'art: Vols, pillage, recels à travers le monde* (Raid on Art: Theft, Pillage and Concealment around the World). I have known Roland for some time now, as our passions have taken us to the same places but at different times. 'Angkor is at the core of Cambodian beliefs and myths,' he continued. 'They derive their sense of identity from Hindu epics. The temples will resonate with meaning when you go there. They have a Buddhist sense of detachment, but at the same time they revere those temples with passion and a sense of attachment,' he had told me.

In the room at my home in London where I write every morning, there is a framed charcoal drawing of *amritamanthan* ("the churning of nectar"), made on rice paper, which I had bought on that visit to Angkor Wat. It depicts the relief of one of the temples. In the story, *devas*, or angels, and *asuras*, or demons, worked together to churn the milky ocean for nectar. Poison spurted out first, followed by mythical animals and heavenly flowers. Finally, the nectar emerged, but the *asuras* ran away with it, reneging their deal of sharing it with the *devas*. God punished the *asuras*, and *devas* got their nectar.

The Cambodian people have had their share of demons and poison. They have waited patiently for the churning to end; they await nectar. Their search is old.

Like the Taj Mahal, the Great Wall, the Statue of Liberty, the Eiffel Tower, and the Big Ben, the world's largest complex of temples—Angkor Wat—has the misfortune of being commemorated by kitsch. You find it on countless badly-produced T-shirts, posters, miniature models, post-cards, and other memorabilia. In Angkor's case, the temple also has the misfortune that its name graces the cans of Cambodia's leading brand of beer.

That sounds odd: temples are sacred; consuming alcohol maybe a spiritual experience for some, but priests hadn't intended that when they recommended that everyone should follow a spiritual life. Many religions frown upon drinking. But Southeast Asia is a practical region, where the sacred and the profane can coexist, and where, as Emile Durkheim suggested, the sacred isn't always holy, and the profane not entirely evil. And the gods of commerce smother all debate.

Many Cambodians resented the diminution, and some would argue, vulgarisation, of Angkor Wat—from being

Cambodia's symbol of supreme pride and glory to a beer can. But Cambodia was poor, and the beer made money. The beer of choice at the Foreign Correspondents' Club in Phnom Penh was inevitably Angkor. The bartender was a devout Buddhist, and by serving that beer, he probably broke some precepts daily. But business came first.

I was at the club, listening to some journalists who had been living in Cambodia for some time telling me how the Cambodian people revered the sacred. We had just seen the screening of Spalding Gray's fascinating monologue, *Swimming in Cambodia*, about his trips to the region and his experiences during the filming of Roland Joffe's 1984 film, *The Killing Fields*, in which he had acted as a State Department diplomat. Cambodia was brimming with the international community that year, as elections were announced, and the United Nations Transitional Authority in Cambodia had set up base and its officials were seen operating everywhere, helping establish the basic political infrastructure to build a state. Four-wheel drives of aid agencies kept driving up and down the streets; and stories—usually rumours—kept landing on the laps of journalists.

Cambodia had suffered enormously during the Pol Pot years of 1975-1979, and the international community wanted to do something to help Cambodia restore its jewel, Angkor Wat. The French restored a hotel; a Malaysian tycoon brought electrical power; Thais wanted their airline to fly there directly. Bringing the temples back to their former glory was on everyone's agenda. Several European journalists were complaining to me that Indians had taken it upon themselves to do it their own way: the Indians were washing, scrubbing, and at times even repairing the haunting sculptures on the walls of the ancient temples (*quelle horreur!*). Broken idols should be kept broken, they felt—authenticity mattered, even if the breaking of the idol may not have been because of the weather, but because of vandalism.

The way they described the Indian effort, you would have thought that India had let loose a bunch of incompetent masons and painters who were turning those temples into colourful pastiche versions of modern temples of the sort you would see on the streets of Malaysia and Singapore. So when I met an Indian diplomat later that week, I asked him what was going on.

'Have you been there yet?' he asked me. 'You should go and take a look first. In our culture temples are living entities. They are not relics. People go to the temples daily with their offerings of flowers or coconuts. We wash our idols—we don't let moss grow. A visit to a temple is part of our ritual. It is not like going to a museum once a year only to take pictures. You go to the temple in the present, not to look at the past. Indian temples live in the present. We want these temples also to live in the present. Cambodian people are like our people. They understand this. We are here to help them.'

In the Indian mind centuries often coexist, but to the European mind, what was firmly in the past had to remain there and be venerated. Many years later, while walking through the Asian section of the British Museum with my sons, I came across a fine, large statue of Ganesha, the elephant-headed God. Next to the statue was an Indian family, suitably reverential and awestruck. They were on their first trip out of India. It was late spring and the weather was pleasant, but it was cold for the visiting Indian family. The grandson, who looked about eight, was wearing two sweaters, which made him look uncharacteristically pudgy. He stood near the Ganesha, as his father told him to go closer to the sculpture, as he prepared to take a photograph of his son. The grandparents stood on either side. The son, playfully, placed his arm along the crossed leg of Ganesha and smiled brightly.

Out of nowhere, a guard emerged, and sternly told the family not to touch the idol. The Indians, used to touching the idol, were unaccustomed to this. In India, the family could have garlanded the same idol, smeared it with vermillion, and if made of clay, carried it on their shoulders, surrendering it in the sea on Ananta Chaturdashi. The god made of clay had ephemeral value. Gods of stone were eternal. But this Ganesha's departure from India was complete. He was a British object, not an Indian idol anymore.

At the museum, Ganesha was cast in stone, and was a work of art—it was not to be touched, nor to be felt. The distance—between the work of art and the visitor—had to be observed and respected. My late mother, who was a tourist guide and took people of all nationalities to the Elephanta Caves across from the Gateway of India, often complained to me about the lack of reverence some tourists showed when they smoked in those rock cutout caves, unaware of the religious significance of the idols there. It was a fine balance: Indians touched their idols but revered them; westerners respected art and placed the idols outside the reach of the human touch—and yet, some would have no perspective of their cultural significance outside the museum, and when taken out of the museum, those objects of veneration sometimes turned into quotidian pieces of furniture, the westerner entirely unaware of the offence that could create. Martand Singh, a former secretary of the Indian National Trust for Art and Cultural Heritage once said: 'Ultimately, a god becomes an ashtray.'

There was an ironical contrast here: I was with journalists who were complaining about Indians washing the Angkor Wat idols clean, as if scrubbing them of their value, while sipping beer from a can carrying the image of the same temples. They found nothing contradictory between what they said and what they were doing. The westerner wanted to see the temples covered with moss, looking like relics, untouched by human civilisation; Indian restorers wanted the temples to have a lived-in look.

Angkor Wat was Cambodian. And it was also Indian.

Even a mass murderer like Pol Pot, who ruled Cambodia between 1975 and 1979, understood that temples are holy places; you don't treat them lightly. Not only did the national flag of his short-lived Republic of Kampuchea have the outline of Angkor's temples, his soldiers were warned not to loot those temples. They protected the site the only way they knew–by planting landmines around the temples, making it impossible for anyone to visit.

When I went to Siem Reap to see the temples, an American Vietnam-era veteran, who was also at my hotel, accompanied me. He was now helping provide artificial limbs to Cambodian victims of mines. He told me that Pol Pot liked mines because they were perfect soldiers: 'courageous, they never sleep, never miss.'

In Siem Reap, our guide had instructed us to follow each of his footsteps precisely. Even a single misstep could be disastrous, he told us repeatedly, because by straying we might stumble onto a landmine.

There were other dangers too, because some soldiers who hadn't yet surrendered continued to target foreigners. To go to the temples, we had to agree to be accompanied by these boy-guards carrying machine guns. The guide repeated that we had to follow our guard step by step, literally. We had to place our feet exactly along the same trail, and follow his footsteps. There were mines everywhere.

To be sure, the mine clearance programme has been active in Cambodia, and it has been more successful than Cambodian democracy. Many mines have been cleared, but many more mines remained buried under the grass. At one time, according to some estimates, there were ten million mines in Cambodia. The Cambodian Mine Action Centre estimates the number to be between four million and six million.The only mines visitors now see near Angkor Wat are in the Land Mine Museum, built by a former Khmer Rouge soldier, Aki Ra, who wants to educate the world about the horrors of that period. The bulk of the remaining mines are near Battambang and the north-west, along the Thai border, the last holdout of the Khmer Rouge. With the surrender of most active Khmer Rouge leaders, the risks of those mines have diminished, as many surrendering troops have helped authorities by identifying the places where they had placed the mines, so that the government can begin the difficult process of deactivating them. The job of deactivating mines is dangerous and labour-intensive. It is also a game of chess, between the sapper and the maker of the explosives. It is poker too, except that the sapper cannot see the face of the bomb-maker. He must unravel, scrape off the paint, and once convinced, cut the wire, in an attempt to break off the circuit that would explode the device—think of the mind-games Kip has to play in Michael Ondaatje's *The English Patient* (1993):

> The tightening of the concrete ball in mid-air, braced with the second rope, meant the two wires would not pull away, no matter how hard he attacked it. He stood up and began to chisel the disguised mine gently, blowing away loose grain with his mouth, using the feather stick, chipping more concrete off...Very slowly he unearthed the series of wires. There were six wires, jumbled up, all painted black. He brushed the dust off the mapboard the wires lay on.
>
> Six black wires.
>
> [T]his opponent had not just concreted the thing but painted all the characters black. Kip was being pulled into a psychological vortex. With the knife he began to scrape the paint free, revealing a red, a blue, and a green. Would his opponent have also switched them? He'd have to set up a detour with black wire of his own like an oxbow river and then

test the loop for positive or negative power. Then
he would check it for fading power and know where
the danger lay.

That necessary painstaking work goes on. And the country is
not yet mine-free—it cannot be so, given the ease with which
mines can be placed and their low cost, sometimes as little as
Rs 150.

As we left that morning, I saw three trucks pass by, each of
them filled with ripe watermelons. A boy sat on the edge of
the last one, his feet dangling merrily from the edge. He waved
at me; he was smiling. The watermelons were shaking mildly,
bumping into one another.

Anywhere else in the world, the sight of a truck filled with
fruit on a country road would have been unremarkable. The
boy's job, it seemed, was to make sure that the watermelons
didn't start to roll over and fall on the road. Or maybe it was a
joy ride for him. The road itself was uneven, and the truck kept
jumping as it sped away.

It was a happy moment for the boy. At that time in that
country, it was also an unusual moment. A few years earlier,
there would have been no trucks on that road. If any did pass
by, it would have been a military truck.

Looking at the truck, our guide seemed a bit unnerved. I
asked him if he was all right. He tried to speak, but he stopped.
I stopped. Then he looked at me, and hesitantly told me the
story of how as a little boy he had walked once, and seen a
truck drive by. Excited by the truck, he started chasing it. But
the truck was going fast. He was panting, when the truck's
back-flap opened suddenly, and out fell two severed heads. A
guard saw him running towards the truck and reached for his
gun. The boy fell on the ground, rolled over to the ditch, and
hid behind a large tree. Terrified, he howled.

I reflected on the image I had just seen, of the boy in the truck who had been smiling at me, his feet dangling. The same boy, barely a couple of decades earlier, would have been a child soldier carrying a sub-machinegun. Had he stood straight with the gun by his side, the gun would have reached his chest or higher. The goods inside the truck would have been jade or timber. Or, as my guide once saw, there would be dead bodies. And the boy would not have smiled, because he had probably been taught not to smile. He had learned to trust no one. In Pol Pot's Cambodia, they denounced their teachers and parents. If I had tried taking his photograph, he'd have aimed his gun towards me and killed me.

The temple complex that makes up Angkor Wat is nearly a thousand years old. In the twelfth century, Suryavarman II expanded the city of Angkor and built many temples, including Angkor Wat. His empire weakened with successive invasions from Chams in what is now modern Vietnam, and later from what is now Thailand. By the fifteenth century, forests shrouded the temples and thick vegetation hid them from view until Henri Mouhot "discovered" the site in the nineteenth century. In his 1983 work *A History of Cambodia*, David Chandler points out that the temple is the only major building to open to the west. The visitor is to follow its bas-reliefs by moving counterclockwise; the customary way of reading a bas-relief lies in moving in a clockwise direction, known by the Sanskrit term, *pradakshina*. Scholars have said that the reverse direction is associated with the dead—Angkor Wat could be a tomb.

Mathematics is also involved. Chandler continues:

> The distances that a person entering the temple
> will traverse coincide with the eras that the visitor
> is metaphorically living through en route to the

statue of Vishnu in the central tower. Walking forward and away from the west, which is the direction of death, the visitor moves backward into time, approaching the moment when the Indians proposed that time began.

In the 1860s perplexed French colonialists, following the legends told by peasants, came across Angkor Wat, and what they saw stunned them. Mouhot made the temple complex popular in the West, after which a steady stream of fortune seekers, engravers, scholars, explorers, archaeologists, and historians made their way to Angkor. The undermining of Cambodians was a recurrent theme: some maintained that Cambodians could not have built such sophisticated temples, arguing that only an invading army could have constructed them. Others helped themselves to its treasures, including the famous French writer Andre Malraux. He was later to become a minister of culture in France, but in the 1920s, he was arrested in Cambodia for trafficking antiques. It is odd to think of a mass murderer like Pol Pot guarding Angkor Wat, and half a century earlier, a Paris sophisticate like Malraux, talking of culture and humanity, stealing Angkor's statues. Ironies occur in the unlikeliest places.

Cambodia was a French colony, and French administrators and Thai rulers had drawn up a series of agreements in the early twentieth century to mark the vague frontier between Thailand, Cambodia, and Laos. Under the 1907 delimitation protocol, Thailand ceded the territories of Battambang, Siem Reap (which happens to mean "Thai defeat") and Sisophon to Cambodia in exchange for Dan Sai and Krat. France tried to secure these pacts in late 1930s, but the Second World War broke out before the agreements could be signed.

The Thais took advantage of this. Ostensibly claiming to be neutral during the war, they offered the Japanese access through its territory to attack the Allies (which the Japanese dutifully did) and in return the Thais got access to vast parts of Cambodia and Laos. When the war ended, victorious Allies disregarded the Thai agreements with Japan, and the 1907 agreement came back in force. The Thais protested, but in 1962, the International Court of Justice granted sovereignty over Angkor Wat to Cambodia.

Then the Vietnam War intensified, increasing the strategic importance of Thailand. Lon Nol's regime collapsed in Cambodia, and in 1975, Pol Pot ascended to power, just as North Vietnamese forces took control of Saigon. Cambodia emerged from Pol Pot's bloody Communist rule in 1979, only after Hun Sen's rebel forces, assisted by the Vietnamese, overran the Khmer Rouge positions. Ten years later, Thai Prime Minister Chatchai Chunhawan would talk of turning old battlefields into a prosperous marketplace, as part of his policy of transforming Southeast Asia into a *suwannaphume*. However, the Cambodians, wary of the Thais, encouraged the Malaysians to invest in their country.

'Malaysians are welcome here because they are not Thais,' I remember the late Southeast Asia scholar, Michael Leifer telling me one evening in Phnom Penh. We were walking along the main boulevard, and Leifer was lamenting that the cycle-rickshaw drivers, whose tinkling bells you could hear once again, no longer spoke French.

But was French ever their language?

The night before I went to see the temples, I saw a performance of *Reamker*, the Cambodian version of the Hindu epic, *Ramayana*. The narrative had reached Cambodia a thousand years ago, when South Indian kingdoms extended their reach in Southeast Asia. In *Reamker*, Rama is known as Preah Ream, and Ravana is called Krong Reap. Sita is Neang Seda, and Rama's brother Lakshman is known as Preah Leak. We saw a part of *Reamker* on a moonlit night, as little boys, dressed in blue tunics and yellow pants that looked like loose *churidars*, danced, their heavily made-up faces cheerful. They were part of the *vanar-sena*, or Hanuman's monkey-brigade, building the bridge to Lanka. In a variation from the Sanskrit *Ramayana*, in *Reamker*, the monkeys would place the stones to build the bridge, but mermaids stole the stones. Hanuman arrives at the scene, determined to defeat the mermaids. Instead, he falls in love with their princess. She is also smitten. The mermaids cooperate, the monkeys dance, the bridge is built.

Cheered by the simplistic tale of good and evil, we left the next morning to see those stories on the walls of the temples of Angkor Wat. These temples represented a peculiar mix of Hindu and Buddhist traditions obviously because the Cambodians practiced Theravada Buddhism. In many of the sculptures, Rama looked more like Siddhartha, the prince who became Buddha. (In another narrative variation, unlike Rama, Preah Ream shunned violence, letting his brother and the monkeys to do what he wouldn't.)

Reality was different. If you scratched any surface in Cambodia, fresh wounds lay beneath, bleeding quietly. Many warriors—dead and silent—lay beneath the surface. As journalists, we routinely heard reports of discoveries of mass graves filled with bodies. The dignified silence of the people concealed enormous pain.

'Almost every place in Cambodia has a ghost story attached to it,' Loung Ung was to tell me in an email conversation several years later, when I was reviewing her book *Lucky Child* (2005) for *Newsweek* magazine. 'I think it's because we practice Theravada Buddhism: our gods are able to cross between the borders of the world. And we believe that our ancestors are always with us. When so many people died in our country in the '70s, we ended up with a lot of haunted, unresolved lives. We don't fear ghosts. We respect those spirits, still wandering in our country.'

॰॰

Negotiating grief and consoling one's self isn't easy. Consolation is the process of fighting grief through acceptance. Greek and Latin cultures recognise it as the middle and concluding stages of coping with grief, a part of mourning. It is where the mind tells the heart to accept the inevitable, and offers solace, to make it calm. Consolation helps repair the heart when the loss is unbearable. Comfort becomes the substitute for loss. Consolation recognises the loss.

The adjustment is not emotional; it is intellectual. Does Buddhism, with its emphasis on detachment, assist the process? Does stoicism help? Is the pain less, and the hurt assuaged? Or are those wounds buried deeper?

How does a nation console itself?

The reality surrounding the temples and the cities is harsh. Drive outside Phnom Penh, and the guide will casually point out a paddy patch, saying there, that was a killing field. Stop the car at what appears to be a road shrine, and you see a mountain of skulls, a monument to the victims of the Pol Pot years.

The numbers pile up, like those skulls. The poet James Fenton is also a renowned foreign correspondent, and he spent time reporting in Cambodia during the war. I stood by the side of one such shrine, looking at the field, imagining people being lined up before being shot—particularly those who wore glasses (which meant they could read and were intellectuals), who had smooth hands (which meant they worked in offices, and not in the fields), or who spoke French (which meant they were tinged by the colonial experience, and would challenge and ask questions, instead of obeying the leader). Joffe's film, *The Killing Fields* had coloured much of my imagination. But Fenton's chilling poem was more vivid:

One man shall smile one day and say goodbye,

Two shall be left, two shall be left to die.

One man shall give his best advice,

Three men shall pay the price.

One man shall live, live to regret,

Four men shall meet the debt.

One man shall wake from terror to his bed,

Five men shall be dead.

One man to five. A million men to one,

And still they die. And still the war goes on.

The killing field itself looks like any other expanse of land. The grass is green; you see some telegraph poles; there are blue hills far beyond. We are outside the city. The grass sways in the mild breeze. It is bright and sunny. The presence of a few tiny saffron flags is the only way you can find the shrine. It looks like a small, road-side *wat*, with the conical crown on top. And then you face it, and you see that mountain of skulls.

There is a more permanent memorial in Phnom Penh. It is a former school. As far as schools go, there is nothing remarkable about Tuol Sleng. The building stands unobtrusively along an avenue in Phnom Penh. But it is in its ordinariness, in the way it becomes an indistinguishable part of the city's landscape, by not drawing any attention to itself, that the school gives meaning to Hannah Arendt's chilling phrase, the banality of evil.

At one time, Tuol Sleng was the torture chamber of the Khmer Rouge—its own little shop of horrors. In July 2010, the Cambodian tribunal adjudicating war crimes found Duch, an officer of the Khmer Rouge, guilty for his tyranny in Tuol Sleng. The sentence wasn't going to offer salve to the wounds of thousands of victims who had been in the jail. But the intent of the verdict was to offer a sense of closure, or completeness, to those who were taken to that building, and then jailed, beaten, tortured, and killed for crimes they didn't commit.

The rooms inside were filled with ordinary objects—a bed made of iron, on which victims were tied and their arms and legs stretched to inflict maximum pain. The beds were rusted. There were dark blotches on the wall. I didn't need a guide to tell me it was blood—and not one person's blood, but of many, mingled together in pain, splattered on the wall, frozen in time. There were other tools—some used to dig, some used to cut, some used to sharpen, a few to drill walls, some to push nails through walls. But in this school none had been used for those intended everyday purposes; each had been used instead to savage human bodies, to cause wounds, to puncture skin, to let blood pour out.

To avoid that pain, people were willing to admit to anything. I read confessions, written in crooked, shaky handwriting that looked like a child's scribbles. The confessors were young men, many of them foreigners, saying they had plotted to overthrow the government. The sheets on which the confessions were written had faded, as had the ink, but the desperation was apparent—the unsteady hand suggested how the people were willing to confess to whatever the man with the iron chain demanded, if only to stop the beatings. But the pain only ended with their death.

I recall reading outrageous confessions written by stranded Indian sailors working on merchant ships admitting to being spies; a backpacker owning up to being an agent of the US Central Intelligence Agency (CIA); another Thai national saying he was going to blow up an army truck; and an interminably convoluted account about the seizure of the American marine vessel, Mayaguez. As Chandler noted in his book, *Voices from S-21: Terror and History in Pol Pot's Secret Prison* (1999), the torture methods deployed at the prison were inspired from a veritable chamber of horrors—the Reign of Terror in eighteenth-century France, the 1930s show trials of Moscow, the land reform and "reeducation" campaigns in China in the 1940s, and in Vietnam a decade later:

> Torture was widely inflicted at S-21.... Few prisoners maintained their innocence for long. Considered guilty from the moment they arrived—the traditional Cambodian phrase for prisoner, *neak thos,* translates literally as "guilty person"—thousands of these men and women were expected to confess their guilt in writing before they were taken off to be killed. .... The severity of practices at S-21 and the literalness with which interrogators went about their business also reflected prerevolutionary Cambodian punitive traditions, by which prisoners were never considered innocent and crimes of *lèse-majesté* were mercilessly punished.

Indeed, nobody was safe at Tuol Sleng. One guard was killed for burning a wasp's nest, another because he shouted, 'The house is on fire,' in his sleep. Typically, there would be three interrogators at a time—one to interrogate, one to write it down, and one to induce responses by torturing the prisoner. People were beaten with bare hands, sticks, and electric wires were used and placed in particularly vulnerable and sensitive parts of the body. Fingernails were pulled out, and prisoners were forced to eat their own faeces and drink their own urine. Bugs, some carrying venom, would be let loose on their naked bodies.

Peter Maguire and Mike Ritter wrote in *Thai Stick* (2014):

> A manual found at S-21 discouraged torture that ended with death, or what it called "a loss of mastery." The objective was "to do politics," to extract all the information possible before killing the prisoner. The goal of the torture was... to

loosen memories: "Beat until he tells everything, beat him to get at the deep things." To find out if the prisoner was lying or not, the Khmer Rouge put a plastic bag over the suspect's head, and if his or her carotid artery throbbed, the person was considered guilty.

There was no purpose or logic to the arrests the Khmer Rouge made. Mike Deeds and Chris Delance were in a boat and trying to escape from a Khmer Rouge patrol boat chasing after them. They surrendered, the Khmer Rouge boat smashed into theirs, and they were blindfolded and brought to port. The reason: Khmer Rouge had recently fought US Marines in the *Mayaguez* incident in May 1975, when they had seized an American merchant ship. The US Marines had retaliated without knowing that the ship's crew was released. In the three-day battle that followed, fifteen Americans and thirteen Khmer Rouge soldiers had died.

Deed and Delance were taken to Tuol Sleng in December 1978. Their confessions sound almost surreal; both became imaginative, crafting narratives that were implausible in the hope that it would convince the interrogators and they might free them. Deeds claimed to have been received training in Virginia and California and become an operational officer. He created an elaborate yarn, about tracking down a Colombian drug dealer and revolutionary, and attempting to subvert an environmental group in Hawaii. Delance would claim he penetrated student groups and in Maui he infiltrated a cult called "The Source" and Hare Krishnas. He wove a fantasy of pretending to be a hippie learning about arms smuggling in the Caribbean. He was in Cambodia to turn local fishermen into spies for the United States.

Still reeling from the confessions I read, and trying to imagine the pain the prisoners suffered, I followed my guide to our last stop in the prison—a hall where I saw a large map of

Cambodia made entirely of skulls. Words were not necessary to describe what I saw; silence—out of respect for those who died, and out of the sense of horror over those responsible— was the only possible response. And yet, what I also recall is the way some tourists from Singapore behaved there. They posed in front of the map, smiling cheerfully, flashing the V sign, as if they were standing next to Mickey Mouse in Disneyland. Flashbulbs popped regularly.

'This is not unusual,' my guide told me. 'Western tourists often cry here, but the Asians—the Koreans, the Japanese, the Chinese, the Singaporeans—they smile and wave; they talk. We say this is what happened to us—we lost our families— but they don't seem concerned. They don't respect our dead.'

The western response to a tragedy of this scale is of guilt. Ian Buruma writes about it in *The Wages of Guilt*. Asian response is often burdened by shame. That also leads to denial. Many Japanese continue to believe that Japan was a victim in that war, and point to the American atomic bombs that razed Hiroshima and Nagasaki. Comfort women (as women used as sex slaves were called) from Korea and elsewhere, forced to serve as prostitutes during the war, continue to demand recompense and justice. But successive Japanese ministers find it astonishingly hard to say "sorry," or to do anything to relieve the hard lives of the victims of Japanese adventurism in Asia. Buruma, who has lived in Japan, says this unwillingness partly stems from an overwhelming sense of shame. That shame prevents Japan from acknowledging the past, offering redress, and moving on.

Acceptance of guilt allows for atonement; part of that atonement lies in cleansing of the soul by expressing remorse, and seeking forgiveness. Shame, on the other hand, prevents remorse to emerge; pride gets in the way. Acute embarrassment shrouds other emotions, not allowing the self to acknowledge the harm done, leaving those emotions unattended, dormant.

There is a difference. The responsibility for the killings in Cambodia rests primarily with the government of that time. It wasn't Japan's fault, nor did the Singaporeans or Koreans carry out the killings, even if they were callous enough to flash those V signs. But the genocide was in their neighbourhood. Many people in this part of the world consider themselves Buddhists. The enlightened one is their spiritual inspiration— the Buddha of the Middle Path, of non-violence, of compassion —but also of detachment. Why did they fail to respond to Tuol Sleng at a more human level?

Part of the answer lies in the notion of shame. You feel it when you believe you are responsible and the matter of honour is involved. You know you have done, or are doing, something wrong. But you don't want to draw attention to it. You don't want to talk about what happened in the past, if it is shameful. Pride is the stumbling block. While Japan, Singapore, or Korea were not responsible for those deaths, and Pol Pot was singularly the architect of the genocide, many governments in East Asia had continued to support Pol Pot-backed rebels till the early 1990s, considering his government legitimate, because they opposed Hun Sen who had come to power riding on Vietnamese shoulders. That Cold War calculation silenced more rational views. They were not executioners, but at some level, they were accomplices. The tourists I saw were unlikely to have been involved in any of those decisions. But they came from partially open societies, and their worldview was probably formed by what they read in their national dailies and saw on their local television channels. Fed on the idea that Communist regimes are bad, that external invasions are always wrong, their elite opposed Hun Sen. And in the binary view of universe, if you opposed Hun Sen, you supported Pol Pot.

Guilt requires the maturity to acknowledge; shame prevents the acknowledgement of guilt.

The end of the Second World War, and later, the fall of the Berlin Wall, led Europeans to identify that which is common to them all, and binds them. They searched for universal values within their cultures, their ethos. And they could recognise what was wrong and move on from there. Many years later in Berlin, as I walked through another memorial built to mark another colossal atrocity—the Holocaust—I felt the silence that cries out for some sound, of love or hope. I saw large pillars of uneven heights, which made them look like waves that rose and fell. Their height reduced, the ground beneath your feet seemed to rise, making you feel as though you were sinking in a tunnel that was getting narrower, squeezing you. But just as you adjusted to a particular level, it would change again, altering the topography, confusing you about where the ground lay, where the sky reached, and where you stood within that space.

Disorientation is a complex idea, but most of us have felt it sometime. What that spatial experiment achieved was something no photograph, or testimony could: it disturbed your sense of certainty, of your moral universe. This was Germany, the land of philosophers such as Kant and Schopenhauer, and authors such as Goethe, Mann, and Schiller, the home of abstract ideas. But also the land which, driven by an insane, messianic zeal, devoured millions of lives. That space symbolised the lives cut short, destabilising one's moral universe, as if you were all alone aboard a ship tossing in waves.

Despite the decades since the end of the Vietnam war, Asia hasn't undergone a cathartic re-evaluation. Shame is an overwhelming Asian emotion because of the importance Asia attaches to "face". That face prevents us from confronting our past. In his 1983 novel *Shame*, Salman Rushdie called "shame" inadequate to describe the range of nuance that the word *sharam* implied: 'Embarrassment, discomfiture, decency, modesty, shyness, the sense of having an ordained place in the world, and other dialects of emotion for which English has no counterparts.'

ॐ

Recently, at a conference on genocide, I met Youk Chhang, who lives in Phnom Penh and runs the centre documenting the Cambodian genocide. For a custodian of such brutal tales, he is remarkably sunny in his disposition, and showed us a film that meticulously puts together the story of a killing.

The film is about Mon, who was part of Pol Pot's militia. The interviewer asked him what happened during the war. A man had died in the neighbourhood. He was old and lame; needed a crutch to walk, as he had lost one leg to a landmine. He had been a soldier in Lon Nol's army. He was taken away and killed. Did he know about that?

'Yes, I remember him. He lived near those trees. We killed him,' he says calmly.

'Did you tie him up before you killed him?' the interviewer asks.

'No, he had only one leg; he could not escape,' he says, smiling. Somebody thrashed him, he says. They made him sit down and tied his hands. He was soon killed, and his body dumped in a ditch, filled quickly.

His daughter was able to identify him after she dug the grave with her bare hands. She identified him because of his gold tooth and amputated leg.

The interviewer asked her: 'Do you know why he was killed?'

'I don't know; they were killing everybody,' she said. Tears welled up, and she played with her beads, pursing her lips. She maintained her dignity. 'What can I do?'she asked.

She has seen the killer, as he lives in their midst. The killer knows who she is, but has not said sorry to her.

'Do you regret what you did?' the interviewer asks him.

'Yes I do,' he says, but still showing no emotion. 'At that time I was tricked to follow orders, so I followed them. Today I realise that my life and theirs are all the same. But it is now too late.'

'Do you believe in karma?' the interviewer asks the murderer.

'Yes, I do.'

'You killed many people. Are you afraid of the next life?'

'I don't know,' he says. 'If there is no karma, maybe it is all over. If it is, we'll torment each other in the next life,' he says.

But is there life after death?

'I understand the Buddhist precepts but don't know what to make of that.'

The victim's daughter, on the other hand, says she no longer believes in those precepts.

I think of Savet Akrun, the woman with dry eyes looking for her lost son in Margaret Drabble's haunting novel, *Gates of Ivory*. Mme Savet Akrun is 'sitting there so patiently with the sorrows of thousands resting on her thin, unbowed shoulders, asking, "where is my son?"'

Where is my son? That's her question, appearing frequently, like a leitmotif. Drabble writes:

> Mme Savet Akrun, mother of four, was held in Camp Site Ten, on the Thai-Kampuchean border. She had walked over the border in 1979 with her three younger children, from the countryside of Seam Reap province, where she had been living and working in a village. Her husband, her parents, her parents-in-law, her sisters, her brother and several of her nieces and nephews had all died in the terror, some of illness and some by violence. Her husband had owned garages and owned a small cinema in Phnom Penh. She had taught in an infants' school and was now employed in a camp by the Khmer Women's Association Centre for Adult Education. "I

am one of the lucky survivors," she was quoted as saying, "but my life can give me no joy until I find my son." She had last seen him in a small village near Battambang. He had been marched away by a group of Khmer Rouge soldiers…. "Is he still alive? How can I find him?"

ॐ

Understanding the horrors of the past century is not easy. The twelfth century temples of Angkor Wat carry on their walls mythological tales of good triumphing over evil. When the French explorers awakened the temples from their slumber in 1860s, they supposedly revealed a civilisation far ahead of its time. Or was it a continuing story that they told? Did they in some ways presage the Cambodian conflicts of the last century?

The walls of those temples, scrubbed, restored and cleaned, unveil stories that celebrate the triumph of good over evil. But the walls also honour wars, with their own paradigm of cruelty and violence. How were those prisoners treated at that time? Did they have Tuol Slengs? Lao Gais? Gulags? Concentration camps? Did those gods treat civilians better than the way victors have treated the vanquished in the past century? When Lanka burned after Ravana's fall—an iconic image in some of those temples—did no innocent Lankan die? Was everyone who died evil? Was there any targeted killing? Collateral damage? And do we read that mythology in a particular way because the author of the story was an admirer of the victor, Rama?

Not all heroes are perfect. When you stray too far from myths and histories, the questions that emerge are often uncomfortable. You have to tread carefully; there are landmines. And that's why it is safer to follow the boy with the AK-47, instead of walking on the road not taken.

WALK LIKE AN EGYPTIAN

In the beginning there is the fragrance. Of fresh, soft, round bread, hundreds of them, bread which looks like rotis, far tougher than the *roomali* but much softer than the *tandoori*, not flat, but like a flying saucer or rugby ball, not perfectly round either, piled high in a cart, smelling of flour and smoke and fire, emerging fresh from the bakery. The bread is not stacked in rows; it is dumped in the cart as it is prepared, and people pick it up casually, pay the baker, and carry on, munching, their first meal of the day. Its smell is sweet. You hear the gentle pounding of the dough, which will soon take the spherical shape of heavenly delight.

It is not yet hot—it is the hour after the first prayers, and the street is full of old men walking these uneven streets, wearing their long gowns—pale blue and green, pieces of olive or cheese wrapped within the bread, as they meander past shops opening for the day. They pat children leaving for school, avoiding the holes on the sidewalk, ignoring the tourists who are out with their flashy cameras and large telephoto lenses, busy capturing the slow unfolding of rhythms of a street in old Cairo in the morning.

I had seen the old city from a garden the previous evening, before the sun went down. Minarets had sprouted on the horizon, and under that pale, fading sun, the domes had shone, making the twilight hour magical. The next day we are in al-Gamaliya—the long road that formed the central artery of Naguib Mahfouz's life in Cairo—near the mosque of al-Hakim, close to the *sabils*, or fountains built by devout traders for people thirsty for water, at the *suq* (market) and the *hamam* (public bath), and those shops, past the persistent hawkers of Khan al-Khalili. There were women in *niqabs* quietly inspecting lacy lingerie, concealing their excitement shrouded beneath their veils. We saw fresh olives and garlic and tomatoes and mint piled high for sale. A milkman poured milk in steel tumblers and sold it to women who looked away from me, hiding their faces when I tried to photograph them. Then my friend Steve took me past the shops with *Qur'an* and carpets. There was a chicken seller, an old shop selling palm leaves, an ironing shop, and cafés with their fresh coffee and more bread. There, a store selling cotton by the sack, and toy stores now flooded with Chinese goods. Beyond, the wholesale market, where traders sell copper, coal, and steel bars; and still beyond, the street with jewellery and perfumes. Across that, there was another store, as if stuck in 1919, the year of the uprising against the British, where I could buy large clocks and watches, each showing a different time, as if each were frozen in another age. A donkey cart passed by, oblivious of us.

This was the heart of *Bayn al-Qasrayn*, the Arabic title of Naguib Mahfouz's novel, called in English, *Palace Walk*, or literally, between two palaces. *Bayn al-Qasrayn* was the first in Mahfouz's *Cairo Trilogy*, written in the 1950s and set at the time of the nationalist revolution of 1919, revolving around the el-Gawad family. The two palaces symbolised the milestones pointing out the political changes Egypt underwent. *Qasr el-Shoak* (Palace of Desire) followed, bookended by *El-Sukkareya*

(Sugar Street). Each a location of old Cairo, each resonating with the calm mood of the city, encompassing the quarter century between the Egyptian uprising against the British and the end of Second World War. The three novels captured the essence of Egyptian transformation, solidifying Mahfouz's reputation, ultimately leading to his winning the Nobel Prize for Literature in 1988.

This part of Cairo represented the soul of Mahfouz's writing. 'The shadows of the place, the voices of those gone, and the clamour of the passers-by,' Mahfouz wrote once, remained with him for long. He further wrote:

> Everyone has a place in time and space, everyone has a point of departure for which he longs and adopts as a refuge, to go back in times of difficulties or when he is away from it. My place is in old Cairo, in al-Gamaliya. My soul is there always, in spite of the passing of long years.

Then in *The Journey of Ibn Fattouma*, Mahfouz wrote:

> However much the place distances itself from me it will continue to let fall drops of affection, conferring memories that are never forgotten, and etching its mark, in the name of the homeland, in the very core of the heart. So long as I live I shall passionately love the effusions of the perfume vendors; the minarets and the domes; the radiant face of a pretty girl illuminating the lane; the mules of the privileged and the feet of the barefooted; the songs of the deranged and the melodies of the rebab; the prancing steeds and the lablab trees; the cooing of pigeons and the plaintive call of doves.

I stepped into Mahfouz's interior landscape that day with friends Steve and Sumita, who had made Cairo their home at that time, and we walked into Mahfouz's world. In the trilogy, the youngest son of el-Gawad family is Kamal, who according to critics is Mahfouz's alter ego. He is a philosophy student grappling with the clash of his faith and science. He is a child in the first novel, grows to a university student in the second, and becomes a teacher in the final novel. As he grows older, he gets bitter, losing the certainties that childhood has taught him, and yet he is not at ease with tradition. The gradual progression is redeemed at the end, when Mahfouz ends the novel on a note of quiet optimism, but its overall mood is unremittingly bleak.

Change is inevitable, but certain things remain the same. Time, and its pace, are at the heart of those novels. Modern Cairo represents some of that—in the old Cairo, in the area around Khan al-Khalili, the activity is paced evenly, where nobody seems to be in any hurry, and each walk is a stroll. Life goes on, as it always has, gently, the child going to school now will inherit the family home, and his children will wear the same sort of clothes, go to the same school, wake up to the sound of the muezzin's prayer and the gentle thump of the dough being pounded for bread, the smell of fresh coffee wafting through the air. And they shall step beyond the markets, to Cairo's busy streets, where the traffic is snarling, cars weaving through the mess impatiently, the driver's palm never too far from the horn, the driver pressing the accelerator the moment he can see a bit of open space between his car and the one ahead, desperate to beat the traffic light about to turn amber. We are near Tahrir Square.

The most striking aspect about Tahrir Square when I saw it the first time was to notice how small it was. Television images can be misleading. At the time when thousands had congregated at Tahrir Square to seek the removal of Hosni Mubarak as Egypt's president, the square seemed enormous; at night, from my hotel window, it looked as if it had shrunk.

Perhaps it was the midnight hour when I saw it first, and perhaps it was the utter lack of traffic at that hour, which meant that when our driver took us along the periphery of the square to give us a feel of the location, it ended just as we thought it had begun.

Later, when I woke up in the morning and looked at the square from the window of my hotel room, it looked like any busy area of a city, largely unremarkable, except for the large Soviet-era government building on one side, and the oasis-like old campus of the American University in Cairo, on the other.

Tahrir means liberation, and in Arabic, the square is called Midan-el-Tahrir. Midan, the word which Egyptian writer Ahdaf Soueif recalls with great affection in describing the square in her account of the Egyptian Revolution of 2011, *Cairo: My City, Our Revolution*. She writes:

> I prefer the Arabic word 'midan', because like 'piazza', it does not tie you down to a shape but describes an open urban space in a central position in a city.... The central point of Cairo is not a square or a circle but more like a massive curved rectangle.

The square is central and indeed pivotal. People seeking to change governments have often attempted to occupy it, and the government has cracked down routinely. The part of Cairo where the square takes central space was built in the 1860s, modelled on Paris's Etoile, with six roads leading out, which in turn lead to six more squares, the city spreading organically beyond. While not as grand as Haussmann's Paris, which was being built around the same time, it has a peculiar continental charm, marking it as distinct from the old Cairo of minarets and muezzins.

To understand the square's centrality better, you need to walk along the busy roads that spread outwards. There are hawkers selling plastic bottles, children's clothing, trinkets for tourists, and books, including a few intriguing biographies of

Hitler and Stalin. But go further along, and the babble ceases, the stock market is visible, and a mall emerges, with an ornate exterior that looks like the headgear of a pharaoh.

Right across, on the other side, is the famous Cairene Café, Riche, which has for over a century been the draw for the city's intellectuals. It is here, in 1952, it is believed, that Gamal Abdel Nasser plotted the coup that removed the rotund king Farouk. Three decades earlier, there was an attempt to murder a prime minister at this café. And it is also here that Mahfouz held court. The afternoon I went there with my friends, an old waiter in robes greeted us and left us alone until I went to the counter where an old man was reading a newspaper by the cash register. With some reluctance I interrupted him, and reluctantly he motioned to one of the waiters to come to our table. We had lemonade and coffee, and if we hadn't asked for the bill, he'd have let us stay there as long as we wanted. The lush, warm colours of the restaurant were comforting after the harsh sunlight outside.

Parisian cafés where Ernest Hemingway and Jean-Paul Sartre held forth carry small plaques with their names on seats which we must believe they sat on. At the place where Mahfouz held court on Fridays, there is his large portrait; you half-expect him to start talking to you as he sips his sweetened coffee. He had the odd habit of ordering two cups, drinking half of each, leaving the rest. His novel *Karnak Café* is based on Riche, and draws on stories he heard at the café.

I walked back to the old campus of the American University in Cairo. Its walls were splattered with expansive street art, mocking the government of the then President Mohamed Morsi. There were some large images showing the Muslim Brotherhood, the political base of Morsi, to be the equivalent of the erstwhile military-backed regime. The murals were huge and painted with great revolutionary fervour and gusto. There were other large murals, red blotches of colour, carrying the names of the martyrs, written in white.

I saw many students at the campus, earnestly discussing politics. One of them giggled shyly after she saw that I had heard her criticising her president. Café Riche was perhaps too old-fashioned for these students, many of whom assembled at Tahrir Square not after listening to a rousing speech, nor after a cardamom-scented coffee-filled evening, but by following tweets and signing up on Facebook. The murals reminded them of what was possible, and what they had achieved— but not alone. If you relied only on western newspapers, you would think this was a revolution brewed on the Internet; if you spoke to men and women who fought for human rights in Egypt, you realised that there were many more foot-soldiers in that revolution. They were united by their revulsion of Mubarak but divided on most other issues.

When I was in Cairo they were disgruntled with the government again, and believed they had the means to change it. They began congregating at the square, banished cars, and magnified this space of urban openness into the vast theatre of regime change that captured the world's imagination. They made Tahrir Square a global metaphor. As I walked around the square, it was pulsating with life, and the men and women, young and old, teachers and students showed, for a brief moment, what it took to walk like an Egyptian.

But to the older town, it would seem, this bustle didn't matter.

Those different cities coexist as if barely acknowledging each other. I was back in Mahfouz's Cairo, which is the old city, where couscous vendors sit by the façade of a seminary; minarets shoot up into the sky; domes are lit in the glow of light; and the parapet has statuettes, like spears bunched tightly together at the mosque of al-Husayn. There are the shrines of al-Sayyida Zaynab and al-Husayn, with an intricate green pattern; quaint Arabic characters look like lattice-work, carved on pieces of stones adorning the walls of a Sufi mosque. At a café yet to open, I see chairs stacked high, one straight, one upside down. And there, I see Fishawi's café.

Fishawi's is an institution, a necessary respite under the hot sun, like an oasis after a trawl through the desert, its couches looking worn, the al-fresco seating area taken up by tourists, who are busy consulting their large maps and placing their guidebooks on the small tables, fanning themselves. Young boys pester them, emerging out of nowhere, pointing out the tourists' dusty shoes, promising to make them shine with their polish, their rag, their energy, and their smile. You look inside Fishawi's, with its lamps and marble-top tables, the arches and the imposing seats for families so that they can sit undisturbed by other patrons, the trays on the table with the delicious lemonade, the large mirrors, the light blue china teapots, the mild yellow light from the large bulbs, the electric fan moving from left to right and then back. You can spend hours at Fishawi's, and like in a café in Paris, the waiters will understand your need for solitude, and they would take their time to come to your table, replenishing your coffee only when asked, letting you at peace with your thoughts. Mahfouz came here often—it is a clean, well-lighted place.

There is Kirsha's, too, another café that Mahfouz wrote about in *Midaq Alley*, its entrance so narrow that you might miss it as you pass by, surrounded as it is by stores selling carpets, shishas, clothes, and board games. Across us, on a table, old men play dominoes. Other men are smoking the shisha, the water-pipe with the base of glass, with scented tobacco, sometimes peach, sometimes strawberry, at other times mint, and often apple. There is the *goza*, made of stainless steel, with its bamboo-like pipe for smoke, firm enough to transport it easily, and easy to use. There is *narghile*, as it is known in Syria, slimmer, and originally, it is said, made of coconut shells. The air thickens with smoke; our pace quickens.

The old shops have lanterns—some made of iron, with intricate carving, letting the light out not in one clear glow, but serrated, making the light shimmer, the lanterns swaying slightly, the landscape around you shifting, revealing what remained in darkness only moments ago.

We pass by a mosque—the faithful come out, looking content and pious, putting on shoes they'd left outside the mosque, and a man walks towards us with a censer, its smoke wafting, and he lets that smoke surround us, and we pay him, and he leaves. The man guarding my shoes asks where I'm from. 'Turkey?' he guesses. 'India,' I say. His eyes light up, as he holds my hand with both hands, and says: 'Amitabh Bachchan!'

We go into the old home of a merchant. The inner courtyard is large, with a small garden and invitingly large space. Its intricate windows are made of dark wood and they jut out on the street, with tiny holes no bigger than the human eye, offering a view of the world beyond. This is the women's quarter; this is where they can look out from, but remain invisible to the strangers on the street, secluded from the world in their own inner space. You could picture the daughter of a merchant, standing in the morning, her eyes wandering down Hamam al-Sultan, taking in the ancient building with the public cistern. I think of Madhabi Mukherjee in the opening scenes of Satyajit Ray's film *Charulata*, looking at the world beyond her window through her opera glasses, and mildly amused by the sights she sees. Here in Cairo, perhaps that merchant's daughter will see a young man that she will fancy; perhaps she might run into him in the market, perhaps she might go to college, and find the young man in her class; perhaps they will meet in a café. And perhaps, they will fall in love. In Mahfouz's trilogy, Kamal does meet, and then loses his love, embittering him further. Mahfouz recounts the pain quietly, as a matter of fact, with an air of inevitability.

Later one evening Sumita and Steve take me on a felucca, the traditional sailboat which plies the Nile. We are now far from the old city; some minarets are visible, but so are the skyscrapers and hotels that dot the banks of the river. The felucca can take up to ten people and the man who sails it plays music, and the children of our friends dance merrily, we share a large pizza, watching the sun turn orange, and then pink, as it lowers itself, hiding behind the skyscrapers, its light settling on the Nile, disturbed by the flow of water, the singular image of the orb disintegrating into a million little fireflies. The breeze is now gentle, the harshness gone, the Cairo day ends.

AH, BUT YOUR LAND IS BEAUTIFUL

This is where Africa ends.

You could argue that Africa ends wherever the land meets the ocean at its farthest point. And if you see as far as your eye can, then any furthest point at either end of your line of vision would be the place where the landmass ends. But there is that end of the road from Bereeda, where Somalia meets the Gulf of Aden. Then there is Cap Blanc in Tunisia, which looks north to Sardinia. Or you go to the west, at the beach off Ngor, in Senegal. Each is an extremity, and each can claim to be the farthest point of Africa.

And then there is the Cape.

The spot we are headed for is in the south, where the land narrows like a funnel to an end point. As it reaches its southern tip, it shrinks in size. You hear the roar of strong waves lashing the shore even though the windows of your car are shut tight.

We are in a car moving briskly, and we can see the vegetation turning rougher. The green of the shrubs looks darker, the land flat and dry, the ground coarse and brown. The few trees sway rapidly. The trees are short, dwarf-like, their strong roots clinging firmly to the ground even as their branches bend at impossible angles. They swing back promptly, like rhythmic wipers. The vegetation too leans in a disorderly way, and for a while it seems as if I'm watching an underwater movie, the vegetation on the surface of the ocean trembling constantly. The wind pushes them around.

It is when we get off the car that we realise the force of the wind. We have to hold on to the car to ground ourselves firmly. Later, when we will reach the top of the point where the lighthouse is located, a tourist with a contraption that can measure the wind's strength will tell us that the speed is 102.5 miles (165 km) per hour. That's faster than the speed at which the Australian fast bowler Brett Lee bowls in a cricket match. But there is a crucial difference: when a batsman faces a bowler hurling the ball at such speed, his eyes are fixed on the hand and on that delivery coming sharply towards him; and he has his sturdy bat to ward off that ball, or take an evasive action to protect himself. But with this wind, it is as though we are constantly targeted by hundreds of such balls, of different shapes and sizes, from different directions, and nothing is visible. The force is exceptional; the winds are from the South Pole.

It is impossible to walk without holding on to the railing as I climb to the top, where the lighthouse is no longer in use because low clouds have routinely shrouded it, leading to shipwrecks. Taking each step is an effort, at the end of which you feel as if you have reached a milestone. With one hand I hold the railing, with the other, I hold on to my glasses— there is no guarantee they will remain on their perch, the bridge of my nose, or that my ears will be able to provide a convenient niche.

The magnificent stretch of land shrivels. The cliff falls steeply, as it descends into the ocean. To my left, beyond the mist, is the hazy blue-grey outline of mountains, which look primordial, untouched from the day the planet was born and continents emerged. Beyond those mountains is the False Bay, which Bartolomeu Diaz called "the gulf between the mountains" and which seafarers mistook for Table Bay. To my right, the Atlantic churns violently, forming foaming waves that come crashing on the serrated edge of the landmass. And in front of me, the waves continue their lurch, as if seeking the unmarked boundary where the Atlantic ends and the Indian Ocean begins. That boundary, which is not marked by any border post, is barely visible to the eye. On less windy days, you can see the blue of the Atlantic and the dark grey of the Indian Ocean—one warmer than the other.

At the top of the lighthouse, the point where the land ends seems dramatic because, for miles, on all sides, all you see is water—dark, blue-grey, thrashing and agitating; your hands hold the railing tight, the wind hits your face with full force, your eyes, desperate to stay open, are filled with tears. You look ahead, in the direction of the South Pole, searching for the horizon where the sky becomes the ocean.

This is where it ends, you think. Couples wrap their arms around one another as they walk, huddled, taking their steps slowly. The descent is harder—the elemental image of that expanse of water is mesmerising. The wind pushes me hard, forcing me to run down.

In *The English Patient*, Ondaatje wrote about the poetry of warm winds—a whirlwind so strong that you have to defend yourself with knives; winds that can knock down the horse and the rider; winds that bury villages; winds that make you nervous; a dust storm that brings rain; winds that are silent, which are fragrant, which are nameless, like 'the secret wind of the desert, whose name was erased by a king after his son died within it.'

This wind is not warm; it is cold. It is different. It can lift you and send you flying, for such seems to be its power. In Manhattan during snowstorms, the wind attacks you as you walk through the stretch between two high-rise buildings. Its ferocity is such that you feel it can slice you. Or the wind with the rain in Bombay, when you are on the waterfront—it is not cold, it is not warm, but it is powerful, turning your umbrella into a cubist sculpture. This wind howls—it is like the sirens in the sea, warning you, pushing you back to the continent.

To defend myself against this wind, I would need a shield, or body armour. I'd need to envelop myself with steel. This wind does not whistle, nor does it blow. It rushes at you like an army, and collapses on you, trying to take you down. This wind is no respecter of structures—and realising its ferocity, nature has surrendered to it.

Later that afternoon, we drive towards Simon's Town, to keep the appointment we have made with penguins, which congregate on a sandy beach. The same wind—though now considerably weakened—sweeps this land. It still has the strength to disrupt the sand, lift it, sending it towards us to attack us, hitting our eyes, clogging our ears, invading our mouths if we try to talk.

By twilight, we are back in Cape Town, and it is calm. I have a glass of Chardonnay for company. Clouds surround Table Mountain which looks like an old man smoking the hookah. The crescent moon looks so delicate, and the sky is pink.

I think of the many evenings I have spent looking at this harbour. The sailboats parked at the bay, the buskers singing to tourists, the seagulls chirping cheerfully, the flags fluttering, and the breeze mild. Bliss.

Ah, but your land is beautiful. That was Alan Paton's title for one of his novels. That it certainly is—South Africa is beautiful. But there is that "but". And that one word tells quite a different story.

To understand that, I must take you to a garden.

ॐ

I had gone to Kirstenbosch Botanical Gardens in Cape Town on a sunny day. The sky was clear and the air mild. Teenagers were playing frisbee on one side; mothers walked along the manicured pathways, pushing strollers; a group of elderly nuns stopped me to ask me where I was from, and told me how much they had enjoyed their recent holiday in Bombay.

I was in that garden looking for a hedge of almonds. A week earlier, in Johannesburg, the South African writer Allister Sparks had told me about the hedge: that's where it had all begun, he had said.

The hedge was not a natural formation—it was deliberately planted as a wall, to keep people apart. Jan van Riebeeck, the first Dutch colonial administrator who founded the western settlement in that fair city, had it built as a barrier between the colonial settlement and the khoikhoi people, the original inhabitants of that area. The Dutch empire was in full bloom at that time, and Van Riebeeck was not going to let a khoi rebellion change his plans. Battles followed, and the khoi were pushed back, their final humiliation coming in 1659.

Good fences make good neighbours, the Dutch thought, and planted the hedge. The National Party may have made apartheid a governing policy after its election in June 1948; the idea of dividing people has a far longer history in South Africa.

Describing the hedge, Sparks wrote in his engrossing history published in 1999, *The Mind of South Africa:*

> Here against the eastern slopes of the Table Mountain, where three amber-coloured streams cascade down from the gray-green crenellation of Castle Rock and flow together to form the Liesbeeck River, is some of the rarest fauna in all the world: a botanist's paradise.... Here, too, is a line of short scraggly trees whose ancient limbs are twisted together into an untidy tangle. A metal plate pinned to one of the trees states that it is *Brabejum Stellatifolium*, or the Wild Almond. They have a long,

blueish leaf and the nut, encased in a furry shell, is dry and bitter. The trees are the remains of the hedge… to keep out the khoikhoi cattle herders who inhabited this southernmost tip of the African continent….The bitter-almond hedge lives on, institutionalized in a thousand laws to exclude the dark-skinned indigenous people and preserve the illusion that South Africa is really a "white" country.

Sparks, who I met at his home in Johannesburg in 1992, went on to describe the landscape—the Cape Flats, the Hottentot's Holland Mountains, the wineries, and the shanty towns— ending: 'There, before you lies apartheid in all its obscenity, to be gazed upon from one of the most beautiful vistas on God's earth.' When you go to Cape Town, see the hedge—it began there, he told me.

The hedge was difficult to find, and when I got there, it was remarkably and disarmingly banal. It looks like any piece of unkempt, wild, disorganised vegetation. When I started taking pictures of that hedge, a group of curious tourists paused, wondering why I was paying attention to this piece of ugliness, when so much beauty lay around me.

Ah, but your land is beautiful.

That was the point: that hedge is a piece of ugliness. As I went to South Africa more often, through the 1990s and beyond, many aspects of that man-made ugliness confronted me with astonishing regularity, influencing human behaviour, with people rejoicing and cherishing small pleasures that the rest of the world took for granted—even the simple pleasure of making friendships with people who looked different from you.

Separateness was at the heart of the apartheid project. It was visible the moment our aircraft began its descent at any urban airport in South Africa. On one side, you saw identical homes in leafy suburbs, surrounded by greenery, with cool swimming pools reflecting sunlight; on the other, teeming slums on sun-baked, brown landscapes, where the majority of South Africans lived. You didn't need to be a genius to figure out which homes were black and which white. Every country has inequality; in South Africa, it was artificially constructed, by erecting barriers. It was also visible, a physical relief map that did not require colour coding to tell you who was rich and who wasn't; who had better access to services and who didn't; who was well-educated and who wasn't; who could protect themselves against crime and who couldn't. I would meet young bureaucrats, keen to drum up tourist arrivals and business in the wake of the lifting of sanctions against South Africa, who would tell me in all innocence: 'We have the third world and the first world in one country,' as if that was a freak accident of nature, as if it was an attraction in itself.

It is now a quarter century since Nelson Mandela was released from prison and South Africa increasingly looks like a normal country. But in those days of apartheid's twilight, when that odious system had not yet officially ended and democracy had not fully taken hold, I recall the evening when my friend Dee showed me around Johannesburg. Her excitement was palpable as she drove me to a fantastic restaurant where we had delicious king clip and fruity sauvignon blanc. She explained why she was excited: a few years earlier, what she was doing—taking a non-white person with her in her car, going to dinner with him—would have been a crime. But we were in new South Africa, she said; the barriers were crumbling. The past was ugly. Ah, but her land was beautiful.

Dee took me to Exclusive Books and introduced me to South African writing that did not begin and end with Nadine Gordimer and Andre Brink. She insisted I read anguished contemporary accounts like Marq de Villiers's *White Tribe Dreaming* and Rian Malan's *My Traitor's Heart*. She spoke to Sparks so that he would see me, and took me to meet Helen

Suzman, Zach de Beer, Thabo Mbeki, Albie Sachs, and Nadine Gordimer; she was by my side when I heard F W De Klerk and Nelson Mandela speak to journalists; each time she would tell me about these people and their histories that I wouldn't find in any history book, and revealing to me aspects of the country that only someone who grew up there and seeking peaceful change would know. She also introduced me to the haunting sounds of Miriam Makeba, Hugh Masekela, Mbongeni Ngema (years before he sang a frankly racist song against Indians), and the Ladysmith Black Mambazo. In return, all I had brought for her from Singapore was *ikan bilis* (dried anchovies).

A few years later on another visit, she drove me to meet my old friend Kirti Menon. She was keen to meet Kirti, who is a great-granddaughter of Mohandas Karamchand Gandhi. Her grandfather was Manilal Gandhi, the second son of the Mahatma, and Manilal ran the newspaper *The Indian Opinion* from 1918 to 1956. Kirti too lived in Johannesburg. Seeing them meet was special—in a sense, it brought together two parallel histories of South Africa. Dee's ancestor was Johannes Rissik, the city's surveyor-general, and the city derives its name partly from him (it is named after Johannes Rissik and Johannes Joubert, an early mine prospector).

The city of gold, or *eGoli*, as the Zulus called the city, was built on the prosperity of the mining industry. Johannesburg is a young city—it came into being as a mining town after gold was discovered in the Rand Belt in the late nineteenth century, and prospectors moved to the place. Mining companies needed a cheap workforce, and for that young black men were brought from the interiors, housed in hostels, and made to work in the mines, their rights to enter the "white" city restricted severely. The blacks lived in townships far from the city. Makeshift and presumed temporary and without character, one was simply called south-west township, which later got abbreviated to SoWeTo, or Soweto. Van Riebeeck's hedge was made solid at last.

The man to challenge the unjustness of such a separation was a young Gujarati barrister, Gandhi. Johannes Rissik had never met Gandhi, and had they met, they would have been on opposite sides of the argument, opposite sides of the almond hedge. Many years later, Gandhi's descendant, Menon became a trenchant critic of many injustices. Rissik's descendant, unknown to Menon, also challenged apartheid in her own way—through her journalism. It was my privilege that evening, to bring them together, forging links that should have got formed organically. The ease and happiness with which Dee and Kirti talked filled me with optimism about the country.

The good cheer of the rainbow nation conceals many wounds, including some fairly recent ones. But it seems as if collective amnesia is forced on the people. They feel it is required that they set an example for the rest of the world, to convince everyone that it is a better, and not a bitter country. One way South Africa addressed the idea of dealing with its past was by setting up a widely-praised Truth and Reconciliation Commission. The country got just praise for moving beyond revenge. But a member of the Communist Party I met, who named her children after Soviet heroes, said many don't know the truth yet, and nor do they feel reconciled. During the apartheid years, she and her husband would drive into Mozambique carrying weapons to underground South African Communist Party or SACP activists, seeking violent overthrow of the apartheid regime. Had those instincts been allowed to prevail, South Africa could have witnessed a bloodbath. But the Anglican Archbishop Desmond Tutu wanted otherwise— he wanted the Christian notion of forgiveness to prevail. As my good friend, the South Africa-born British novelist Gillian Slovo explained to me: 'Lots of countries like the idea of truth commissions because they look at South Africa and think of the miracle. But I am not sure if it was entirely miraculous; it had its flaws, too. The commission was a compromise to stop people from fighting. When people say that a commission should be established to settle a conflict, they need to see if the two sides want to stop fighting first. It is impossible to start a process that goes so deep without deciding that violence must stop. There is a difference between an individual's response and the collective response to the past. South Africa's experience reflected the thinking of an archbishop whose church believed in forgiveness. But real reconciliation only happens when it is possible to acknowledge the terrible, so that you can't say that it did not happen.'

Many South Africans want to put that past behind. But many also want to remember the past, and its shame.

Let me take you to four places, of which one that survives only in memory.

First, the suburb called Triomf, which used to be the dynamic Sophiatown. In his 1992 memoir, *A Good-Looking Corpse*, a fascinating book about South Africa of the '50s, the writer Mike Nicol recounts apartheid's early years. Nicol wrote about the musicians, artists, writers, and journalists resisting the creation of apartheid. He also wrote about the magazine *Drum* and celebrated how they told a story of 'bathos and paradoxes which rule our lives as much now as then. Theirs is a record of naivete and optimism, frustration and defiance, courage, exile, and death.' *Drum* chronicled that era, where Sophiatown had seedy *shebeens* and lively jazz, an undercurrent of crime and the cheerful mixing of races and sexes. It was razed, making way for Triomf, a town deliberately named after the Afrikaans word for triumph. (When I asked Meshaek Mekona, who drove Dee and me around Johannesburg during my first visit more than twenty years ago if he could drive us to Sophiatown, he laughed hysterically. 'It doesn't exist,' he said. 'It died.' Sadly, so did Mekona, an early statistic among the lives lost to HIV in South Africa.) Triomf is a disaster, in fact—a suburb with nothing to distinguish it from other neighbourhoods. But Sophiatown lingers in memory—it has now regained its name, but not its character.

The apartheid regime had passed the Group Areas Act in 1950, and the aim of the act was to remake South African cities. The hedge was becoming a wall. There were earlier acts, passed in 1915 and 1940s, restricting land access to black and Indian populations by preventing them from certain parts, but the Group Areas Act formalised the haphazard legislation and arrangements. The first world could remain first only if the third world was out of sight. To do this, communities which were integrated needed to be torn apart. Homes were razed and families were removed, all with the intention of freeing up space in the city centre for businesses—always white—and the many workers who were not white would have to depend on poorly-run public transport, and live miles away from the city. In Cape Town, all the people of colour—blacks, coloureds, and Indians, were forcibly moved to Cape Flats, an extensive stretch of land which is sandy and windy. Blacks settled in Gugulethu and Khayelitsha, the coloured in Bonteheuwel, Manenberg, Heideveld, and Mitchells Plain, and Indians, in Rylands. District 6 was cleared for whites again.

Today, District 6 is a metaphor of what was, what could have remained, and what must be remembered. There is a small, privately-run museum commemorating the district, and on one recent visit, I walked around the museum, talking to volunteers and staff who were former residents in the area. They show no bitterness, but the wrinkles on their faces show the agony they have lived through. Much of the city is now unrecognisable for many of the older residents who come looking for the neighbourhoods in which their memories lie buried. The day I was at the museum, I saw families hunting for some remnant they could share with their teenage grandchildren, who had grown up in the new South Africa, scarcely aware of the kind of injustices their grandparents had experienced. On the floor of the museum is a vast, sprawling map of the district, with each of the old streets named, and I see an elderly woman, with tears in her eyes, reliving her past, showing her granddaughter the street where her home was, where her memories lie buried. The granddaughter takes some interest; the daughter, bridging generations, takes a photograph of the grandmother and the granddaughter, sitting on the floor, on the map, where that miniaturised street is still named and exists.

More chilling is the Apartheid Museum, in Johannesburg. It is set far from the city centre, in the suburb of Ormonde, and forces you to face apartheid at its doorstep. The randomly-issued tickets separate you from your companions into whites and non-whites. However well-prepared you are, it is a sobering experience to get a ticket with a race category not yours, and then be divided from your friends as you enter the museum through different entrances. In the end, all of you will see the same exhibits, but you don't know until you meet them inside. The same experiences, different entrances, and the perception of artificially-induced separation give a false sense of exclusivity. In a telling way, the museum achieves this before you are inside, where you are reunited with your friends (most people smile with relief when they see their friends inside) and the depressingly familiar history of contemporary South Africa follows, with giant screens showing video footage, sound recordings, famous speeches— including Mandela's defence speech, "I am prepared to die," at the Rivonia trial—and a real hippo, as the large armoured personnel carriers (APCs) were known, which imperviously levelled homes, people and animals, on its way to establishing its authority in violence-prone or defiant black townships. Those "hippos" are scary. In 1991, when I was in a township reporting about the referendum, I saw a group of black men coming dancing down the street. Their dance is called *toi-toi*, and it looks menacing, as people come running rhythmically, raising their fists—and at times, it can turn worse. Suddenly they started running in all directions—a large "hippo" was following them, moving rapidly, spraying dust, white soldiers looking out from the top, sun reflecting on their dark glasses. It was a cliché image of apartheid; it was also terrifying.

But yes, your land is beautiful.

Last year, I went looking for the old fort where the regime kept its most troublesome prisoners. An empty jail cell cannot convey the sense of isolation, nor can it make you feel the claustrophobia. However small the cell is, when it is without prisoners, it gives a false sense of openness and space. And when it is filled with people, as the photographs on the walls of this jail indicate, it is overcrowded.

I entered this jail knowing that I would get out when I wanted to. Others have not been so lucky. The wall honours some of the individuals who were held here against their wishes, often for crimes they hadn't committed, or for acts which weren't crimes.

This is the old jail in Johannesburg. It is set on a hill, and it shows South Africa's inspired attempt to reconcile the story of its inhuman past with its optimistic present. The place is called Constitution Hill, and part of the property has made way for the country's constitutional court. It is a deliberate choice.

Symbolically, the walkway between the jail and the court is made of bricks taken from the building, which was part of the holding area for prisoners before they were processed and dumped into those cells: from the past to the future. The court exudes openness with its tall glass windows and cheerful art; the cells are constricting and narrow. The dim interior and the grey mattresses are bleak.

When you enter the Number Four prison, the wall carries a statement of Mandela's: "No one truly knows a nation until one has been inside its jails." And the picture of this apartheid-era jail isn't pretty. The guide tells me about the food the prisoners got: even the rations were racially divided.

The first drum had beef or pork, to which only the whites were entitled. The second drum was for Indian and coloured prisoners. It had porridge or boiled vegetables over which the cooks tossed some fatty meat from the discarded bits for the white prisoners. The third drum was for black prisoners—it was without meat, and it had porridge, boiled mealies (corn), and beans.

The prisoners were humiliated often. Upon arrival, they went without shower for months; weekly showers were contingent upon good behaviour. The recalcitrant ones were sent to *Emakhulukhuthu* (the deep dark hole) as the isolation cells were called. There, their staple diet was rice water.

The only black prisoner separated from other black prisoners, and kept in the white prisoners' jail, was Mandela—not out of respect, but to keep him from influencing or inspiring—or inciting, as the authorities saw it—fellow blacks.

I was interested in another prisoner—Gandhi. When Gandhi challenged the government to live up to the ideals the British claimed to live by, the police used force—and Gandhi willingly took the blows. By not retaliating, he confused the Government. By insisting upon truth, he unleashed a new weapon—*satyagraha*—which shamed his adversaries.

There is a permanent exhibition for Gandhi inside the jail. Gandhi was born in India, but South Africa made him: to counter the injustice he faced, he opted for the morally superior alternative to violence, of civil disobedience, which he would deploy so skillfully against the British, after he returned to India in 1915. Explaining what South Africa did for him, Gandhi was to say: 'It was after I went to South Africa that I became what I am now. My love for South Africa and my concern for her problems are no less than for India.' You find those words inscribed in this exhibition.

The walls tell Gandhi's South African story without any adornment. You see the simple cap he stitched. You see the life-size image of Gandhi on translucent fabric, as if he is standing in front of you. There's the prisoners' uniform of the kind he wore. And on the side there is a table, upon which sits the typewriter that he used when he wrote for the newspaper he owned, *The Indian Opinion*. The typewriter is accessible—I felt the tactile urge, to feel the keys, to press them, but thought the better of it. I felt unworthy.

I wanted to see the sandals he had made for General Jan Smuts, whose job it was to tame Gandhi. In many ways, Smuts was a reluctant adversary. Gandhi could separate his opponent from his actions, the individual from his power. Smuts understood that, he knew how Gandhi left him powerless. When Gandhi left for India, he presented Smuts with a pair of sandals he had made for him. Smuts accepted the gift. Many years later, on Gandhi's seventieth birthday, he returned the sandals to Gandhi with a note saying: 'I have worn these sandals for many a summer since then, even though I may feel that I am not worthy to stand in the shoes of so great a man.'

The sandals were at the end of the room. They are kept in a glass case, and they have the look and feel of simplicity and comfort.

The heels of the sandals are flat. But you know that whoever wore them, would get a lift that can't be explained or understood easily. And that elevation had nothing to do with the wearer, but with the maker.

Their scale was human, and sliding one's feet in those sandals would seem so simple. Walking like Gandhi, however, is a different matter.

One man who followed Gandhi's footsteps—although not with perfection—was Mandela. I first went to Robben Island, where Mandela was jailed for eighteen years, about a decade ago. The cell was painfully small—I had met Mandela in 1991, and the most striking impression of the man was how tall and imposing he was, in an avuncular way. To imagine him in that restricted space was like squeezing the universe into a ball.

And yet, the real punishment for Mandela was the limestone quarry, where blinding white sunlight hit his eyes—and of other inmates—who had to face that sun day after day as they broke the stones, with Sisyphean perseverance. There was no point to that exercise, and yet they did it, uncomplainingly. It caused permanent damage to Mandela's eyes.

Ah, but your land is beautiful.

I returned to Cape Town after the visit to Robben Island, with the familiar, reassuring Table Mountain providing neutral certainty to the divided landscape. Beyond were the wineries of Stellenbosch. Seagulls twittered around us. The colours of the city returned, emerging slowly, like an image in a dark room, revealing richness.

But this was the city with a scar, the almond hedge. And at the same time, to the city's south-west, where the land met the sea, was the region they called the Cape of Good Hope.

There is enough man-made ugliness in South Africa—the harsh limestone quarry, the wild hedge, the missing Sophiatown, District 6 which only exists in a museum, all reminders of separateness. But there is also incomparable beauty. And there is good hope.

We are headed for Vergelegen, a Cape Dutch wine estate in the Stellenbosch region outside Cape Town. I am with my friend David. We are teaching at a seminar organised by a British university. David has been there before. Earlier in the morning, he had told me how the clouds there had a delightful habit of resting on the peaks and then gliding down, creating the illusion of a waterfall. David should have been a poet.

That evening we left for Vergelegen. The foothills of the surrounding mountains were filled with colourful flowers, the grass green. A river ran through it, and it looked like a painting come alive.

The house is at the end of a vast lawn and, inside, there is a library, rooms with large portraits of white men and women, and deep sofas and solid carpets. Vergelegen means "lying far away", and by the standards of the late seventeenth century, Vergelegen was indeed far from Cape Town, with the Cape Flats separating the two. The bay lay beyond; the mountains sheltered the area from the idea of "Africa". Beyond those mountains was the African flatland, stretching forever, with no clear indicators in sight of what began here, and what was there.

The Dutch liked order and precision; they made rules. Here they had space, something which they lacked in Europe. Their homes in the Cape became grander versions of their European homes.

They had come from elsewhere but, arguably, so had the blacks. The Khoikhoi were here first, from the beginning of time. They were cattle herders and farmers, and they moved across the land, looking for pastures. That upset the rules the Dutch wanted to live by, with clear boundaries. So the Dutch created markers like that hedge at Kirstenbosch Botanical Garden.

Three hundred years later, who was the original inhabitant and who was the outsider? In *White Tribe Dreaming*, de Villiers's haunting memoir of eight generations of Afrikaners (as white South Africans of Dutch origin came to be known), he asks an Afrikaner in the Veld about his birthplace. 'I am from here,' he says, underlining the confusion about who is local and who isn't. The Afrikaner felt rooted; he considered this land his, just as the Zulu did, the Xhosa did. The Afrikaner didn't mind the African on his farm, so long as he worked for him, followed the rules, and lived in his quarters, even as his family remained miles away. He wanted Africa around him, feeling its presence unobtrusively. There were bells in these houses—they were there for the masters to call the slave when necessary, David explained.

Each estate had a troubled, complicated history, and Vergelegen's story was no different: except that it took a remarkably pleasant turn.

The sun was setting when we reached the estate, and the mountain blushed a deep red. Sunlight rested on the mountain's hard contours, and the moon was already out, beaming. We saw two large trees with trunks that looked like the feet of a prehistoric elephant. Inside, in the garden was an even bigger camphor tree, 300 years old, which was the favourite tree of Nelson Mandela.

It was an odd moment and an odd place to think about Mandela. He would not have been allowed into an estate like this a quarter-century ago. A system that made a prisoner, an outsider, of Mandela had to collapse, and it did. But as Whoopi Goldberg asked in that marvellous film, *Sarafina!*: 'Nelson Mandela is free. Now what?'

How was a new nation to be created, which respected all ethnic groups, language and cultures? While there was an African National Congress (ANC), it needed to think through policies to assure markets, assure the whites who were staying behind, and assure their own constituents of all races, that they had a creative way to build a just society. There were many views within the movement: some believed in violence—"one settler one bullet", the graffiti *Umkhonto we Sizwe* (Spear of the Nation) would scrawl on the walls of South African cities carried a certain resonance; some knew how to agitate, but not build—they had organised the boycotts in townships and not sent children to Afrikaans-medium schools; some had lived in exile, and knew how to sabotage the state by bombing bus stops and courthouses; and some had been in jail for decades. How would these individuals, united by a common goal, but divided by tactics, who had not been able to meet openly and legally during the apartheid era, come together?

This is where Vergelegen estate played a modest role. Its new owner was the mining company, Anglo American, which took over the estate in 1987. In late nineteenth century, it was the mining industry whose need for cheap and pliant workforce and the desire to maintain exclusivity for the wealthy had made apartheid possible. A century later, another mining company opened its doors to the ANC, and Joe Slovo, Aziz Pahad, Thabo Mbeki, and Mandela himself met there, away from the limelight, to think of the country's future. It is easy to picture them here: sitting in the garden, talking of matters of great importance, while seagulls flew towards False Bay, defying those strong winds, their animated conversations interrupted by the shrill sounds of the Hadeda ibis, the brown bird which insists on having the last word in every conversation.

As I walked in the garden, reflecting on an estate designed as an enclave of exclusivity where black slaves once worked, I thought of the irony, of how the ANC leaders met here as free men. They were angry about the injustice they had faced, and yet they were thinking of ways to bring their sick and dysfunctional nation back to its feet. They would heal its wounds by showing the kind of magnanimity that would shame their erstwhile oppressors. It was dark outside: the evening had a quiet beauty and the shade of the trees caressed the wounds.

A gentle breeze blew, far less ferocious than the wind we had encountered at Cape of Good Hope. It was possible to walk without searching for railings. It was a full moon night and the moon shone brightly, lighting the path ahead of us, ahead for the nation.

SINGING IN A CAGE

The last rays of the setting sun spread a golden sheen over the reservoir in Seletar. Across the water, we saw giraffes amble from tree to tree, munching leaves. No cage stood between us and the animals, and yet they knew where their freedom ended, as did we. You didn't cross the line on this island.

We were on the other side, sitting by the lake on a table in an open area, eating greasy fishcakes and slurpy *mee goreng*, the fried noodles that Malays make, blending Chinese and Indian cuisine, much the way the two cultures permeate through the Malay Peninsula, adding turmeric in fried rice and making curry milder by adding *tahu*, or beancurd.

We were listening to those animals: there, that's the cry of hyenas, this is the whine of a jackal, and the trumpeting sound is of an elephant. The ceaseless drone of crickets prolonged our silence. The animals had come to this island from different parts of the world; here, they put up a show of exemplary harmony; each animal knew its place, almost as if living out a patriotic song that they sang on the national day in August during each of my eight years in Singapore: 'Every creed and every race, has its role and has its place.' Like at those mass national day rallies, there was choreography to their movements, the feel of an orchestra.

There was no rule requiring us to stay quiet, but this was Singapore, and one thing you learned here was that you didn't do something spontaneously. Everything was planned. Elsewhere, you did what you wanted to do, when you wanted to do it, unless you knew there was a law against it; in Singapore, you asked first, and did something only if it was allowed; you didn't do what others didn't or hadn't, lest there was a law against it. This is the city where rules were followed so obediently, that joggers waited when the traffic light said "do not cross" even if the road was empty and without cars, in case they get arrested for jaywalking. It was called a fine city, with a fine for everything—it took the former Prime Minister Goh Chok Tong to repeat that joke, at which point loyal Singaporeans realised that it was OK to laugh a bit at themselves. In Singapore, you learned the hard way that the nail that sticks out gets hammered; the bamboo shoots that grow tall are the first to get cut.

It was hard being a journalist in that city. Few people responded to your phone calls. Fewer wanted to say something on record. And far fewer were willing to share anything that might remotely be controversial. 'Why you so like that?' if you asked Singaporeans that question innocently with the disdain for grammar implied in the question, and those friends would smile nervously, and say: 'Because we are Singaporeans, *lah!*'

I knew little about Singapore before I went to live there. There was an old song from a Hindi film—*jeevan mein ek baar ana Singapur,* exhorting me to visit Singapore at least once in my life. In 1960, the Indian filmmaker, F C Mehra had produced a film called *Singapore,* a murder mystery in a rubber estate, and looking at some of the scenes from that film recently, I noticed how much of that city no longer existed by the time I reached there in 1991. The neon lights brightening the buildings were gone because Lee Kuan Yew, the republic's first prime minister, found them cheap and garish; jaywalkers were punished, because the city must look orderly; the mess had been removed, because the city had to be squeaky-clean. And singing and dancing in public parks was out of question— you would need a public entertainment licence which the authorities would not give you.

When I came, the city was making plans for infrastructure needs a decade ahead, and by the time I left eight years later, had accomplished most of its targets. Nothing stood still—it was the age of videotape players and Walkman equipment. You felt they lacked the pause button; most people liked their lives in fast-forward. A bureaucrat responsible for the island's economic development used to keep a copy of *Only the Paranoid Survive*, the autobiography of Intel's founder Andy Grove, on his desk. There was purpose to the city's restlessness: this was a Chinese island in a Malay sea; it had to run to stay ahead; it had to leap-frog over its competitors; it had to become, within a generation, a first world state, with what planners described as the Swiss standard of living. And within a generation, its people had moved from living in kampungs, as villages are called in Malay, into identical high-rise public housing blocks. Old names no longer carried meaning—neighbourhoods were almost forced to forget their distinguishing characteristics, and all blocks and flats had numbers.

The transformation of the country from the third world to the first, as Lee titled the second volume of his memoirs, was actually a fine myth. Singapore's economic progress was impressive, but the island hadn't started from miserable poverty, although it did have many people who were poor. It did suffer hugely during the Second World War being a British garrison town defending the Malacca Straits, and when the Japanese imposed a harsh rule after defeating the colonial British masters the Chinese were singled out for cruel punishment because of their loyalty to the British. But when the war ended and the British returned, the city still had battered and bruised versions of its port, its airfield, its banks, its harbour, and they later became the sources of its later prosperity. Lee's genius rested in his realisation that his small island would prosper if it would be useful to others, by being an efficient middleman.

I had read one novel about Singapore before my move there—Paul Theroux's *Saint Jack*. Written in 1973, it was about a man called Jack Flowers, who worked along the quays of Singapore for a Chinese businessman. The official business was providing services to ships, but the unstated service included procuring and providing women to sailors, or for that matter, anyone else. Written in Theroux's early years as a writer, the novel was laconic and satirical, with brutal but often funny stereotypes of all ethnicities, including washed-out white men. Flowers was a cynical man, and dreamt of the day when he could create his own pleasure empire. The Singapore he wrote about was exactly the Singapore Lee hated. It wasn't a surprise then, to find that the novel was banned in Singapore. When Peter Bogdanovich made a film based on the novel, he had to shoot it surreptitiously in Singapore, not revealing what he was filming, to prevent the authorities from stopping the filming. He succeeded, and so the film, too, got banned, and remained so until 2006.

If there was any part of Singapore other than the quays where such carefree attitudes existed, it was in Bugis Street. In the early 1970s, some of my school friends had visited Singapore, and told me about the transvestites and buxom women who performed at clubs there. By the time I reached Singapore, it had all gone. Singapore had become a straitlaced, straight-forward businesslike republic, whose bureaucrats would get excited rattling statistics of the turnaround time at their admittedly efficient port. Businesses like certainties, and Singapore offered that.

In my eight years, I had got used to some certainties, such as the familiar sight each Sunday of Filipina domestic workers at Lucky Plaza shopping centre, and Indian construction workers flocking to the temples at Serangoon Road; like rains falling punctually each afternoon, sometimes staying a hundred yards ahead of you, as you drove along a road, making you feel you were chasing away the monsoon so that your sons could play in the park; like the *Straits Times* telling its readers that while the economy was growing and Singapore was doing well, it must stay ahead of competitors; and how Singapore prized symmetry over wild abandon (like the equal distance between each tree on East Coast Road along the waterfront, as arriving passengers were driven from Changi Airport to the city).

When I returned twelve years later in 2011, I found much of the geography changed beyond recognition. There were more subway stations, a light rail, taxis came in different colours, and familiar landmarks had vanished—like the patch of greenery between Orchard Road and Orchard Boulevard where on warm Sundays, the Filipinas would set up picnic. New ones had emerged, like the casino on the Marina waterfront, looking like cricket stumps, slightly askew and at an angle, as if intimidated by a fast bowler.

What had disappeared was Furama Tower, the high-rise apartment which was my last home in Singapore. It was a perfectly fine, functional, modern apartment with breeze coming through its large windows on higher floors. We lived on the eighth floor, a number the Chinese considered auspicious. It had its own swimming pool and car park, but it was torn down to make way for an even more posh condominium. The slope down which my sons walked to their school was gone, and so had the swimming pool in which I exercised to recuperate my broken leg, watched over by my wife, who was worried that I'd take the easy way out by floating in the pool, instead of recovering quicker, since I was not in a hurry at that time, being between jobs.

In those intervening years, so much of my life would also change.

If the Singapore of *Saint Jack* was one extreme, the puritanical garb it had taken on to wear was another. Concerned by the criticism that the city was becoming too sterile, Singapore's leaders were willing to allow some entertainment, and so, slowly they began opening up. They allowed Michael Jackson to perform there, although *Cosmopolitan* magazine remained banned; they gave approval to build an arts centre on the waterfront, even as local artists complained about a lack of resources. Bugis Street became Bugis Junction, the first glass-covered shopping mall built while preserving old architecture, its stores selling everything from Danish ice cream to showing films, and whose public square had those spontaneous eruptions of water from a concealed fountain that would squirt pedestrians, catching them unawares, offering a pleasurable, wet respite on a warm day. It was fun but wholesome; as William Gibson was to describe the island, it was a "relentlessly G-rated experience". He also wrote: 'If IBM had ever bothered to actually possess a physical country, that country might have had a lot in common with Singapore. There's a certain white-shirted constraint, an absolute humourlessness in the way Singapore Ltd. operates; conformity here is the prime directive, and the fuzzier brands of creativity are in extremely short supply.' (Singaporean officials probably saw that as a compliment.)

I tried to imagine the seediness of Jack Flowers's quays, but when I went to Clark Quay, Robertson Quay, or Boat Quay, there was more G-rated experience. A mild breeze wafted over the quayside, and water taxis ferried evening passengers from one quay to another. If there was any hint of crime, it was the fact that at Harry's Bar, in one corner, some years ago Nick Leeson would meet fellow-traders over beer, relaxing after another day in front of computer terminals, buying and selling futures. Those were the heady days before he brought down Barings Bank. Ties and tongues were loosened, elbows rested, and gossip got traded, and as the evening turned to night, shirt buttons were undone and skirts got shorter. Waiters at the Thai, Japanese, Indian and Italian restaurants lay cutlery on the tables along the waterfront, observing everything, saying little.

Sure, Singapore is a human habitat, and there are indeed streets where you can find what some think of as pleasure and others call it vice, but those streets are indistinguishable from the rest of the city, and that is perhaps the point. If there is anything unusual, or dirty, or sinful, it stays hidden. What the island's puritanical government would find repugnant can't be known ahead of time—whether it was the seamy nature of Theroux's plot or the prescient metaphor about Jack being "the middleman" who was willing to do anything for anyone. But things would change surprisingly. In 2009, *The Blue Mansion,* a film which offers a thinly-veiled metaphor of Singapore, was screened and nobody banned it. The Republic was beginning to let its hair down. On my visit to Singapore in 2011, I could buy books like *Beyond the Blue Gate,* by the lawyer Teo Soh Lung, who was arrested in 1987 under the Internal Security Act over allegations that she was involved in a Marxist conspiracy to overthrow Singapore government. (She was finally released in 1990.)

By 2006, even *Saint Jack* (the film) could be shown in Singapore, and Singapore granted permission to businesses to open casinos, something Lee abhorred. Casinos are places where people gamble, but then Singaporeans gambled on stocks anyway. They even gambled on the price at which permits to buy cars would get auctioned. (Singapore restricted the supply of cars, for environmental and traffic management reasons, the effect of which was high prices for the few cars allowed into the city each month.) At Chinese funerals, Singaporeans gambled all night in void decks, as the open area of public housing is called, with its stone chairs and tables and letter-boxes. They gambled on state-permitted lottery. And they gambled in boats, which would go three miles out of Singapore's waters, and once in international waters, the wheels would spin and roulette would begin. When I saw the odd architecture of the casino—a ship on top of three towers, I wondered if the architect meant to remind patrons of those gambling boats I remember from the past.

There was freedom in Singapore, but there were limits. In the early 1960s, the poet DJ Enright, a lecturer at what became the National University of Singapore, bemoaned government-sponsored attempts to create culture in his inaugural lecture. 'Art does not begin in a test-tube, it does not take its origin in good sentiments and clean-shaven upstanding young thoughts,' he said. For his efforts the culture minister rebuked him, calling him a mendicant professor, adding: 'We have no time for asinine sneers by passing aliens ... [who are] beatnik professors.' Enright titled his 1969 autobiography *Memoir of a Mendicant Professor*.

When Singapore's arts centre on the waterfront—the Esplanade—opened, the world class lineup of artists included Kurt Masur with the London Philharmonic Orchestra, Wynton Marsalis with the Lincoln Centre Jazz Orchestra, Lorin Maazel with the New York Philharmonic Orchestra, the Singapore Dance Theatre staging *Reminiscing the Moon*, a ballet choreographed by Indonesia's Boi Sakti, the world premiere of *Portrait of an*

Empress, directed by Steven Dexter, and the National Ballet of China performing Zhang Yimou's *Raise the Red Lantern,* besides artists from Japan, India, Norway, and South Africa.

The Esplanade was a triumph of Singapore's planning skills. It showed the culmination of another journey towards a target. The rationale to develop Singapore into an arts hub was entirely unsentimental. Singapore attracted some fifteen million tourists annually, but they stayed barely three to four days. How could the republic make them return or stay longer?

The republic's mandarins moved in with characteristic efficiency. Transforming Singapore into an arts centre was an audacious idea. The Economist Intelligence Unit ranked Singapore below Tokyo and Hong Kong as a desirable place for expatriates. Singapore took such findings seriously, and began inviting foreign acts: in my time, we had seen Ravi Shankar, Michael Jackson, *Les Miserables,* and Phantom of the *Opera* perform, and an international film festival, which outspent Manila. Incentives were offered for creative businesses like art galleries and auction houses (Sotheby's and Christie's came promptly), and international broadcasting companies were wooed, bringing in teenybopper channels like MTV Asia. Culture follows prosperity, Singapore's leaders said; now that Singapore was rich, it could afford art. Deepak Chopra turned up, offering his mumbo-jumbo of spiritualism, which he claimed, only the middle class and wealthy could afford, because the poor had too many other priorities. That he was born in India, where the poorest Indian had a sense of spirituality about him and yet could laugh happily, made his claims even more ridiculous.

In such an environment emerged the Esplanade. Its striking, futuristic design has been likened to bug's eyes, Chinese dumplings and *durian* (the foul-smelling local fruit that looks like a spiky cannon ball and is banned on the subway). But the buildings are splendid. The complex includes a 2,000-seat theatre, a large concert hall and other smaller venues. More positively, the complex has been compared to the Sydney Opera House.

But can it match its spirit? Ong Keng Sen, a theatre director in Singapore, told a newspaper that he feared the complex would sacrifice art for commerce. Singapore-based columnist Lee Han Shih, my friend and former colleague, believed that such preference was inevitable. In an article in *Business Times* (Singapore), he estimated that the Esplanade's cost would grow to £600m, making each of the 4,000 seats worth a five-room state-built apartment. To keep those seats filled, the complex would have to invite top international artists regularly. To keep it affordable to Singaporeans, subsidies would become necessary. As a prestigious national project, large companies would have to direct their grants to the Esplanade, depriving the small, local arts groups without which Singapore's arts scene would become entirely imported. Lee pointed out that in 2001, Singapore's National Arts Council gave $4 million to local groups, and spent $5.76 million on an annual arts festival. The opening of the Esplanade itself cost $9.6 million.

Art not for art's sake, but for its commercial spin-offs was the agenda. Unlike great arts cities of the world, Singapore worked on a Faustian bargain, which swapped political and artistic freedom for profit. In the 1949 film *The Third Man*, Orson Welles had ad-libbed: 'In Italy for 30 years under the Borgias they had warfare, terror, murder, and bloodshed, but they produced Michelangelo, Leonardo da Vinci, and the Renaissance. In Switzerland they had brotherly love—they had 500 years of democracy and peace, and what did they produce? The cuckoo clock.' Apply that to Singapore, and you might hear him say: 'Indonesia had a bloody revolution, a militant insurgency, and three decades of Suharto's dictatorship and a million died, and yet it produced *Balinese* dances, *wayang kulit*, and the fiction of Pramoedya Ananta Toer. Singapore had 30 years of peace and stability, and what did it produce? The disk drive of personal computers.'

The plan to become a global arts city clashed with Singapore's firm rules governing what could be said and what couldn't, and distrust of dissidents and artists who challenge the established order. But that contradiction didn't appear to worry officials. The list of films, books, magazines and plays banned in Singapore was long, and local artists weren't spared. Elangovan's play, *Talaq* (Divorce), about rape within an Indian Muslim marriage, was banned following local protests. At the Singapore International Film Festival, a short documentary about opposition politician J B Jeyaretnam, called *A Vision of Persistence*, was withdrawn after the filmmakers were advised that they could be charged under the Films Act, which banned the making, distribution and showing of films containing "wholly or partly either partisan or biased references to or comments on any political matter".

A few years ago, in the case of performance artist Josef Ng, the authorities went a step further: his controversial production staged after midnight to a handful of people at an avant-garde theatre was enough for the government to ban the genre entirely. In his show, Ng caned slabs of tofu (phonetically, the word can mean gay in some Chinese dialects). He then turned his back to the audience, bared his buttocks, and quietly snipped off some of his pubic hair. Ng was charged under obscenity laws for a staging a show which protested against a police operation in which twelve gay men were arrested and punished by caning (Singapore retains Victorian-era colonial laws against homosexuality). Ng was banned from performing in public, and the group that backed him was denied National Arts Council grants. An official statement said that art forms without scripts that may encourage audience participation 'pose dangers to public order, security and decency ... the performances may be exploited to agitate the audience on volatile social issues, or to propagate the beliefs and messages of deviant social or religious groups, or as a means of subversion.' Such rules were common in Jacobean England and medieval-era Europe. But we were now in the twentieth century.

Since then, performers played it safe. In a play that had partial nudity, one company installed a red light at the corner of the stage to warn the audience that a risque scene was coming up, so that anyone offended could shut their eyes. Another director clothed his artists in skin-coloured tights during a lovemaking scene. People were happy to swallow their words. Garry Rodan, director of the Asia Research Centre at the Murdoch University in Australia, told me once: 'The tension between promotion of the arts and limits to free expression is manageable (in Singapore) precisely because the curbs are not generalised and are often achieved through self-censorship.'

The boundaries of transgression were not defined. Singapore's leadership bemoaned the lack of creativity among its people, and exhorted them to be different. But when some did, the establishment came down upon them, because it feared spontaneity.

Singapore's *raison d'etre* was, after all, to be an efficient business centre where people were expected to trade goods and services, not talk about politics, or debate sensitive or artistically challenging ideas. Business centres thrive on certainty and predictability, not on spontaneity.

Boundaries and markers. You place them, and you earmark an area. You get a zoo, and you know where you can stay, and where you mustn't stray. Remove the boundaries and markers, and it becomes a jungle. Singapore offered the freedom to the goldfish to swim inside a large bowl. The fish could swim round and round, but there was always that awareness, of the glass at the edge which formed the boundary, and if you tried to cross that, you hit the wall, and you retreated to where you began, and started again, much slower. A cabinet minister called that boundary "OB Markers", using a term from golf for out-of-bound markers. But the difference was that those markers kept changing, and you never knew when you were too close to the edge, and when you were comfortably in the middle. It was safer to stay within limits.

However, you could sing in your cage. In fact, elderly Chinese men trained their parakeets and bulbuls and other exotic birds to sing in their cages, and they held competitions in those void decks. But the winning birds could never flutter their wings and fly.

To see birds, you went to a bird park—the falcons would come and rest on your arm; the peacock would walk besides you. The macaws would display their brilliant colours and you could walk through an African aviary, with a reassuring waterfall behind you, while the birds flew around you. At the same time, the city hired staff to shoot crows, whose ugliness and noise were a recurring menace in Singapore. The central idea behind the Singapore project was to lift yourself from your region and be part of the modern, western world, but with distinct Asian values. The hearty virtues of Minneapolis on the Malay Peninsula—but with mandarin policies.

Birds too must obey, and mustn't be encouraged to flutter their wings. Doing away with dirt and filth was an obsession. During our first year in Singapore, we lived in public housing, in Eunos. Old men used to sit in void decks of car parks and they would feed seeds and nuts to pigeons. The food drew more birds to that area. Someone got so angry with the feeding, that the person laid poisoned seeds on the ground early one morning, before the old men had woken and come down for their tea and noodles, before they could feed their seeds to the pigeons. And the pigeons ate the poisoned seeds the stranger had left, and they died, one by one. In this undramatic city that was a story for the newspapers the next morning. The reporter speculated that someone upset with the filth of pigeons' droppings must have done this.

As Stan Sesser notes with wry amusement in *Prisoner in a Theme Park*, his essay about Singapore published in *The New Yorker* magazine in 1992, Singapore's obsession with cleanliness went to absurd lengths. Newspapers named and shamed toilets that were unclean; one newspaper photographed a man who had left the toilet without flushing it, and even named him. Sesser's title of his essay was an accurate metaphor: Chia Thye Poh, an opposition politician, was in jail. The Government wanted him to admit that he was a Communist agent; he refused, because he said he wasn't a Communist. His cell was near one of the stations of the monorail on the island of Sentosa, Singapore's pleasure ground. The tourists looking for dolphins and Mississippi riverboats and fake volcanoes would neither know, nor believe, that the playground was also a prison. Chia was released after spending more than a quarter century in detention.

For another metaphor, I'd turn to Gibson, who called Singapore "Disneyland with Death Penalty", reminding readers that the faux-cheer of Singapore has a sinister undercurrent. (On a per capita basis, Singapore used to have one of the highest rates of executions, although the actual numbers have fallen in recent years.)

The birds could sing, but there was the golden cage, and the bird wasn't allowed to fly. If it did, the consequences would be unpredictable. In his novel, *Love in the Time of Cholera*, García Márquez had written that caged parrots forget everything they have learned. And in his poem from the collection, *The Gardener*, Tagore writes about a conversation between two birds, one in a cage, one free. The free bird wants the cage bird to fly; the cage bird wants the free bird to join him in the cage. The free bird points out the bars and asks where he could spread his wings; the cage bird fears, not knowing where he could sit on a perch in the sky. The free bird wants to sing and soar; the cage bird wants to speak and listen. They yearn to be together, but they won't fly together.

*The free bird cries, "It cannot be, I fear the closed
doors of the cage."
The cage bird whispers, "Alas, my wings are powerless
and dead."*

But sometimes opening the cage is the only way to know
what one is capable of—and to discover if what was inside
was ever yours.

The zoologists who designed the night safari didn't have a
political project in mind, and yet the safari ended up mirroring
the city it was part of. The zoologists had been scrupulous
and meticulous: only 12 per cent of the native trees were cut
to create the game preserve, and hundreds of new trees had
been planted. Along with the majestic sight of the rain forest,
the landscape was dotted with rare trees such as the aquilaria
and the jelutong, also known as the chewing gum tree, from
which gum can be extracted for commercial use (and despite
its name, the tree was not banned in Singapore—which had
famously banned chewing gum in early 1992, on the eve of
President George H W Bush's visit to Singapore).

Safaris are meant to be wild. I had been to Sabi Sabi in
South Africa where, over twenty-four hours, we were able
to see the big five animals—elephant, lion, rhinoceros,
hippopotamus, and buffalo. But the forest rangers there had
made no promises. Then again, in Kenya one afternoon, I saw
flamingos take off from a lake like ballerinas on cue, with the
breathtaking synchronicity as if they were expecting to be
featured in a *National Geographic* spread. It was unplanned,
unexpected, and hence more memorable. But Singapore was
the city of certainties.

A wild national park was never on the cards here—the
amount of space such a park would need did not exist, or, if

it did, the land had more profitable uses. And while there was a solid, professional zoo that you could see in broad daylight, you knew it was a zoo, a park, and not a forest. There were cages, moats separating you from the animals, and there were signposts.

A night safari, on the other hand, would conjure the illusion of appearing to be a jungle, but one where everything ran according to plan. So very Singaporean, *lah*. The night safari guaranteed what you saw, that you saw what you paid for, that you didn't return disappointed, a sort-of trouble-free what-you-see-is-what-you-get experience that its shopkeepers were accustomed to provide. It is what businesses expected—quick turnaround time and minimum disruption to make for a reliable, satisfying experience. And you got that in spades. The world was on offer, like at the shopping malls on Orchard Road, like at the food alleys of Singapore—not just the hawker stalls of Newton, Geylang, or Chinatown, but also at the restaurants at Clarke Quay and Boat Quay, with cuisines from around the world. In the same vein, the night safari had the African giraffe, the Indian barasingha, the North American deer, the grazing mountain goats and bharal (blue-coloured sheep) from the Himalayan foothills, the South-East Asian seladang (wild ox), and the banteng, or the Bali cattle, a species of wild South-East Asian cows, whose large white spots on brown rumps prompted our guide to remark, 'They look like they're wearing diapers.' This being Singapore, that would be in character, where even cattle must wear diapers. You had to know your toilet manners.

The safari is spectacular at night—concealed lights illuminated the animals and their habitats, casting a gentle bluish glow almost convincing enough to make you believe you were strolling through a jungle on a moonlit night. Nocturnal animals have different habits, and the only time to see many animals in action is at night. Only mad dogs and Englishmen go out in the mid-day sun, as Noel Coward sang, sagely, referring to the British habit of stepping out when the sun was at its most merciless, when all the native Asians wisely took siesta. Animals needed lots of hours to sleep during the day, but were willing to come alive at sundown. When the lights dimmed, they began to hunt for their prey, to graze, and mate.

But it was a make-believe world. In the real world there were rules if you tried doing any of that. The safari recreated the reality—like Second Life—of a jungle, but without its dangers, without the scents, and made it a wholesome experience, eliminating surprises. In the city-state where the jungle is made of glass and concrete, where the national bird is the crane, and where wildlife means everything that's banned, the safari adds a new dimension to its urban vocabulary. It transports the island back to its tropical roots. But the experience is strictly "parental guidance".

There is something to the make-believe nature of the island, I thought, reflecting on the prevailing myths about its origins. In 1811, Temenggong, a local chief, arrived to resettle Singapura, as the island was known, with about a hundred Malays. A medieval city had once stood there, called Temasek, over which the Javanese and Siamese had fought, and Temenggong wanted to reclaim it for the Malays. He held it for six years, before Stamford Raffles took over the island for the British East India Company.

Another myth was that the city got its name after Sang Nila Utama, a local ruler, saw a lion, although later story-tellers say he very likely saw a tiger or some other big cat. But Singapura, or lion city, it became. Then there was a more modern myth, about Singapore's last surviving tiger being shot in the Long Bar or the Bar and Billiards Room of Raffles Hotel in 1902. The tiger had hidden beneath a raised structure—was it a bar? A billiards table? There is no evidence about either—and it was shot. Other writers have claimed that it was a large cat that the inebriated patrons had mistaken for a tiger.

Tiger, cat, or lion: when it came to creating its national symbol, Singapore wanted a feline motif, and an advertising executive came up with the bright idea of a Merlion—part fish, part lion—which had never existed: not only in history, but nor in Singapore's past or its myths. But Singapore's tourist promotion board didn't think that such a minor detail was a problem, and the Merlion became the island's symbol. On Sentosa Island now stands a large statue of a Merlion, giving the island no time for history.

When I was at Sabi Sabi at night, our jeep had to pause when a herd of buffaloes thundered past. We were told to stay quiet when we passed elephants. We were told not to get near the hippo—there was no safe buffer zone. And we had to drive slowly when we saw a lion, sitting quietly and ignoring us, blood trickling from its mouth.

The Merlion of Singapore was also immoveable, because it was a statue. And when the right switches were pressed, it emitted fireworks, its eyes turning colourful. Nothing could be left to chance to make for a happy family experience.

Birds can sing, but only in the cage; you open the cage and they fly away; they were never yours anyway. But the golden cage becomes the city's metaphor, a city whose folk tales are made up, and where even lions are prisoners in a park.

PRAISE THE LORD AND BUY INSURANCE

Within moments of landing at the Murtala Mohammed Airport in Lagos, I see a tall man, not particularly friendly, coming towards me. He is matter-of-fact, shows no identification, he is not wearing any uniform, and asks for my passport. I have no time to decide if he is for real: everyone else gives in, so I comply.

It turned out he is indeed from the immigration department, but I don't ask why he is not in uniform, nor carrying any identification. Then, with karmic acceptance I move towards the front of the queue, hoping to be reunited with my passport.

It seems only two kinds of foreigners arrive in Nigeria these days: burly oilmen sweating profusely, their Scottish and Texan accents announcing their identity before their passports are seen, and meek-looking men wearing dark suits, their collars suggesting they are men of God. The first lot wants the oil, the next lot is keen to save souls, but both exude piety. A talkative Scottish man has spent the better part of the long flight from London explaining to me how he does his bit for the poor children who live near the oilfield where he works. Before returning to Glasgow for home leave, each time he asks the children what they'd like, and then faithfully complies with their requests, buying Manchester United T-shirts at bargain prices. 'They had nothing, now they are happy,' he tells me. The man of God—the one with the collar, has Bibles to give, not T-shirts—and he expects to float over the crowds in the queue because of that collar. Miraculously, he does.

I'm wearing a collarless T-shirt, and it doesn't carry the Manchester United logo. With my bulky Indian passport, I'm not of much interest to the immigration officials either.

There are people idling about aimlessly throughout the airport, as in any poor country, eagerly sizing up the new arrivals, hoping that contact with one of them just might lead to a better future—a cab ride to the hotel, offer of services legal or otherwise, willingness to partner in a business deal. There is probably that idiot from abroad, who has responded to the offer of a fortune from someone in Nigeria. Legions of enterprising Nigerians have posed as widows of dictators, children of dead ministers of petroleum, and nephews of dead generals, willing to share part of their ill-gotten fortune with you, if only you would provide them with your bank details. That many succumb to such outlandish offers only proves the old saying attributed to the showman who gave Americans the circus—P T Barnum—that a sucker is born every minute. That Barnum did not say this multiplies the irony.

In the baggage hall, oversized bags have been dumped between the conveyer belts, and the bags sit there, immovable, like stubborn cows on an Indian road. And there are assorted overstuffed baskets, as I try to negotiate my trolley through the congested space, like a tuk-tuk driver during rush hour in Bangkok. Some trolleys are without wheels, and they lie abandoned, like cars with open bonnets on a highway. I find another trolley coming my way. It squeaks loudly, as if making up for the missing siren, and while it does not have flashing lights, the determined way it moves towards me prepares me for a showdown. There is a woman behind that trolley, and she is staring straight ahead. 'Get out,' she shouts. 'Get out of my way.' There are people behind me; it isn't possible to turn back. There is a crowd to my right, people eagerly rummaging through bags, and the crowd will miraculously race towards the carousel the moment the chute starts dumping more bags, randomly, as another flight arrives. To my left, there is a huge pile of unclaimed suitcases which another crowd is busy examining.

It is impossible for me to step aside and make way for the woman. It would be simpler for her to move back; there is nobody behind her. But she advances menacingly towards me.

I try suggesting she let me pass instead, politely. She begins banging her trolley with mine. 'Get out of my way, you bastard. This is not Pakistan. This is not India. This is Nigeria. This is my country,' she roars, glaring angrily, continuing to hit my trolley hard, like the child who won't listen, who has never been disciplined, and who will keep knocking down tricycles in her way.

A British Airways attendant notices this and swiftly creates space to my side and removes my trolley from her path and moves in front of me. I step aside. Noticing my abject surrender, she sways by, not even looking at me. She is wearing gold jewellery. Her *bubu*, white with a black border, looks lovely on her. Her hair is tied neatly in a tall bun. She has dark eyes and she looks like someone who must have broken many hearts in her teens.

Later, the attendant tells me: 'Some General's wife. Best stay out of their way, sir.'

In her outward beauty, in the promise she represented in her youth, in her willingness to knock anything that's in her way today, and in the childish petulance she has retained in her adulthood, she personifies the arrogant, swaggering Nigerian elite. Her rage and her impatience train me well for what to expect on the roads over the next few weeks.

୬୬

As I leave the terminal, the full force of humidity greets me. Our driver is amused as I buckle up. He reluctantly agrees to do so only because I insist. The sky is already dark and it is the middle of the night, confirming the cardinal rule of aviation— the poorer the country, the more unearthly the time of arrivals and departures.

We see traces of smoke from fires lit in the slums which can't be seen in the darkness. Our driver is from Benin, and his name is Sunday. I prefer to call him Dimanche, since he speaks French. He actually likes that. Nigeria has unusual names—its most recent President was called Goodluck Jonathan, and that's his real name. Dimanche drives fast—that you can tell from the rattling sound. There is no way to know how fast he is driving, because the speedometer is among the several things in the car that have stopped working. The window in the front won't open, and the window in the rear won't shut. The radio periodically emits static, between evangelical sermons and Yoruba incantations.

It is night: not only are the slums without lights, so are many of the buildings. The streetlights do not work either. The driver honks periodically to warn the people, because they cross the highway without any warning. He drives fast, as if he is late for an appointment, but we are only headed to my hotel and there is no need to rush. But he does not listen. The bridge has no lights either; the car's headlights don't work; children from the slums on either side dash across the bridge, disregarding the cars; and the air smells of smoke. It is not an easy ride.

We get onto the Third Mainland Bridge, Africa's longest. The next morning, we will be able to see the slums, precarious on stilts, with skyscrapers on the horizon, visible in hazy light, and the grey waters of the coast will be covered by mist.

Reading Chris Abani, I discover there are more canals in this city than in Venice, except that many were not intended as canals. 'Gutters have become waterways and lagoons fenced in by stilt homes or full of logs for a timber industry most of us don't know exists. All of it is skated by canoes as slick as any dragonfly,' he writes in an essay about the city.

As we near the city, I can make out the dim outline of a billboard, which says—This is Lagos. That's it. It doesn't say "Welcome to…" or "Enjoy your stay in..,," or "… the city of smiles," or any other cheesy slogan tourism ministries dream up. Abani writes that the slogan reminds him of a warning. This is Lagos—Watch out for pickpockets.

Outside the city the highway is full of life: some cars are stuffed with chairs, some with pots and pans, still others with food. We see men on okadas, as motorcycle taxis are known, carrying dozens of wooden cages, full of birds.

It is not yet 8:00 am, and my meeting in a town outside Lagos is at 12:00 pm, but we have set out anyway. This is the city of go-slow, as traffic jams are known. There are bottlenecks of all sorts—a diversion because of construction, a burst oil pipeline, a police checkpoint, or cars queuing up to buy petrol in a country that's sub-Saharan Africa's biggest oil producer but still faces fuel shortages.

We join our first go-slow, behind a trail of red tail-lights. This is commonplace; no one honks, no one complains. Drivers wait stoically. Hawkers have emerged, selling us magazines, cell phone cards, soft drinks, biscuits. When I notice we haven't moved in twenty minutes, I ask the driver if it is normal. He asks one of the children selling napkins, who tells us there is an overturned lorry ahead. A lot of flour lies on the road, and cars have to drive through the flour.

We lurch forward; an evangelist on the radio promises salvation if we attend a rally at a stadium that weekend.

The enterprising Nigerians have made way for the desperate ones—beggars now surround us. They point the infants they are carrying (unlike in India, they aren't maimed), and they are certain many passengers will succumb and pass with their naira notes.

At last, we reach the overturned truck. Hundreds of kilos of flour and grain sprawled on the street. Other cars drive by nonchalantly, disturbing the dune each time, creating an oddly pointillist image, as the flour rises up, making the landscape hazy. On the side of the road, a woman desperately attempts to protect the eggs she plans to sell. Two policemen try in vain to preserve some order. One waves his arms enthusiastically, as if conducting an orchestra. The other stares at the traffic, thinking how pointless it is to keep waving his hands when nobody is paying attention.

Better roads would make life easier for the inveterate traders, like the woman selling eggs. The only authority they fear is of the men in green, who we meet later, as they walk around with AK-47s slung casually on their shoulders, demanding papers. If they find someone who has had a good day at the market, they'd like to share her fortune—like that woman who sold eggs.

Corruption swallows a huge chunk of Nigerian income. According to Transparency International, Nigeria ranks 136th out of 175 countries evaluated under its corruption perception index in 2014. A few years ago, London's Metropolitan Police questioned a visiting Bayelsa state governor because he could not explain how he was travelling with so much cash. He escaped from a British jail dressed as a woman. Another governor runs an airline, imposing stiff costs on competing airlines; the idea of conflict of interest doesn't occur to him. A senior naval officer accuses his commanders of permitting an entire oil tanker to disappear from a port, after the tanker is seized for investigations of stolen oil. And the police nonchalantly demand bribes from aid workers.

Later that week, as we fly over the estuaries in a helicopter, we see the riverine landscape dotted with flares, burning twenty-four hours a day, like men smoking incessantly. Oil companies had promised they would stop the flaring by 2008. The target had been pushed back to 2011. And then again. By day the rivers glisten, as if reflecting a rainbow— but it is not a rainbow over a beautiful sunset; the colours are on the water, illuminating the trail from the oil leaking from the engines of boats.

We were going to an oil facility facing the ocean, and we flew by helicopter because my host, who worked at the oil company, felt that any other way of travelling there would be too dangerous. He mentioned how precarious the unlicensed boats would be, and how their drivers, as the captains were called, would fleece my Swedish colleague Ulrika and me, as neither of us looked like we belonged to those parts.

From the helicopter, the dense forest below us looked stunning. It was an emerald wilderness, but the green wasn't the shining bright green you'd associate with a country blessed with sunlight, lying so close to the equator, but a dull and tired green, as if a grey layer, like ash, was scattered evenly between us and the trees.

It wasn't difficult to guess why. The landscape was dotted with the well-heads and flow stations of oil companies, and you could see the chimneys aflame, like lit cigarettes scattered in a field, sending billowing smoke to the sky, the embers lit bright. Instead of a crisp blue, the sky was a permanent, dull grey, and it was not yet 11 am. The land was serrated by an intricate network of oil pipelines criss-crossing the area, looking like intestines of a dead, prehistoric mammal. The creeks revealed the now-familiar rainbow patterns that boats left in their trail. 'The petrol they use is mixed with spurious stuff, and the boats are very unsafe. That's why I said you should fly, not take the boat,' my host reminded me. We nodded.

Those colours took me back to the time I grew up in Bombay, where I'd see the rainbow pattern in little pools of water after the first burst of monsoon in early July, and how much I enjoyed splashing that water, seeing the disturbed water form concentric circles, before settling back to its placid state, the rainbow returning where it used to be. Here, too, we could see a boat move along the creek, belching smoke, separating the water, the oily rainbow emerging again, regaining its original shape.

The oil plant looked like the innards of a gigantic skeleton. It was lit up. It was surrounded by water on three sides, an island of modernity, with occasional tiny fishing villages nearby, villages that had been there for a long time—before there was the plant, before there was oil, before this place was Nigeria.

With all that oil beneath the surface, there is no reason for seven out of ten Nigerians to live on less than a dollar a day. Some 97 per cent of the country's exports and 80 per cent of the state's revenues come from oil, which, at US$70 a barrel (at the time of writing) can earn Nigeria more than US$43 billion. The journalist Karl Maier, in his book *This House Has Fallen*, pointed out that Nigeria has earned more than US$240 billion from oil in the past four decades. Over that period, its human development indicators have declined.

Such is the state of the country four decades after independence, with billions of barrels of oil exploited, and with another four decades' worth of oil buried beneath its land. Nigeria has had several presidential elections after democracy has returned, but the country hasn't made any progress from the bleak assessment of Chinua Achebe, who wrote in his 1983 tract,*The Trouble With Nigeria*: 'The trouble with Nigeria is simply and squarely a failure of leadership. The Nigerian problem is the unwillingness or inability of its leaders to rise to the responsibility, (and) to the challenge of personal example, which are the hallmarks of true leadership.'

Even democratically-elected leaders don't understand this notion of "personal example". They don't like pesky activists asking inconvenient questions. After the two-term President Olusegun Obasanjo gave a long sermon to activists in the Niger Delta, asking them to be patient, a friend of mine who studies conflict in the Niger Delta raised his hand and asked a pertinent question about the military's links with oil companies. Obasanjo is a former general: he frowned and lectured him, saying the questioner had been rude to him, an elder, his senior in rank, age, and experience, and he should be ashamed of himself for having asked such a question. His question wasn't answered.

Elders demand respect and hope to inspire fear. In the remote village of Odioma, I saw the charred remains of the "palace" of a local chief, destroyed by the army to remind the local residents who was in charge. To humiliate the chief, they forced him to eat sand, as his subjects watched. Nigerian Nobel Laureate Wole Soyinka recalls brutal rituals in *Ake*, his childhood memoir, where the faces of many men and women carried inexplicable scars, to mark one community from another, to establish authority.

The village that disobeys is destroyed so thoroughly that not a trace remains. The executed Ogoni activist and writer, Ken Saro-Wiwa described an evacuated town, Ogale, thus:

A lone lean dog
Scrounging for food
Reaps human skulls
In a shallow gutter

For Ogale out in the dreary rain
Her legs apart like a cheap prostitute
Exposed, utterly exposed.
Ogale is a ravished woman.

Then again, in *Sozaboy: A Novel in Rotten English*, he writes about a village where all the houses have fallen and those left standing have a hole where the roof should be, and rains have flooded the home.

Fear prevails everywhere. Even professionals tremble with fear when they think their actions might disobey authority. Another time, I was in the town of Warri, which has witnessed brutal violence between the Ijaw and Itsekiri communities. I was there with Ulrika to interview the director of a hospital, to verify claims made by a few young men, who had shown me their wounds, and alleged that security forces had beaten them up. They had to make their own way to the hospital.

We had turned up at the hospital unannounced. The doctor was polite in the beginning, but turned pale when we told him what we wanted to know. He asked us to meet his deputy, and while we were away from his office, he spoke to some superior, came back to us agitatedly, and asked us to leave, immediately. He had studied in Pune in India, but the easy early banter—when he spoke a bit in Marathi with me—had disappeared. The young doctor escorting us to our car whispered to us, confirming that the young men's claims were, indeed, true.

As we sat in the car, a bearded man, without any identification or uniform, drove near us in a growling motorbike, and told our driver that we should follow him.

Ulrika has long experience of Africa. She instantly knew he was from the secret service. She told the driver to lock the doors, ignore the man on the motorbike, and drive away—quickly. It was still daylight; it was a calculated risk: we were gambling that he was unlikely to shoot at us or chase us, and it was a risk worth taking. The petrified driver did as we had told him. The man on the motorbike got angry; his motorbike growled; he tried to give us a chase, and then, inexplicably, he turned away.

Later that day I saw him again, when we went to meet the local military commander. He was standing with men in uniform, laughing and exchanging gossip. We froze when we saw him. He laughed at us.

❧

Fear is omnipresent in Nigeria—in his Reith lectures at the BBC in 2004 Soyinka dealt with the theme of fear. He described the Nigerian state of mind as one which has 'a palpable intimacy with fear, an experience that was never undergone even in the most brutal season of the colonial mandate.' And it is easy to understand why: the guardians of the state have looted the treasury wantonly, and those who question anything are asked to mind their manners, as the president did with my friend. Nigerians know that challenging the authority is only for the brave. The Harvard-educated finance minister Ngozi Okonjo-Iweala's efforts to make the economy transparent were resisted at all levels. Dora Akunyili, a fearless food and drugs administrator, who tried to eradicate spurious drug manufacturers, has survived an assassination attempt.

One writer who protested Nigeria's injustices to his region was Saro-Wiwa. Appalled by the military repression, the pollution, the devastation of the landscape in the Niger Delta, and the constant flaring of gas, he organised his community— the Ogoni people—demanding an end to environmental degradation. He made Shell Petroleum companies in Nigeria the target of his criticism because in Ogoniland, Shell was the main oil company, even though other oil majors—Total, Chevron, Agip, and Exxon Mobil also operated throughout the Delta. The Ogoni campaign against Shell took on David vs Goliath proportions.

The communities argued that the companies were ruining their health, their farmland, and their environment. If the community protested, the company was able to get the men in green to protect their facilities. And the army took its role seriously, saying oil was a strategic national asset, and disrupting its production was unacceptable to the government. The oil companies expressed their helplessness in one specific regard: while they made the investment and set up the plants, the majority stake of every operation belonged to the Nigerian state. Company officials said they lacked the power to make the government change its policies. Activists refused to believe companies' protestations. The antagonism worsened: to buy support from local communities, some companies began building primary healthcare clinics, schools, and provided water and electricity to the villages near their operations. That built expectations in the communities in the immediate vicinity, who began to bypass the state and turned to the companies directly for all their needs; and that made other communities, not so close to the oil operations, angry, because they felt they were being denied access to the facilities the communities near the operations enjoyed. And so, the communities which were further away from the oil facility began attacking the company's infrastructure, or the villages that were benefiting from corporate philanthropy.

It is in that environment that Saro-Wiwa launched his campaign. The generals hated him; they implicated him and eight others (now known as the Ogoni Nine—besides Saro-Wiwa, they included Saturday Dobee, Nordu Eawo, Daniel Gbooko, Paul Levura, Felix Nuate, Baribor Bera, Barinem Kiobel, and John Kpuine) in a conspiracy to murder four Ogoni elders. Ten days before his arrest, Saro-Wiwa is supposed to have told his friends: 'This is it—they are going to arrest us all and execute us.' He believed it was for oil.

From his jail, Saro-Wiwa wrote:

> A year had gone by since I was rudely roused from my bed and clamped into detention. Sixty-five days in chains, weeks of starvation, months of mental torture, and, recently, the rides in a steaming, airless Black Maria to appear before a kangaroo court, dubbed a special military tribunal, where the proceedings leave no doubt that the judgment has been written in advance. And a sentence of death against which there is no appeal is a certainty.... The men who ordain and supervise this show of shame, this tragic charade, are frightened by the word,

the power of ideas, the power of the pen; by the demands of social justice and the rights of man. Nor do they have a sense of history. They are so scared of the power of the word, that they do not read. And it is their funeral.... I had no doubt where it could end. This knowledge has given me psychological advantage over my tormentors. Whether I live or die is immaterial. It is enough to know that there are people who commit time, money and energy to fight... If they do not succeed today, they will succeed tomorrow.

In his final statement to the military tribunal, Saro-Wiwa declared:

I and my colleagues are not the only ones on trial. Shell is here on trial... The company has ducked this trial, but its day will surely come... The ecological war that the company has waged in the Delta will be called into question; and the crimes ... will be duly punished.

After a show trial, the government executed them, despite appeals from world leaders. When President Bill Clinton called Gen Sani Abacha, pleading clemency for the Ogoni Nine, the general was conciliatory on the phone with the American president, but then boasted to his followers how he was going to ignore Clinton.

In mid-2009, Shell settled a long-standing lawsuit filed against the company by Saro-Wiwa's family. It did not admit any wrongdoing—it insisted it had tried hard to seek Saro-Wiwa's release. But it paid $15 million to the survivors and select Ogoni charities. It succeeded in avoiding being sued under the Alien Tort Claims Act in the United States in a case that came to be known as *Kiobel vs Shell*, and more recently settled more claims in the Niger Delta, by paying compensation to communities for pollution.

That is not yet the full justice Saro-Wiwa sought. But for many in the Niger Delta, it is a start. *'Let me love and sing and dance; let me dance and sing and love; before the doom engulfs.'*

A year after the executions in 1996, Soyinka wrote in *The Open Sore of a Continent*:

> Ogoniland, alas, only has the model space for the actualisation of a long term dreamt totalitarian onslaught on the more liberated, more politically sophisticated sections of the Nigerian polity, which have dared expose and confront the power obsession of a minuscule but obdurate military-civilian hegemony.

Had anything changed in the decade since? Appearance and reality clashed everywhere, the camouflage more confusing. A woman who called herself a human rights activist was, we found out, the wife of a general, and her job was to spy upon us. Late one night in Port Harcourt, the oil capital of Nigeria, I met a leading civil liberties lawyer, who admitted over dinner that he felt more secure during military rule because, 'at least we could go out in the evening and feel safe.' He had been jailed during dictatorship, and was documenting cases of urban violence in Nigeria. His figures showed there were more random shootings and deaths since the onset of democracy.

Safety was relative. Car-jackings were frequent. A few months before my visit, a car carrying a senior naval commander was ambushed in Lagos. When I asked a Western diplomat if it was safe for us to visit The Shrine, the nightclub of Femi Kuti, the musician son of the legendary Fela Kuti, the diplomat shrugged: 'Sure, if you go with armed guards in a Humvee.' The climate of fear that Soyinka talked about was a permanent state of mind.

We had to go to the Delta one more time. Disregarding the oil executive's warning, Ulrika and I boarded one of the local boats. The journey to the village was uneventful. Once there, we met a well-fed village chief, surrounded by unemployed men who called themselves the local youth (which meant anyone under forty). A hungry man is an angry man, one of the young men said, quoting Bob Marley. He looked well-fed, but insisted on calling himself hungry. They said they were desperate for jobs, that they were hungry, pointing at the oil company we had seen a week earlier. You didn't have to be a Marxist to realise that such a contrast couldn't survive for long. When we prepared to leave, the whole village had turned out to see us; women wearing colourful *bubus*, carrying plantains for the chief, their children sleeping snugly and secure on their backs, tied tight, rocked gently by the rhythm of their mothers' walk.

A loud, ominous cloudburst greeted us at what passed for the pier. The driver told us to hold on the edges of the boat tight. Within moments of our taking off, it started to rain. The sky looked menacingly dark, like the sky off the Indian west coast, but the rain was a different matter. Instead of falling vertically on our heads, it lashed at our bodies, our faces, attacking us horizontally. It felt like pinpricks first, but as the boat speeded up, the raindrops pierced us like little arrows, stinging sharply. The boat shook vigorously, like an aircraft in turbulence: without any warning, the driver bent low, and tossed a dark tarpaulin sheet over us, shrouding us, as if we were contraband goods.

The journey that followed is probably the scariest I have ever made: we could hear the rain hitting the sheet above us loudly, and it sounded like bullets. We could not see anything. Lisa Margonelli, an American writer who was there to research and later wrote the book about the oil industry, *Oil on the Brain*, was sitting next to me—all of us were afraid; we held each others' hands tight; Lisa held on to the edge of the boat on her right, as my left hand made sure that the sheet covering us did not fly away. The boat kept swaying, as if we were on the high seas. Here, despite the fact that you could see nothing, you felt forced to shut your eyes. I thought of my family and wanted to see them again. This was no way to die.

I have no idea how long it lasted. But stop it did, and then suddenly, the boatman took off the tarpaulin. We were all perspiring. The temperature rose, we cast aside the sheet, and the boatman looked visibly relaxed. Ulrika and Lisa began talking, making light of the experience, when suddenly, the boat swerved again as it sharply turned left, taking a different direction from the one intended.

'What happened? Why did you turn so suddenly?' I asked the driver with some annoyance.

Shh. He asked me to stay quiet.

I looked in the direction of the stream we had not taken. A large tree lay there, as if it were a roadblock.

'Is it the tree? Didn't you see? You could have turned slowly and gone from the other side.'

The driver said nothing. After a few more minutes, when we could no longer see the spot where we had taken that sharp turn he told us why. And what he told us was scarier than the boat ride.

'They were bunkering there,' the boat driver said. 'They had cut the tree and left it lying as a warning. If we had gone there, they'd have shot me and kidnapped you.'

"They" were the armies of the night, members of a local militia we had heard about. And "bunkering" is a unique Nigerian term for stealing oil. The Delta is littered with such groups, which make a living by stealing oil from the pipelines. If you interrupt the groups, you are kidnapped—if you are a foreigner and worth a ransom—and killed—if you are a local. Companies often pay up to secure the release of their staff. Nothing can stop this trade, unless there are real jobs in the area. The rebels justify what they are doing, saying, at least this way their families won't go hungry. Hungry men are angry men.

These gangs fill up ramshackle barges and supply tankers that take the oil to neighbouring countries like Cote d'Ivoire, where local refineries process the oil and the resulting petroleum products are sold to Nigeria. Armed guards protect the thieves, and it is not wise to cross their path.

As Nigerian crude goes abroad for refining, its own refining industry decays, operating at one-third of its capacity. And when some enterprising business thinks there's an opportunity in refining, so that some of the value-added profits can remain in Nigeria, the refinery gets mysteriously sabotaged. Millions of dollars of state wealth is siphoned off this way. And so it is that Nigeria, Africa's biggest oil producer, and OPEC's seventh largest, has economic indicators that would make a state like Bihar, often maligned as the poster-child of Indian poverty, blush.

Saro-Wiwa called one of his books *The Darkling Plain*. And ignorant armies do clash here by night. After his death, there is no one who can inspire the youth with a moral message. The youth have taken arms; they follow different strongmen—men like Alhaji Dokubo Asari who claimed the Delta's oil resources—he wanted all of it, not the 13 per cent of the revenue due to the oil-producing states once, nor the 17 per cent that the government was willing to offer. One hundred per cent: nothing less. And what if the state says no?. I stayed the rest of the night in his room while he went to sleep.

I find no poetry in slaughter fields

No lyric grace; redemptive passion, no.

Only that which came and went, as others –

The blaze of empires, salvation's ashes,

The crunch of cinders in time's cul-de-sac.

The communities attack the pipelines and claim damages because of the pollution that results from the sabotage, and companies refuse to pay up, saying the damage was due to a sabotage, and not because their pipelines were old. The military is everywhere. And everyone fears the military, and nobody trusts the authorities or the companies. Even those with power are cheated. Lagos has an area called Badagry, a beautiful stretch of land which blends into the sea. The place gets its name from a transaction between the local king and the colonial masters. It was a bad agreement—hence *bad agree*, and the place gets its name—Badagry.

To set those bad agreements right, people break rules. In Lagos, too, the poor attack the pipelines, hoping to steal fuel. If the city is the body, its veins are those pipelines, and as Abani puts it, the communities turn into vampires:

> Someone somewhere bored a hole into the pipelines to steal some oil—a drum here and there. Then it began to grow and the people like hungry mosquitoes began to drill more and more holes, taking greater and greater risks. The city bled thick sweet crude into containers that were sold and resold and then the city rebelled and the veins, tapped too much, too quickly, too dangerously, began to explode. Like a victim reclaiming its body from a deadly virus, the city began to kill its parasites, its succubae.

There are much simpler and less risky ways for people to earn money here. Stop those flames darkening the sky; let the sky be blue again. Let the creeks become a wetland that can draw tourists looking for lagoons. The tilapia fish will taste nice, and the boat ride will be less dangerous, as if in Disneyland.

In the land of Soyinka and Saro-Wiwa, one can dream.

On another journey outside Lagos, our driver was a cheerful Ghanaian man called Armstrong, named after the first man on moon, who listened to the same Yoruba rock group throughout our journey.

Armstrong may have been named after the man who advanced science, but our driver firmly believed in black magic. He probably thinks the Apollo mission to the moon was a miracle. In Port Harcourt, I was woken up one night by some screams from Armstrong's room. I knocked hard on his door, which was not locked, and saw him walking up and down his room, wearing only his underwear, shouting something incomprehensible. I shook him, and he stared back at me, as if he had woken up from deep sleep. I stayed in his room while he went to sleep. I stayed the rest of the night in his room. Later, I saw him wake up, grab a notebook, take out a torch, and write something furiously.

After breakfast, as we drove towards Lagos, I politely asked him what was going on.

'Angels and spirits,' he said, matter-of-factly.

'Angels?' I asked.

'Angels are speaking to me. They look after me. They are also looking after you. We've driven from one end of Niger Delta to another. Has anything happened to us so far?'

'No...'

'That shows the angels are looking after us.'

I let him drive. He is singing to himself.

We returned to Lagos in daylight, and saw many large billboards praising the Lord. Repent, seek forgiveness, confess, and God will help, we were told. Telegenic preachers like Benny Hinn offered a "healing crusade", whereas home-grown ministers Mike and Peace Okonkwo promised to listen to your confessions at the Redeemed Evangelical Mission. Across the road, the Redeemed Christian Church of God assured us that "God Still Answers". Grace Assembly, on the other hand, reminded us that "Jesus Transforms, Don't Conform". And for naira 400 (about eighty rupees), you could register for the Mountain of Fire's Global Prophetic Conference.

Pentecostal and evangelical churches grew during military rule, when all hope seemed lost. As Nigerians felt they could not control their lives, they sought hope through divine intervention. Electoral politics has returned, but hope hasn't, and evangelism continues to grow. Life is still hard for many and miracle workers are everywhere, promising redemption through healing and prayer. On Sunday mornings you wake up to loud hymns sung in makeshift churches. White-robed members of the Order of the Cherubim and Seraphim Church dip themselves in the water, invoking the Virgin Mary and Yemeya at the same time.

But people want to aspire and there is hope. In a country with post offices but no stamps, and telephones that sit on desks like paperweights, people communicate using cell phones and through Internet cafés, bypassing the state infrastructure. While people grumble about corruption and violence, they feel they can regain control by trusting temporal, not spiritual powers. They might still communicate with the Supreme Being through an intermediary, but they are also buying cell phones and talking to each other. Between 1999 and 2003, digital mobile telephone lines grew from a handful to 3.1 million, and Internet Service Providers have doubled to thirty-five. The software education company, NIIT, has opened computer schools, promising "the guide to a successful future". That could mean jobs. Kirloskars, another Indian company, is selling its generators for home use, to keep those computers running.

Big billboards promising miracles remain, but many Nigerians don't want to wait for angels to transport them to the kingdom of heaven—Chinese motorbikes with brandnames like Zongsheng, Nangang, Qing Qi or Jingcheng will do. As for wealth, fewer Nigerians seem to think praying harder will earn them riches. Their eyes are set on how the rich live on Victoria Island, in fancy houses that advertise wealth. In Ikoyi, the money is older, shown off by the size of land, the trimmed lawn, and perhaps a boat anchored at the lagoon. Across the bay, a village of millionaires sits in the hazy mist. Wind rustles through the palm fronds—it sounds romantic to those who live there; a poet listens to the moans of the mother whose child was crushed by a Humvee. Many Nigerians drive their friends from abroad through these parts, as if to show what they hope to achieve. In the land of Soyinka, people do dream.

To fuel those desires, companies and banks are offering shares to investors, banks are offering loans and seeking deposits. Thirty-seven banks were listed on the stock market when I visited Nigeria last, and their capitalisation had risen to more than US$81 billion. Some Nigerian banks advertise their services at London's Heathrow airport, in ads on London's buses.

On our last night in Lagos, at a Lebanese restaurant in Ikeja, a lawyer notes that middle-class Nigerians are increasingly buying financial products, including insurance policies. I see that as a good sign: you buy insurance when you want to hedge against risk. And you do that if you see a future for yourself in Nigeria. It is an important step away from fatalism. On our way to the restaurant, I have seen billboards selling cement—right above slums. Maybe, that's the future—made of concrete, not stilts. As Abani notes: 'Somewhere in another Lagos slum, a child is peeping through a crack in the wooden wall of a shack built on stilts in a swamp. In the distance, a line of skyscrapers rise, like the uneven heart of prayer.'

Nigerians want to own their space, not to keep borrowing it. In another poem, Saro-Wiwa had written:

Nigeria you like to borrow borrow

You borrow money, cloth you dey borrow

You borrow motor, you borrow aeroplane

You borrow chop, you borrow drink

Sotey you borrow anoder man language

Begin confuse am with your confusion

Anytin you borrow you go confuse am to nonsense

Idiot debtor, wetin you go do

When de owners go come take dem tings?

This time, they will own, not borrow. The churches pull them one way; *juju* magic another way; but some Nigerians now don't want to pray. They see a sign in those skyscrapers. They will invest in stocks and not in prayers, build homes and not only hopes, and then, maybe, dream again.

When the centre cannot hold, things fall apart. Borrowing from Yeats, Achebe acknowledged as much, when he titled his 1958 novel, *Things Fall Apart*. Some Nigerians are now beginning to hold their own centre together and taking charge of their lives—if enough of them do it, maybe, the country won't fall apart.

UNTIED AND UNITED

I have seen water shimmer on the Mekong, where a lonely boatman wearing a conical hat sails away into the river, his silhouette lengthening in the water in the evening; on the Arabian Sea, turning immensely golden and bright, blinding me, off Salalah in Oman; on Windermere Lake in England, a stark, sharp glimmer of autumnal glow one afternoon.

None of that had prepared me for the magical, quivering light of the Bosphorus, the strait that makes you think it is a river, blending one sea into another, keeping two continents apart, or bringing them together, depending on how you look at the world. People in this city refer to it as Boğaz. Here, East meets West, but not the way Rudyard Kipling intended.

How we describe locations is conditioned by where we are. When I had told a friend I worked for a magazine called *Far Eastern Economic Review,* he asked me: 'Far from where?' In India we used to call West Asia what the world liked to call the Middle East. The mother of an American friend once asked me if I lived in "the south" when I told her I lived in Bombay, because her daughter was spending a year in India, in Delhi. And therefore, for her, Bombay was to the south, and not the west, as we had been accustomed to referring to the city in India.

So where does the west meet the east? When Konrad Adenauer crossed the Elbe on his way to Berlin, he said, "*hier beginnt Asien,*" much like Metternich did once, for whom Asia began on the Landstrasse, east of Vienna. But I am in Istanbul, one-time Constantinople, the city where the fall of an empire once shaped the trajectory of world history. You can see the two continents on the horizon tantalisingly close, like lovers whose lips are about to meet.

Istanbul oozes passion. Here, some clerics and politicians want women to wear veils, but many men sit, their jaws dropped, mesmerised before a belly dancer at night. Here the East looks like the West, but behaves like the East, and the other way around. You are never sure if the Bosphorus signifies the division of continents, or their mingling.

Borders set apart differences; they divide people into clearly-marked territories. Borders operate at political levels and have human implications. As the Indo-Pakistani-British poet, Imtiaz Dharker writes:

It is the women who know

You can take in the invader

Time after time

And still be whole.

Whether they enter with loaded guns

Or kind words

You are quite intact.

The fact is

Each one has a borderline that cannot be erased.

Every borderline becomes a battlefield

And every night an act of faith.

જી

Istanbul has indeed been one kind of borderline: in 1453, the Ottomans vanquished the Byzantine Empire, making Constantinople Istanbul. In the new order, Christian ships could no longer navigate the waters. It stopped trading routes and forced Europeans to look for new ways to discover spice. Today, ships from around the world pass through the waters.

Istanbul carries the burden of that history, and the cloud of melancholia that hangs over the city has much to do with the collapse of the Ottoman Empire in 1922, after the First World War, when the sultanate was abolished. For many Turks that was humiliation. The Turkish Nobel Laureate Orhan Pamuk has a word for it—*hüzün*, which describes the city's unique and shameful post-imperial melancholy. It continues to weigh the city down, and Istanbul lives with its past by letting it blend with its present. You discover astonishingly beautiful doors and buildings emerging out of nowhere, behind bus stops, flanking the funicular, alongside the trams, mutely witnessing the city's transformation, revealing the city's past grandeur. And you do feel sad at the loss.

Kipling's "twain", east and west, do meet here. Women wear veils and jeans; men wear jackets without ties, but sport the unshaven look of the pious. "East" and "West" are often used as mutually exclusive categories. But as the novelist Elif Şafak writes: 'In Istanbul, you understand, perhaps not intellectually but intuitively, that East and West are ultimately imaginary ideas.'

This may be because much of Istanbul has embraced modernity—witness its high-rise towers, its public transport, its freeways, its easily accessible, clean and safe toilets for women—and the old city's crumbling walls, palaces and churches. They coexist, tolerating the other, often blending with one another, making it difficult to mark the boundaries between the spiritual and the temporal, the spirited and the abstinent. 'Like a pendulum, Istanbul swings obstinately between cosmopolitanism and nationalism, memory and amnesia—between a weighty past we can never fully shed, much as we like to try, and a hopeful future we can only run after but never quite grab hold of,' she continues.

In such confused places, boundaries remain undefined. Şafak mentions her own experience to describe how the state and the society are not the same. She experienced this first-hand a few years ago, when she was prosecuted under Article 301 of the Turkish Penal Code, which makes it a crime to insult "Turkishness." In her novel, *The Bastard of Istanbul,* an invented character refers to the millions of Armenians "massacred" by "Turkish butchers" who "then contentedly denied it all." In its official report, the Turkish Historical Society refers to the killing of at least a million Armenians between 1914 and 1918 as "relocations" with "some untoward incidents," with the sort of understatement that British bureaucrats too would find it impossible to make with a straight face. When Şafak's character said that, the government sued her—just as it had sued Pamuk earlier, for telling a Swiss journalist that '30,000 Kurds and one million Armenians were killed in these lands, and nobody but me dares to talk about it.' (Make that at least two—Pamuk is not alone, as Şafak's story shows, and there are over sixty such other cases, though many have been dropped subsequently.)

The Bastard of Istanbul was seen as a threat by ultranationalists, but welcomed, widely read and discussed in Turkey. This happens because, Şafak says, there are many Istanbuls—the city whose passing is marked by churches, chapels, synagogues, a Jewish cemetery, an Armenian Catholic hospital, an Assyrian church, and a Greek school without a pastor. Then there is the city of the latecomers who have migrated from remote villages in Anatolia for economic reasons. They aren't concerned about the past; they want to make their own future. There is the Istanbul of those born and raised in the city; and the city of tourists, hippies, mystics, secret agents, journalists and other sojourners, on a stopover before they go someplace else.

These cities live side by side, touching each other, but not always meeting.

> Just like water and oil. Yet in truth, East and West are not water and oil. They do mix. And in a city like Istanbul they mix intensely, incessantly, surprisingly. That can leave the city confused about its identity. We Turks like to brag about straddling past and present, East and West, but we are not quite sure what we mean by that. We think of these two civilizations as boroughs we can go in and out of randomly.

At one end of the Bosphorus Bridge, she notes, it says WELCOME TO EUROPE; at the other, WELCOME TO ASIA. 'But under the bridge, deep beneath the waters, there are two tides that pull the city in opposite directions,' one pulling towards Europe, the other nationalist and anti-western.

Who will win? Şafak sees that struggle as the defining one for modern Turkey. She writes:

> In a world where too many assume that Islam and Western democracy cannot possibly coexist, Turkey has been trying to keep a foot in each. One day— perhaps when Turkey joins the EU—the two signs will be removed from the bridge, and we will be able, once more, to re-imagine what East and West mean. Until then, however, many remain fearful of being made unwelcome on either side.

If borders divide people, bridges unite them. Another great unifier is trade, which is why the fall of Constantinople and a ban on Christian shipping forced Europe to think of new routes

to India, sending Vasco da Gama and Christopher Columbus in
opposite directions; one reaching India, the other, America.
    As I sit with a Danish friend one late evening, watching
the Bosphorous, she remarks how stunning it is to see so
many tankers. Here, ships sailing at night are noticed. And
they are welcomed, because they connect the world. There
is something special about the body of water separating
Istanbul, besides the light it reflects.
    In his melancholic and meditative reflections on his city,
Istanbul, Pamuk notes that the onetime sleepy fishing village,
Tarabya, where the poet C P Cavafy once lived, was known as
Therapia, because of its fresh air. He further writes:

> To be travelling through a city as great, historic and
> forlorn as Istanbul and yet feel the freedom of the
> open sea [is] the thrill along a trip on the Bosphorus.
> Pushed along by its strong currents, invigorated by
> the sea air that bears no trace of the dirt, smoke and
> noise of the crowded city, the traveller begins to feel
> that ... this is a place in which he can enjoy solitude
> and freedom.

    Is this a European city with an Asian soul, or an Asian town
with European manners? The haggling in the bazaar is straight
out of Asia, with salesmen pushing carpets and hookahs and
coffee and precious jewels onto you, making tall claims of how
they originally belonged to a pasha's princess or a sultan's
son, their shops carrying large photographs of Bill Clinton in
the souk, and you see Clinton's photograph in so many shops
you begin to wonder if he did anything else while in Istanbul,
besides buying carpets. And on the cobblestoned streets,
where pedestrians walk on a chilly night, huddled together,
cuddling one another, the clip-clop of their feet breaking the
silence of the street—now, that's so Europe.
    Around the corner of the mosque, the mood is distinctly
Asian when a friendly Turk starts chatting us up. He asks

where we are from, and talks of football with my friend John, who likes to remind anyone who presumes that he is English that he is Scottish too. And then with me, about Raj Kapoor, assuming that I must like India's greatest unacknowledged ambassador. And it is European when we are in the alfresco part of a restaurant, with musicians serenading the diners, while Juan, my Spanish friend, carves the delicate fish with thin bones so beautifully that the skeleton that emerges looks like fine filigree art, like French lace.

The church Hagia Sofia has Byzantine-era motifs on its walls and uneven stone paths, and it was once a mosque, and it is now a museum. Conquerors rename monuments, appropriating them. In Córdoba, I had seen both Muslims and Christians claim a particular building to be a mosque and a church. Here, the church-mosque has changed hands often, but nobody has thought of razing it down. In London where I live, an old church made way for a synagogue and now a mosque in East London, and there was no force used, but because the population had moved elsewhere, making way for a newer set of immigrants. Another church, not far from where I live, is now a Hindu temple. But in India in 1992, in Ayodhya, Hindus who believed that a god they revere was born at a particular spot decided to tear down a mosque that a Muslim conqueror had built in the sixteenth century on that spot. Perhaps Istanbul has found the way by making it a museum.

The mosque itself is huge and inspiring, making you feel so small as you walk inside; its dome hushing you into silence. The precise geometry of Islamic calligraphy on its walls, the patterns and the latticework, connect you with an aspect of the faith that's open, inviting, spiritual and ennobling. Walk through the large hall, and you think of peace; you shed the images the faith has acquired—of bearded men in swords glaring angrily at the enemy, their women invisible in black cloak-like outfits, making them look like shadows—and think instead of the elegance of the calligraphy, or the chants of Sufi dervishes that I heard from a corner store later in the afternoon. Those sounds did not have the same uplifting effect for me as Nusrat Fateh Ali Khan's singing tended to do, but the spiritual feeling was unmistakable.

I find manifestations of faiths coexisting side-by-side elsewhere, too. From an apartment window on an island I see a church and a mosque, near enough to each other. But there is competitiveness too, raising its head: the bell tower of the church is slightly smaller than the triumphant minaret. And yet, earlier that morning, on the same island, I see supporters of a traditional Islamic political party, all men, dancing arm in arm celebrating a victory, ignoring the young couple wrapped together as if they are stuck by glue, their mouths sealed, as though it is the last kiss before their parting, like a rare, G-rated fully-clothed Rodin sculpture, frozen in time.

This confluence and coexistence makes Istanbul romantic like Venice, but without its picture-postcard imagery; magical like Paris, but without its intimacy; and alive with history like Delhi, but without its disregard of ruins.

When I travelled in the Bosphorus, I was with my friends Mark and Claire. Both journalists, they were on vacation in Istanbul and I was also visiting and so we met. As our ferry left the terminal, I could hear the city's noise ebb and the chatter of seagulls surrounded us. The waves tossed our ferry around a fair bit, and the water was unexpectedly buoyant, splashing us often. I turned around to look at the city, fading slowly. And I saw the waterside mansions and villas that Pamuk writes about so movingly in *Istanbul*, recalling:

> Old ladies watching you from balconies as they sip their tea, the pergolas of coffee houses perched on landing stations, children in their underwear entering

the sea just where the sewers empty into it and sunning themselves on the concrete, people fishing from the shore, others relaxing on their yachts, travellers gazing out to the sea through bus windows while stuck in traffic, cats sitting on the wharves, waiting for fishermen, trees you hadn't realised were so tall, hidden villas and walled gardens you didn't even know existed, narrow alleyways rising up into the hills, tall apartment buildings looking in the backgrounds, and slowly, in the distance, Istanbul in all its confusion—its mosques, the poor quarters, the bridges, minarets, towers, gardens and ever-multiplying high-rises.

As singular passages go, in which the writer encapsulates the vistas of many lives in continuum along the stretch of water, Pamuk's description of Istanbul here is not unlike Hemingway's description of the people on Seine in his nostalgic memoir about life in Paris, *A Moveable Feast*. There is so much life along the waterfront. When Pamuk was a child, he went with his mother on a bus to Bebek, from where they would walk the shore and meet a boatman who'd be waiting for them, and climb into his caique, a traditional fishing boat used in Ionian and Aegian Seas, and, in the Bosphorus, smaller, more like a skiff. They would make their way through the narrow space between rowing boats, pleasure crafts, city-bound ferries, mussel-encrusted barges, all the way across to the lighthouses, leaving still waters of Bebek to meet the wilder currents of the Bosphorus, rocking in the wake of passing ships.

There is a certain distinct type of luminosity that this water has, as if it comes from somewhere deep within. On a late summer evening as the sky turned pink and the water itself became a rich red, the foam of its waves looking creamy and frothy. But the further away you went from the city, the deeper the water became, for you reached what Pamuk calls 'a smoother part of the sea whose colours do not change so much as undulate, like Monet's pool of water-lilies.' Pamuk celebrated the waterway in its various moods—the misty spring evenings when not a leaf rustles; the windless summer nights when a man walking alone along the shore after midnight can hear his own footsteps and reaches the lighthouse, 'when he hears the happy roar of the current, and notices with apprehension the flaming white foam that seems to have come from nowhere, and he cannot help but wonder, as [the poet A S] Hisar once did and I too have done, whether the Bosphorus has a soul.'

Some of the villas we saw had tall iron gates even as the paint on their walls had peeled away; some walls had turned green with moss. Some had darkened. The woodwork of the window of one villa cast a shadow on its wall.

We reached Princes' Islands, or *Prens Adalari*, the chain of nine islands in the Sea of Marmara. Cars are prohibited at the largest island, Büyükada, where princes and royal families were often exiled. The stately mansions were imposing. The only mode of transport was the horsecart—or your feet. We walked to the top of the hill, from where, it being a clear day we could see as far as the island called Imrali, where in 1961, in spite of global criticism, a military regime executed the country's first democratically-elected prime minister, Adnan Menderes.

When we returned, it was late evening and the sky was dark. The lights of hundreds of ships travelling through the straits lit up parts of the sky. The city looked bright, its mosques and churches aglow. The water shivered, disrupting the reflection of the lights and the moon.

I thought of an earlier time, when poets would see moonlight play on water. Here's Hisar: 'When there is no breath of wind, the waters sometimes shudder as if from inside and take on the finish of washed silk.'

And what of the city itself, of the east and the west? Burdened by history, trampled upon by armies, seized by generals, defaced by charlatans, appropriated by demagogues, reformed with the zeal of a missionary, and stubborn as a grandmother sitting on her favourite chair? Its essence is its Turkishness, being neither wholly eastern, nor entirely western. The mosques' minarets reassure the devout; the sweet wine in the café nearby comfort the sybarite.

Istanbul has had history, too much of it. It lies concealed beneath its placid exterior, and as Şafak has observed, you stir a little, and the past returns. The djinns emerge—some may be benign, like dervishes, others may be scary, like ghouls. But there is always the Bosphorus. As Pamuk writes: 'If the city smells of defeat, destruction, deprivation, melancholy and poverty, the Bosphorus sings of life, pleasure and happiness.' It is a small waterway, short and sweet, but its currents are strong, with enough life in it to keep you going when the night is young, like a tiny cup of Turkish coffee.

That piece of baklava besides the coffee will help forget the bitterness.

WORDS

&

IMAGES

BAMBAI MERI JAAN!

We walked by the sea along this arc called Marine Drive, as if forming the outline of the friendly arm the city seems to extend to strangers. Look at the map again—Bombay is that arm extended, offering a firm clasp in the deep blue sea. We knew it all along; it was a teacher in my second grade who had first drawn the city's shape on the blackboard, and pointed out how it resembled a human hand, but it took Salman Rushdie, the city's finest chronicler, to make it vivid, noting how the hand extended, almost achingly, to touch another hand.

We'd walk along Marine Drive, with the orange sun scattering gold dust across the ripples of the calm sea, towards that stretch of land that ends at Nariman Point, where high-rise office towers rose from what we liked to think of as winter mist, until I learned what winter really meant when I lived in New Hampshire. For what we had in Bombay was smog, with pollution settling on the city during its mildly cooler months.

Many years later I saw a similar, shinier arc along Cote d'Azur. To me it looked like Marine Drive after its art deco buildings had been scrubbed and given a fresh coat of paint.

During the months before the monsoon came, the Arabian Sea would roar, the seagulls would chatter as they flew in front of the reddish-pink setting sun, giving countless people with cameras that perfect moment to click, making them think that they were better photographers than they really were. But then the city was like that, it made you feel better in spite of your limitations; you could claim to be what you weren't; and if you did what was expected of you, others didn't really care whether you had lived in the city for five generations or arrived only the week before. It was a trading city.

That image of the seagull with the sun outlining its silhouette created one of the many images you wanted to capture because it looked beautiful and honest but not profound and could easily pass for an image on a poster along which you could write an inspiring quote from someone like Richard Bach if you were from my generation, but Paulo Coelho if you were from the next, just the kind of authors who you found motivating when you were in your teens.

The reality at the water's edge was quite different. Where the waves lashed the shore, there was never a quiet moment. You went there on a date, walking besides the one you thought you loved and who you thought would love you for the rest of your life and be by your side, and you'd hold her hand and hold her tight when the breeze would get colder. But the same thought had occurred to dozens of other couples, and there was no quiet spot left facing the sunset, and there would be entire families near you, whose children would stare at you, their mothers lightly slapping them, telling them not to look, while young men and boys brazenly implored you to buy their sugarcane juice and peanuts and grams and bhelpuri and coconut water, denying you that perfect quiet moment, for in this busy and crowded city there were no perfect, quiet moments. And just then the performance would end at Tata Theatre, and among the people emerging from the audience would be several people who'd know your parents and who would reach their home before you would, and call your parents to tell them that they had seen you with a young woman who they didn't know, and, you know, not that it was any of their business, but that you were sitting along the parapet facing the Arabian Sea, admiring the sunset, as if you were already married and all. Children these days!

Countless men and women who grew up in south Bombay, now trendily called SoBo, could relate to that experience, and I had been there and done that, but what I remembered most was that image, of that arc, that stretch of land reaching the sea, looking so much like an outstretched palm. It was a palm extended with affection, which you wanted to hold.

Bombay was a city by the sea. When you live along water, your relationship with the outsider is different. You welcome a stranger. My friend Guy, who was a French diplomat in Bombay, once told me that the reason he liked cities by the sea was that the sea calmed the people. To reach a city by the sea, you needed to come in a boat, and the boat would need to anchor, and it would need the guiding hand, the extended arm, of people who lived in the city, so that it could find the spot to stop, and disgorge the goods and people it carried. Cities that were landlocked had a different relationship with strangers. Here, the strangers came on horses or camels, with swords, to loot the shops, to kill the men, to steal the women. Cities by the sea welcomed the outsider, the foreigner, because in that contact they saw the opportunity to trade. Other cities have gates and fortifications; cavalries have attacked them. But Bombay looks at the world beyond with a sense of wonder. Its symbol is not a gateway without doors that can be shut or locked. You look through its gates, and you see the wide sea and an open, blue sky. Give a little, get a little, and both would gain—the resident and the outsider.

In his epic biography about Bombay, *Maximum City*, Suketu Mehta writes:

In the crowded suburban trains, you can run up to the packed compartments and find many hands stretching out to grab you on board, unfolding outwards from the train like petals... And at the moment of contact, they do not know if the hand that is reaching for theirs belongs to a Hindu or Muslim or Christian or Brahmin or untouchable, or whether you were born in this city or arrived only this morning. All they know is that you're trying to get to the city of gold, and that's enough. Come on board, they say. We'll adjust.

In the past two decades, Bombay has been knocked about much, but it adjusts. Its train network has been bombed; its famous landmarks like Air India Building, Stock Exchange Tower, and Passport Office have been shattered; and men have come by the sea and audaciously gone to two of the city's finest hotels and its main railway station, and killed nearly two hundred people over forty-eight terror-filled hours, before Indian special forces killed them.

In spite of those attacks, the city carried on, shrugging off those assaults. The spirit of Bombay? Many of my friends who still live there become livid when someone utters that phrase. As if we have a choice, they argue. Praising Bombay for taking blows is callous, they say. Tens of thousands have no choice but to lead their normal lives anyway. The next morning they will have to take that crowded bus again, even if there may be a hijacker in it; they must cling from that train, even if it might have a bomb; the day-wage earners must return to push the handcart the next day, otherwise there may be no food to feed the children at night. Such little acts of everyday bravery were often the only choices for those who have none left.

ॐ

We will adjust. That is what Bombay does very well, even in the face of terror. Other cities go quiet immediately after terror—but it is the lull before the storm. An Ahmedabad or a Delhi goes berserk in retaliation after the outrage, spilling more blood. Bombay, ever pragmatic, returns to normalcy, hums with activity. When the city's stock exchange index, called Sensex, shot up days after terrorist placed bombs made of Semtex, a stockbroker said: 'It takes more than Semtex to shake Sensex.'

For Bombay is where people come from all over India to live out their fantasy, and that's what terrorists have sought to change. In *The Moor's Last Sigh*, Salman Rushdie had warned: 'Those who hated India, those who sought to ruin it, would need to ruin Bombay.'

Rushdie was writing about the threat the city faced from the Shiv Sena, a Right-wing party of Marathi chauvinists, who turned Hindu nationalists when they found that if they wanted to expand politically beyond Bombay and into Maharashtra they needed a rallying cry besides language chauvinism. They went about being Hindu nationalists quite seriously, and systematically tried to destroy the city's inclusive, welcoming character. They even changed the city's name from Bombay to Mumbai, claiming that Mumbai was its original name. (If you really want the city's original name, it is Heptanesia, which is what the ancient Greeks called it, and the singer Tanuja Desai Hidier gave it new life by composing a song by that name. Mumbai, Bombay—Like Louis Armstrong singing about the potato, most of us shrugged, saying, "You say Mumbai, I say Bombay.")

If Shiv Sena's founder Bal Thackeray hounded "Madrasis" in the 1970s, the Sikhs in the 1980s, and non-Marathi speakers all the time, his followers have continued beating up "outsiders" whose presence makes the city what it is, or was, before it was forced to retreat into this narrow identity called

Mumbai. Scratch that, and you will find that old good bay, *Bom Bahia*, Bombay.

Rushdie was right when he said that those who wished to destroy India would need to attack Bombay first, because Bombay represented what India could be, if the many narrower identities (which gave the country its richness) weren't allowed to jostle with other identities in a race to dominate, but instead to intertwine and intermingle, and get submerged in a bigger humanity, one as vast as the sea itself. Tourists travelled in its motor launches to the Elephanta caves, traders dealt in shares, tycoons set up businesses, shoeshine boys worked hard and dreamt of striking it rich, dabbawalas kept the city fed, performing their astonishing daily choreography, of taking hundreds of thousands of home-cooked lunches to the right office worker, making sure that the Jain trader won't end up opening a box with tandoori chicken in it, and the meat-eating banker won't find an onion-and-potato free Jain vegetable curry with dal fried in ghee but without using ginger in his box, and the Christian typist will get his Mangalore prawn curry; just as starry-eyed girls coming from the hinterland to make it in the Tinseltown would look at those large billboards and imagine their own faces smiling at the traffic below. The city's absence of majority was demonstrated in its plurality— the Zoroastrian philanthropist, the Punjabi film producer, the Malayali clerk, the Konkani bookseller, the Jewish bookkeeper, the Anglo-Indian model, the Gujarati stockbroker, the Marwari wholesaler, the Marathi bureaucrat, the Tamil lecturer, the Bengali MBA, and the cab driver from Uttar Pradesh. The city belongs to nobody, and to everyone. Not interested in the past, Bombay was where, Rushdie would write, 'All Indias met and merged... Bombay was central; all rivers flowed into its human sea. It was an ocean of stories, we were all its narrators, and everybody talked at once.'

When the Pakistani terrorists attacked Bombay, that's what they wanted to tear apart—the city's harmonious cacophony.

Those two hotels, the majestic Indo-Saracenic railway station, are but symbols. They wanted Bombay to be afraid, so that there would be fewer people at Nariman Point, fewer couples on that parapet, fewer hawkers bothering them, fewer nosy relatives looking at the young men and women sitting by the sea.

Crowds had watched the drama as Bombay lay bleeding in 2008. They were transfixed; hundreds held candlelight vigils; but in the end, they went about their business. Bombay, after all, is the city for business. It has little time for politicians; when they are not arranging sightseeing tours of scenes of crime for filmmakers on location hunting, they are busy trying to keep "outsiders" out of the city. This is a city that cares for its cricketers and movie stars, businessmen and stockbrokers, not its politicians—it doesn't need them; they can only do harm. When politicians drive the agenda of cities, those cities erupt. Politicians divide people; they remind people of their narrower identities.

If you follow the perverse logic of India's eye-for-an-eye riots, there was ample provocation in Bombay. The terrorists were Pakistani; they claimed to be acting in the name of their religion; and they wanted to kill as many as they could, caste no bar, creed no bar. But those who live in the city understood instinctively the difference between the individual and the collective, between those from within and those from without. It did not pour its rage on its own.

That's why Bombay did not go the way of New Delhi in 1984, where two bodyguards who happened to be Sikh had assassinated Indira Gandhi. Congress party workers, guided by some of their leaders, went around from ward to ward in the nation's capital, looking for Sikh families, destroying property, killing people. Three decades later, those victims still await justice.

Nor did Bombay react like Gujarat did in 2002. There, its chief minister failed to protect Muslims who had nothing to do with the burning of a train in Godhra, but who ended up losing their lives because Hindus in Gujarat decided that the state's Muslims must bear the collective guilt and face the punishment for what had happened in Godhra. When frightened Muslims sought help from the authorities, the police apparently told them: 'We have no orders to protect you.'

In 1993, when terrorists struck Bombay with simultaneous bomb blasts at several locations that killed two hundred and fifty-seven people, I was in the city, visiting from Singapore. My son Ameya was born a few weeks earlier, in late December. A week after he was born, Bombay was in flames. I recall those gigantic flames, the cloud of smoke choking the city, as I walked on the terrace of my father-in-law's flat, patting Ameya to sleep. Within days, the city was normal again. There is a word in Bombay's street argot, Bambaiya Hindi, about it. It is called *khadoos*. Sunil Gavaskar, who my generation considers the city's greatest gift to Indian cricket, is a fine example. He blocked bowlers trying to get him out until their patience had worn out. He'd then step out effortlessly and drive them straight, so fast that they wouldn't notice, adding another four runs in his long march towards a century. The city was also *bindaas*, like Sachin Tendulkar, the city's greatest gift to Indian cricket a generation later, who would step out and pitilessly unleash aggression on bowlers. That is the real spirit of Bombay—to find it, go to Azad Maidan and Cross Maidan, to Shivaji Park and the Gymkhanas along Marine Drive, and see young boys, dressed in white, working tirelessly to improve their game, in the hope of making it to the city's cricket team, even during monsoon.

You will see the bus conductor telling passengers "*pudhe chala, pudhe chala*" (keep moving forward, keep moving forward). Keep moving forward, that's what the city does.

Rushdie's original love song to the city, *Midnight's Children*, remains vivid—in the city's cinemas, where a Metro Cub Club might be watching a movie and a future Saleem Sinai might be seeing the film. Over at Breach Candy, and you will find Chimalkers and Readers' Paradise—even though it doesn't have Bombelli's and its yard of chocolates anymore. And the pointy tower of Westfield Estate, which becomes Methwold's Estate in the novel. Or visit an Irani restaurant like Pioneer Café, where the dancing fingers of Amina Azeez and Nadir Qasim will float around teacups, coming tantalisingly close, yearning to meet,

> Hands flickering like candle flames... next a woman's hands, black as jet, inching forwards like elegant spiders... hands beginning the strangest of dances, rising, falling, circling one another, weaving in and out between each other, hands longing for touch, hands outstretching tensing quivering demanding to be but always at last jerking back, fingertips avoiding fingertips...

Here's Arun Kolatkar, immovable from his seat at Wayside Inn near Kala Ghoda, writing about an Irani restaurant not unlike that Pioneer Café:

> *The cockeyed Shah of Iran watches the cake*
> *decompose carefully in a cracked showcase;*
> *distracted only by a fly on the make*
> *as it finds in a loafer's wrist an operational base.*
>
> *dogmatically green and elaborate trees defeat*
> *breeze; the crooked swan begs pardon*
> *if it disturb the pond; the road, neat*
> *as a needle, points at a lovely cottage with a garden.*

And Rushdie again, in *The Moor's Last Sigh*, recalling the list of what you can't do at an Irani restaurant, in the restaurant called Sorryno, the two words encompassing what the blackboard said at the entrance:

Sorry, No Liquor, No Answer Given Regarding Addresses in Locality, No Combing of Hair, No Beef, No Haggle, No Water Unless Food Taken, No News or Movie Magazine, No Sharing of Liquid Sustenances, No Taking Smoke, No Match, No Feletone Calls, No Incoming with Own Comestible, No Speaking of Horses, No Sigret, No Taking of Long Time on Premises, No Raising of Voice, No Change, and a crucial last pair, No Turning Down of Volume—It Is How We Like, and No Musical Request—All Melodies Selected Are To Taste of of Prop.

Bombay's bard, Nissim Ezekiel, too found the restaurants' admonitions worth noting. In a 1972 poem he wrote:

Please

Do not spit

Do not sit more

Pay promptly, time is valuable

Do not write letter

without order refreshment

Do not comb,

hair is spoiling floor

Do not make mischiefs in cabin

our waiter is reporting

Come again

All are welcome whatever cast

If not satisfied tell us

Otherwise tell others

GOD IS GREAT

Today, those Irani restaurants are vanishing, and you find sushi bars and Thai restaurants and baristas and bistros and there are high-rise night clubs as the centre of gravity seems to be shifting to Bandra and beyond to places which once seemed so far that those of us who grew up in SoBo would pretend we'd need a passport and visa to get there—anywhere beyond Haji Ali and its onion-shaped dome in the Arabian Sea. But Café Britania still serves its berry pulao, Sardar still fries pao bhaji at Tardeo, bhaiyas from UP make piping, spicy bhelpuri at Chowpatty, the lassi at Jain Dairy remains fresh, the ragda-samosa at Kailash Parbat continues to invite, the vada pav and kala khatta at Bori Bunder beckon, as does the chana bhatura at Cream Centre, and the thali at Thacker's.

Whenver I see a crowded suburban train leaving a platform, with men running behind the train trying to clamber on as it picks up speed, they extend their hands, secure that other hands will reach out and clasp them, lift them up. And think of Suketu Mehta's perfect description of the city's ethos. In any other city, that arm can easily become a fist; in Bombay, it takes you in because it values human contact and interaction. And so the city welcomes all, and doesn't shrink, nor shirks. It encompasses India's big-heartedness; its largeness. When asked about his identity, the cricketer Tendulkar said he was a proud Maharashtrian, but an Indian first. When thugs tried to beat up an elderly Bohra Muslim couple in early 1993 during riots, Sunil Gavaskar rushed down from his apartment and stood between the couple and the thugs—an act as courageous as facing Dennis Lillee without a helmet.

That's the spirit of Bombay that some within and some without keep attempting to destroy. They won't win.

SHIMMERING CANALS, SIMMERING DISCONTENT

I rose early one morning in Amsterdam, this city of clear light and lustrous canals. I left my hotel for Marnixstraat, to look for a house I had remembered seeing on a previous visit several years earlier. That house was across from the hotel I stayed in at that time, and it had, for some unknown reason, a verse by Emily Dickinson on its wall:

> To make a prairie it takes a clover and one bee.
>
> One clover and a bee,
>
> And revery.
>
> The revery alone will do,
>
> If bees are too few.

It was a puzzling poem, about nature, love, and sexuality. It was surprising too, to find it in Amsterdam on a wall, without any obvious reason. Dickinson had no known connection with Amsterdam. When I had asked a shopkeeper why the poem was written on the wall, he shrugged; he didn't know. But I felt an odd kinship with her poetry. Dickinson was born in Amherst, Massachusetts, and lived much of her life there. My wife Karuna had studied in that town, but being an engineering student she had never found the time to visit a museum in the town commemorating Dickinson. On one of my visits to Amherst and Northampton, I had seen the museum. In a childish way, I liked the idea that I knew, and she didn't know a part of the town that had been her home, and she hadn't had the time even to visit it, whereas I had.

When I saw the house in Amsterdam the first time, I was travelling with my family—my sons were then eight and five—and seeing Dickinson's poem there made me feel as though the part of our life that we had left behind—the time spent in America in the 1980s—was joining us on our journey. When Karuna saw that poem on the wall in Amsterdam that autumn afternoon, she had found it charmingly whimsical— the poem itself, and its appearance in a Dutch city. I saw it as reconnection with our younger, more innocent world.

My world had changed substantially when I went looking for that building again. I was in Amsterdam a year after Karuna's death, to see those words again on that wall, to reconnect with a more innocent world.

Light changes magically in Amsterdam. It gives the streets, with its lamps and its tinkling bicycles, a painterly glow. The breeze disturbs the shimmering canal, making the reflections of the solid stone buildings quiver. Amsterdam flickers to life as in a Rembrandt landscape.

How clear is that light, and how well the Dutch painters have captured its many moods! Think of the light falling on Vermeer's milkmaid, standing by the window; the shining face of the girl with the pearl earring; the glow falling on two men in the painting known famously as *The Night Watch*. I saw it at Rijks museum, where it commands large space in a hall. Rembrandt painted it as a group portrait of a Dutch militia company that was fighting to stay independent in the seventeenth century from the Spanish empire. But the painting looks more like a busy street scene without any patriotic triumphalism. Instead of showing moustachioed commanders staring back at the artist, you see a scene that looks like a bunch of men unconnected with one another—a soldier hunched over his gun, a militia captain and his lieutenant walking and talking in a self-important way, a little girl looking at the scene, and no two faces are pointing the same way. An undisciplined unit; a rag-tag army; a militia force made up of part-time soldiers. A soft fog surrounds them and the illuminating light is like a flash. They look vulnerable and eccentric, but they are, somehow, together. If the frieze at Pantheon showed Athenian democracy in a communal procession, *The Night Watch* shows the Dutch burghers and soldiers united together, defying the dark forces, even if the radiance is partial, and highlights only a few.

There is magic in Amsterdam's light. But it is a pale light, as if it has lost its warmth somewhere along the way.

Amsterdam is not a city that likes to pause and admire the light; it is a dour city, and it has to be practical. It is built on mud, always fearful that it might sink. The Dutch writer Geert Mak calls his city "impossible", reminding us that in its struggle for physical survival (the country needs dykes to prevent the sea from swallowing land), 'Holland is kind of Bangladesh—a rich and modern Bangladesh, but still a Bangladesh.'

Rather than let the sea overwhelm the city, the Dutch saw it as the means to reach distant parts of the world. In the seventeenth century, ships of the Dutch East India Company sailed as far as Java, buying and selling goods and commodities. The prosperity that the trade brought created probably the world's first middle class, which lived in affluence but, as Simon Schama describes in *The Embarrassment of Riches*, lived in mortal dread of being corrupted by happiness. Life may have been tough and had to be endured, but the riches had to be displayed.

One of the unusual things about walking on the streets of Amsterdam is the ease with which you can look into people's homes. Unlike England, nobody draws the curtain to keep out sunlight and curious onlookers. Dutch homes have large windows facing the street, and the curtains do not hide the interiors of the home. The furniture, paintings, and tableware are set in full display. You feel you are looking into a set, or a display at a shop. But, my Dutch friends say that these are real homes, with real people; and they don't mind if outsiders look in and saw how they live. In a culture that prizes tolerance above all other values, the assumption seems to be that you accept other lifestyles, even if different, so long as those lifestyles don't intrude your own. Even if the behaviour is mildly illegal—the Dutch word is *gedogen*—you tolerate it.

But tolerance doesn't always work.

To understand why, I went to another house in Amsterdam. It is at Prinsengracht, facing one of the canals. An old house, numbered 263. It refuses to draw any attention to itself. Anne Frank lived in that house.

Anne Frank's story is now part of textbooks. A child in a close-knit family, she was forced to live in hiding with her family for years, not able to even step out and play. But she was observant, and kept a diary in which she wrote what she could see from her window, what she ate, and her hope in humanity. Her writing was important because it was honest and clear and simple and true but not necessarily profound and not intended to be profound either. She was writing for herself, not for posterity. She was setting down her thoughts to make sense of the world around her when it was changing rapidly. She hadn't planned to publish the diary. She would have written less if she had been able to live a normal life. She couldn't, and we have a fine manifestation of a child, an adolescent, almost-young woman, describing her isolation and her hope that tomorrow will be another day.

There were soldiers outside who were looking for her family, not because they had done anything wrong, but because they were Jews. The house is now a museum. I walked through its corridors, looking at the pin-up photographs of film stars that young Anne has stuck on a wall. There is a half-finished board-game which she may have played. Her handwriting can be seen in notebooks and pads. Her letters begin as a lazy scrawl, then grow into straight lines, as if required by a stern teacher, and then mature into a solid firmness and fluidity which, while not necessarily calligraphic, certainly look determined and cursive: exactly the way a teenage girl would write in a journal, which she alone would read. Many of us do this; we know friends who do this, and then discover those adolescent fantasies decades later while clearing an attic. The handwriting doesn't match yours much anymore, and the feelings expressed may seem cloying, but there is a charm to those pages, like the faded pair of jeans that don't fit anymore but feel so comfortable— there, feel that texture again: nice, isn't it?

In Anne's case, such nostalgia can only be imagined— she didn't live long enough to rediscover her writing. But it is that fresh teenage look at life, and the simple clarity that permeates through her thoughts, that makes her writing so honest. And yet, that clarity is pale, like Amsterdam's light; the warmth stolen.

There is ordinariness about her house which makes the experience chilling. There is a certain banality about the street, commonplace evil lurking beyond the lamp post.

The real horror of Anne Frank's story is that her home is part of the city's organic whole, its intricate mosaic; it is not part of a ghetto, for the Jewish community was well-integrated in pre-war Amsterdam. It looks identical to the houses with which it stands shoulder-to-shoulder. But the view you get from inside is quite different. In a brilliantly designed part of the museum, I see through a tall window a tranquil canal, its water turning dark, and a few pedestrians walking by. A cyclist moves past, clad in a glowing leotard, pedalling furiously, as if late for a yoga class. But take several steps back from the window, and the translucent screen turns opaque, and you see the scene as Anne would have seen it. Suddenly, the colours disappear, a hazy greyness covers the window now, and you see a large, black-and-white image of goose-stepping Nazi troops. It is a frozen frame, meant to shock, and that it is in black-and-white accentuates the sharpness of the tragedy.

Almost everyone I see in the museum has found the experience moving; nobody speaks. This is the story of one family, but that family has become the symbol of what happened to many more families. Those stories weren't written, but they were as real. The house itself was once meant to be demolished, but an international effort prevented that final atrocity. The Dutch are proud that the Frank family survived, undetected, for so long. They see that as a sign of their tolerance and stoic defiance of the Nazis. But they are also ashamed that weeks before the war ended, the Franks were betrayed. That reminds them of their complicity. An investigation after the Second World War showed that many Dutch had collaborated in some way with the Nazis, helping send ninety-eight deportation trains with over 1,00,000 Jews from Amsterdam's central station to places like Auschwitz.

Frank's story continues to needle the Dutch conscience, and she returns to Dutch debates at odd, unexpected times. As Ian Buruma, the Anglo-Dutch writer, puts it in the book, *Murder in Amsterdam*: 'Never again, said the well-meaning defenders of the multicultural ideal, must Holland betray a religious minority.'

But what does a society do, when it has a new minority, which it hasn't known well, and which poses challenges that could not be conceived? What do liberalism and tolerance teach the Dutch when one part of that minority—a woman—needs protection from another part of the same minority—a fundamentalist?

In 2004, Mohammed Bouyeri, a Dutch Muslim of Moroccan origin stabbed and murdered the outspoken filmmaker Theo Van Gogh, who had recently completed a short film called *Submission.* The film was based on a script by Ayan Hirsi Ali, a Somali immigrant (and later Dutch parliamentarian), which was highly critical of Islam's treatment of women. Bouyeri had warned that Hirsi Ali would be next. She got police protection initially, but after the government found that she had misrepresented her personal history while seeking refuge in the Netherlands, the authorities threatened to take away her citizenship.

Which refugee does not lie about the past?

Hirsi Ali then left the Netherlands for the United States, pointedly reminding the Dutch that they had let down another young woman who was in some ways different from the majority—Anne Frank—half a century ago. Frank was Jewish, Hirsi Ali was born Muslim; Frank was white, Hirsi Ali black; Frank was the perfect victim—an innocent teenager; Hirsi Ali may have exaggerated stories of her suffering to get to Europe, but by speaking out against bigotry within her own faith, she was reminding Europe of its own values and warning about its future. She was, as Mak puts it: 'A kind of Joan of Arc against "the Islam; in the defence of the enlightenment".'

Frank was the girl-next-door; Hirsi Ali, the strange foreigner walking in their midst. Frank wrote politely; Hirsi Ali's tone was angry. We learn about Frank's agony only later—she didn't leave behind a record of what she suffered while she was in the concentration camp. Hirsi Ali describes, graphically, the sexual torture she underwent, and how she had to flee a marriage she did not want. Both Frank and Hirsi Ali have the right to be protected in a society that makes virtue of its post-Enlightenment traditions. But one is a Jew, the other, a Muslim who has turned her back on her faith. And for many liberals, consumed by anger towards Israel over its policies in the Middle East, championing either is bad form. And so Frank and Hirsi Ali, both victims in their own right, get embraced by demagogues and racists too, besides many committed to women's rights, civil rights, and free speech. In this battle, as in many other battles, you can't always choose your allies.

I know many human rights activists in Amsterdam who had spent their lives fighting apartheid, or Suharto's dictatorship, or Israel's policies in the Middle East. It became hard for some among them to defend Hirsi Ali, because it placed them in the same corner as those defending the Guantanamo Bay camp and the torture in Abu Ghraib prison. To think clearly through this mess is actually quite simple, but the more they thought, the more evidence they weighed, the more that simplicity eluded them.

The Dutch had learned to tolerate the presence of Muslims who lived quietly. But their sense of exclusiveness—their desire to be different, and live differently, compared with their Dutch counterparts—began to irk some of the Dutch, when young Muslim boys insolently began insulting Dutch women sunbathing on a summer's day in a park; or when the Muslims' devout religiousness reminded the Dutch of their own religiosity withering away, about which they didn't wish to be reminded. As the Muslims built mosques, churches were getting empty. In 1958, Buruma points out, some 25 per cent of Dutch were atheists. By 2020, that figure is likely to rise to three-quarters. In the fifty years since that 1958 survey, the percentage of people calling themselves Catholics in the Netherlands has fallen from forty-two to seventeen; Protestants, from thirty-one to ten. Pim Fortuyn, a populist politician who was murdered by an animal rights activist, strongly criticised those who were bringing religion back into the public sphere. The irritation rose because, as Buruma writes: 'They had just painfully wrested themselves free from the strictures of their own religions.' The rise of another populist politician, in the form of Geert Wilders, was inevitable. Wilders preyed upon the sense of insecurity of the new suburbs, whose residents had begun migrating from the cosmopolitan quadrangle of Amsterdam, the Hague, Rotterdam, and Utrecht, with their smells of lamb shawarma, couscous, and Indonesian *nasi goreng* wafting through neighbourhoods. These families were willing to tolerate anyone who looked, thought, and talked like them. Opinion polls in 2006 showed that more than 40 per cent of the Dutch only wanted someone of Dutch origin to teach their children; more than 60 per cent began to believe Islam was not compatible with European life; and half were worried about Islam's influence in Europe.

These aren't easy questions. But after a visit to that house in Prinsengracht, the answer seems disarmingly simple, and pure, and white as snow.

Several years later, I was near that house again, with a Colombian friend called Yadaira, who would discover snow that afternoon. It was Yadaira's first time in Europe, and she had never seen snow before, except in photographs and films. We had told her to bring along warm jackets and sensible shoes, but she had grown up on the Caribbean coast, and could not imagine how cold it might get.

As the flurry gathered force, covering the ground with a white carpet lain evenly, she wanted to step out. Careful, not with these shoes, we told her, but she would not wait. She stepped out of the door, ran across the courtyard, balancing herself well for one who hadn't walked on snow before. 'I have walked on slippery surfaces in Cartagena when it rains,' she yelled loudly, turning back, moments before she slipped, disturbing the surface not yet trodden. A burst of snowflakes erupted, and under that bright yellow light all you could hear was her laughter.

She got up quickly, and we walked towards the canal. She shivered as the weather had unexpectedly turned chilly, and her eyes lit up as she saw the tiny snowflakes falling on and around us, like silent rain, the flakes lighter than the raindrops she was accustomed to, the flakes swaying in the wind. Her feet sank in the fresh snow. Cyclists, annoyed because we were walking on the street, kept tinkling their bells persistently and somewhat furiously, forcing us to step aside and walk on the footpath, not the street. We were the newcomers, intruding in this space, but we had moved aside and now harmony was restored. They raced past us, and the musicality of the bells made their annoyance bearable.

The polite sound of the bells, and the softness of the snow, humanised the city, and offered the hope that the Dutch will navigate the tortuous path amicably, and that tranquil image —of boats sitting on their reflections, of light falling evenly on the canals, and of the pale sky—will return, cooling the temperature, simmering at the moment, but tomorrow, a shimmering memory.

LIGHTING LITERARY LAMPS IN THE CITY OF LIGHTS

As the bells chimed at Notre Dame and the wind whispered through the trees on the banks of the Seine, I sat under a parasol at a café sipping Tavel, a pleasant red wine from the Rhone region. American teenagers walked by, cheerfully bidding bonjour to every passing Parisian and giggling cheerfully, even though *Le Paysan de Paris* had little time for their juvenile pranks. French men at the café continued to smoke, cigarettes stuck in their mouths, ashes smearing their jackets, as their fiercely gesticulating hands did the talking, while they sorted out some issue that bothered them intensely. North African immigrants played their drums with careless abandon, while a young French student played the saxophone to nobody in particular. A painter vigorously brushed her canvas, while a clown mimicked a blonde woman walking precariously, as if she was on stilts, weighed down by parcels she was carrying, containing boxes of clothes she had bought from Galeries Lafayette. The fragrance of Mediterranean soups from the alfresco restaurants wafted through the air.

By early afternoon, the sky had turned pale, and Notre Dame was visible in full glory, its beauty no longer hidden by the ugly scaffoldings that I remembered from my last visit to this city, when the church was covered with a dull net as though there was something embarrassing about its appearance. It was winter: the trees had discarded their leaves, and their delicate branches curved like the curlicues of an intricate window. There was a chill in the breeze, and the buildings along the riverbank lit up in the fading sunlight, and the most remarkable aspect about Paris revealed itself—how modern it was, and yet how changeless it seemed. When I saw the river Seine, and reflected on how Ernest Hemingway had described it when he wrote his memoir—no, love poem—to Paris of his youth, in the 1920s, *A Moveable Feast*, I could have been seeing what he saw and wrote about:

> With the fishermen and the life on the river, the beautiful barges with their own life on board, the tugs with their smoke stacks that folded back to pass under the bridges, pulling a tow of barges, the great plain trees on the stone banks of the river, the elms and sometimes the poplars, I could never be lonely along the river. With so many trees in the city, you could see the spring coming each day until a night of warm wind would bring it suddenly in one morning. Sometimes the heavy cold rains would beat it back so that it would seem that it would never come and that you were losing a season out of your life. This was the only truly sad time in Paris because it was unnatural. You expected to be sad in the fall. Part of you died each year when the leaves fell from the trees and their branches were bare against the wind and the cold, wintry light. But you knew there would

always be the spring, as you knew the river would flow again after it was frozen. When the cold rains kept on and killed the spring, it was as though a young person had died for no reason.

In those days, though, the spring always came finally; but it was frightening that it had nearly failed.

Hemingway was among the first writers who had inspired me. This quiet, descriptive passage, affirming that spring would return, had lifted my spirits during some low moments. I had been visiting Paris for a quarter century now, and in those twenty-five years my life had experienced the moods of all four seasons. Walking the Parisian streets inevitably put wings on my feet.

I sat looking at the river, in front of a bookshop where I had spent many pleasant hours over several visits over many years. Once upon a time the shop was called Le Mistral; for over forty years, it has been called Shakespeare and Co. There had of course been another Shakespeare and Co. earlier in Parisian history—Sylvia Beach had set it up in 1919, and in those uncertain years between the two world wars, her shop had become a haven, a comfortable resting point for writers and artists travelling through Europe, discovering themselves and creating the modern idiom. Many of the writers were American, and the critic Gertrude Stein was to call them *une generation perdue*, or the lost generation. If I have one regret which is way beyond my control, it is not to have been alive and in Paris then, and that too, to be in my Twenties, at that.

After the Second World War ended, George Whitman, a former GI, decided to settle in Paris in 1951, and set up Le Mistral. A few years later, he convinced Beach he was the rightful inheritor of her work, and she let him call his bookshop Shakespeare and Co. He also named his daughter Sylvia. Whitman, who died in December 2011 at the age of ninety-eight, managed to keep Beach's spirit alive. Over the years, Berkeley, New York, Moscow, and Bogotá have also seen bookshops by that name. But it began in Paris, and it survives there.

I had read *A Moveable Feast* in my teenage years and I had always wanted to experience that literary age in Paris. Describing that period in Paris, Hemingway wrote: 'If you are lucky enough to have lived in Paris as a young man, then wherever you go, for the rest of your life, it stays with you... for Paris is a moveable feast.'

This was the time when James Joyce might be dining with Hemingway and F Scott Fitzgerald, and Pablo Picasso might be arguing with an art dealer at Stein's apartment at Rue de Fleurus. Hemingway had portrayed that period so vividly, you felt you were there, sitting across the table, listening to their conversation, and ever since then I wanted to be there. *A Moveable Feast* was the first book of Hemingway's that I had read, and I was entranced. I was to discover his short stories later, but at that time, that short book produced an epiphany, revealing how one should write. This is how you do it, I had felt —write simple, clear prose, without ornamentation, without metaphors, without words that are too big and clumsy when you say them out loud or which would send you to a dictionary, without unnecessary and redundant adjectives, or dangling adverbs that deliberately slow down the pace of the text, so that you gave each sentence its rhythm, its flow, and your thoughts could move smoothly, like the water in the Seine itself, without any interruption, with no one noticing if your sentence was too long. Or short.

I began collecting and reading Hemingway's books; I began reading about him; I began feeling envious of the life he had led. I wanted to go to Europe, to East Africa, to Cuba. I wanted to cover wars. I wanted to distill life by writing about it in Moleskine notebooks. At that time I did not know about Hemingway's underlying depression, his petty cruelties to the women he loved, and his false bravado; I was to come across all of that much later. But like Michael Palin who retraced his footsteps in a documentary, I felt I had to immerse myself into the Hemingway experience.

Paris, then, became the necessary first stop in that quest. In 1995, an American travel magazine in Singapore surprised me by agreeing to let me go and wander around Paris for ten days, following Hemingway's footsteps. The only condition was that I had to go to the bars he wrote about. How could I turn that down? I wore a pair of comfortable moccasins; I carried a notepad; I was young; I had time. I walked the streets of Paris, looking for Hemingway's shadows.

The street where I began my journey was Rue de la Bûcherie, the home of Whitman's Shakespeare and Co. George Whitman was a remarkable man. He was in his Seventies when I first met him. He was delighted to hear that I had come all the way from Singapore to retrace Hemingway's journey through Paris, and took out a large map to show me the various landmarks I should visit. He later took me to the study upstairs, where he told me about his life; he made me a tall glass of delicious strawberry milk shake. Then he left me alone. It was a tiny room, smelling of musty, old books, and from behind its worn green curtain I could hear a retired diplomat speaking in halting French, discussing Rimbaud's poetry with a professor. I looked at the view of the Seine from the window. I wrote two poems that evening.

Looking through the list of writers who had lived at Shakespeare and Co., I spotted several familiar and well-known names that would keep a literary insomniac happy all night. I pictured the writers walking around Paris hoping some of its magic would rub off, and even if they were not part of a lost generation, they'd find something.

The writers who had come to Paris in the 1920s had chosen self-imposed exile to understand themselves better. Men like Hemingway saw bullfights in Spain, they fished in Italy, climbed the Alps, and slowly got sucked into the vortex of European politics when the debates were about such fundamental questions like the rise of Nazism and Fascism which questioned humanity and our existence, and what we would do to influence the events and whether we were brave enough to do something to shape them.

Hemingway had begun writing serious fiction in those years. He'd visit cafés such as Dome and Rotonde, with their red upholstery, gleaming brass railings and lamps, large mirrors, and tiny coffee cups. They were known hangouts for those expatriate writers. In *The Sun Also Rises*, Jake Barnes says, 'No matter which café you asked, a taxi driver will bring you to la Rotonde.' There were also cheap eateries like Café des Amateurs, where Hemingway would spend hours over a cup of café crème, writing about lonely, macho men displaying uncommon valour, or grace under pressure, in windswept landscapes. *The Sun Also Rises* drew heavily from the ambience of the Paris he lived in. At a telling moment in the novel, it also revealed the kind of life Hemingway saw himself living. Bill Gorton harangues Hemingway's alter-ego, Jake Barnes:

> 'There you go. And you claim you want to be a writer, too. You're only a newspaper man. An expatriated newspaperman. You ought to be ironical the minute you get out of bed. You ought to wake up with your mouth full of pity... You know what's the trouble with you? You're an expatriate... Nobody that ever left their own country wrote anything worth printing. Not even in the newspapers.... You've lost touch with the soil. You get precious. Fake European standards have ruined you. You drink yourself to death. You become obsessed by sex. You spend all your time talking, not working. You are an expatriate, see? You hang around cafés.'

'It sounds like a swell life,' I said. 'When do I work?'

I wanted that life. When do I start?

࿐

There is a Paris for everyone—for the art lover, there are the museums; for those who want to admire architecture, there is the marvelous symmetry of buildings designed by Georges-Eugene Haussman; for the gourmet and gourmand a range of restaurants with delectable food; and for the lovers of the written word, there is the rich world to immerse in, reading Flaubert or discussing Balzac on dark nights. Literature greets you in Parisian posters (one invited me to a performance of Bertolt Brecht's play, *The Resistible Rise of Arturo Ui*; another poster, several years later, advertised an exhibition of photographs of my friend Sooni Taraporewala, but the image they had used on the poster was of an old Parsi gentleman in his sola topee at Marine Drive, which had adorned the jacket of Rohinton Mistry's novel, *Family Matters*; other posters told me to check out retrospectives of Federico Fellini, the Italian neo-realist filmmaker, and another, a revival of Satyajit Ray's Apu Trilogy). In the kind of coincidence that can only happen in Paris, one afternoon, as I travelled in the metro, a man grinned sheepishly when he discovered that he and I were reading the same book—he was reading the French translation of Hemingway's posthumous novel, *The Garden of Eden*, which I was reading in English.

I began my journey into the heart of Hemingway's Paris at 12, Rue de l'Odeon, where Beach's Shakespeare and Co. was located. Today, only a plaque remains: *En 1922 dans cette maison, Melle Sylvia Beach publia "Ulysses" de James Joyce.* (In 1922 in this building Ms Sylvia Beach published *Ulysses* by James Joyce.) That was a courageous move, as Joyce's novel was banned in the English-speaking world. Beach challenged those governments, letting that harbinger of stream of consciousness soar above censorship.

Hemingway spent many hours at her shop:

> On a cold, windswept street, this was a warm, cheerful place with a big stove in winter, tables and shelves of books, new books in the window, and photographs on the wall of famous writers. Sylvia had a lively, sharply sculptured face, and wavy brown hair that was rushed back from her fine forehead. She had pretty legs and she was kind, cheerful and interested.... No one that I ever knew was nicer to me.

Brave, she certainly was. During the Second World War, when the Nazis occupied France, Beach was forced to close her shop because she refused to sell Joyce's *Finnegan's Wake* to some German soldiers. Hemingway was not in Paris then. He was a war reporter in the trenches. He was in Normandy soon after D-Day (6 June 1944) and listened to soldiers telling him war stories, and advanced towards Paris with the troops. On Liberation Day, Beach was surprised to hear a familiar voice outside her window calling out her name loudly. It was Hemingway, with some American soldiers. He proudly "liberated" Shakespeare and Co., lifted Beach, gave her a huge kiss, and announced that he must now liberate the Ritz Bar.

According to one account, on 25 August 1944, Hemingway and his entourage arrived at the Ritz, which they found undamaged but deserted, except for the acting director and member of the resistance, the "imperturbable Auzello". Hemingway and the soldiers, intent on chasing Germans, climbed to the roof and blasted away with machine guns, bringing down only a clothesline full of white linen sheets. The legendary reporter then descended on the bar, ordering dry martinis for all.

I went to the bar the first time in 1995, the year of the 50th anniversary of the liberation. It was now called Bar Hemingway, and it retained much of its original décor, with a bust of Papa Hemingway, and black-and-white photographs of other regulars. Not far from the Ritz is the famous Harry's Bar, near Place de l'Opera. With its vast selection of beers and pennants of college football teams, it carries the atmosphere of an undergraduate college bar, where grownup American men go misty-eyed, looking at the pennants, noisily high-fiving friends while the air grows thick with cigarette smoke.

That alcohol-fuelled atmosphere is far removed from Sylvia Beach's Shakespeare and Co., where our story began. That old bookshop is now gone; in its place there is a porcelain and Chinese furniture shop. Next door is another plaque, commemorating the fact that Thomas Paine lived there, and wrote *The Rights of Man* in that building.

Paris is that kind of a place.

The view I saw from the first floor of George Whitman's Shakespeare and Co. brought back Hemingway's description of another scene along the river in *A Moveable Feast*, where he could see a small park at the water's edge with fine chestnut trees. On a bright day, Hemingway would 'buy a liter of wine and a piece of bread and some sausage and sit in the sun and read one of the books I had bought and watch the fishing.' I could never be lonely along the river, he had said.

How could you feel lonely along that river? There were different people now, but they still gathered along the Seine. A busty backpacker with her raucous classmates, a besotted young lover pleading with his obstinate girlfriend, a diligent student waiting hesitantly before stepping into the store, where he will probably blow up his month's savings.

The barges were replaced by modern boats carrying videocam-wielding tourists filming the Latin Quarter from their air-conditioned cabins, drinking chilled white wine while their children ran along the decks. It was late spring, and the weather no longer sharp and bitter and cold, and some brave

Parisian women lay topless on the decks of boats, basking in the sunshine filtering through the leaves of the elms. With the May sun in no mood to set, the water shook gently each time the breeze passed along its surface, and the river shone, as liquid gold was poured on its surface, like a Pissarro canvas coming to life.

Like Beach's shop, Whitman's shop too became the honeypot attracting a new generation of writers, including Beat poets Allen Ginsberg, Lawrence Ferlinghetti, and Gregory Corso. Magazines like *Merlin* made their office in the shop; the first editors of *The Paris Review* had their early meetings here; and Whitman himself encouraged visiting writers to come and stay, or read to the people visiting his bookshop.

He nurtured thousands of writers. Anaïs Nin, who had stayed at the store, sometimes with Henry Miller, describes it in her chapbook, *Paris Revisited*:

> There, by the Seine, was the sort of book store I had known: a Utrillo house, not too steady on its foundations, small windows, wrinkled shutters. And there was George Whitman, undernourished, bearded, a saint among his books, not eager to sell, lending books, housing penniless friends upstairs, a haven bookstore... All those who came for books remained to talk, while George tried to write letters, to open his mail, to order books.

Appropriately, Whitman called the location of the store "kilometre zero". This was the centre of the universe, and a short tour of his bookshop would take you around every corner of the world, covering every topic. That disorganised charm continues, with books piled over two floors, the shelves stacked with new, quirky and difficult-to-get-hold-of titles. You can squat in a corner and read. You come to see books, touch books, drink books, swallow books, browse books, smell books. You also buy books here.

The bookshop is eclectic in its taste: Anthony Burgess, Peter Mayle, Martin Amis, Kwame Nkrumah, and the collected works of Enver Hoxha can be found on the shelves, along with the Moroccan journals of Nancy du Plessis. The store sits on prized real estate, and offers as large as $3 million had been made, but Whitman refused to leave the site. When he had a dispute with the civic authorities who refused to renew his license at one point, he stopped selling books in order to stay within the law, but kept the doors open—people could use his shop as a library. The authorities relented, and renewed his license and you can buy books now.

From Rue de la Bûcherie, I followed a lane that leads up to Rue du Cardinal Lemoine, and I walked all the way toward Hemingway's first home, the building numbered 74. It was plastered by movie posters and held up by scaffolding, and it looked as though nobody had lived there since 1923, when the Hemingways had moved out. A bar below is called Salon de The Under Hemingway's, next to a disco called Le Rayon Vert.

Further along is Place de la Contrascarpe. That place— a square, really—is like something out of a George Seurat painting: a small square, cobblestone roads, people ambling across streets, tiny lanes, and a riot of colours. In *The Sun Also Rises*, Hemingway wrote about his taxi passing the trees and turning onto the cobbles of Rue Mouffetard. There were bright bars and late-open shops along the street then. The taxi bumped often on that uneven road, and Jake Barnes would get jolted, sitting close to Lady Brett Ashley, and in the dark street, he'd kiss her.

From Rue Mouffetard and its overflowing market of flowers and fruit, I walked down to Rue Descartes, went further west toward Pantheon, on to Jardin du Luxembourg. Hemingway writes that he and his first wife Hadley were young and poor in those days, and that he preferred walking through the garden on his daily walk to Shakespeare and Co. because he wanted to avoid the smells of the fresh baguettes from the patisseries, which he claimed he could not afford. Later critics have doubted this, given the lifestyle he describes in *A Moveable Feast* which suggests the Hemingways certainly weren't hard up and didn't need to live frugally.

I then walked along the avenue towards the Observatory. There, next to Fontaine de l'Observatoire, I saw the restaurant La Closerie des Lilas. It is where Hemingway wrote his story, *The Big Two-Hearted River*. Hemingway would sit in its garden on long afternoons, fortified by a regular intake of aperitifs. It was at this café's garden that Hemingway assuaged Fitzgerald who was anxious about the response to his novel, *The Great Gatsby*. The cafés have little plaques at the tables honouring the writers who sat there, and it can get quite intimidating. Joyce here, Camus there, Sartre and Simone de Beauvoir across the corridor... Sitting on that sofa where they sat has a momentary thrill.

Searching for literary landmarks gives your wanderlust a purpose, a meaning. The Sri Lankan novelist Romesh Gunesekera finds it amusing that tourists turn up in Dublin in June each year on Bloomsday, trying to retrace the steps of Leopold Bloom. In my attempts to retrace some of the steps, I've tried to imagine again what they saw, and marvel at how something as apparently inconsequential as a clocktower at Breach Candy might inspire Salman Rushdie to locate his childhood in *Midnight's Children*, or how a host of golden daffodils, embedded deep in memory, might spur William Wordsworth to write a poem months later, capturing the image as fresh as if it was yesterday.

ॐ

I walked towards Rue Notre Dame des Champs, where Hemingway lived over a sawmill, in the house numbered 113, but nothing of that remains now. A more important landmark lay a little further, after Boulevard Raspail, on Rue de Fleurus—the home of Gertrude Stein. After the way Woody Allen has caricaturised that charmed circle in his film *Midnight in Paris*, it may seem difficult to imagine the kind of conversations the writers and artists had in that apartment. But when arguments went unresolved, revenge was swift. When Stein made the famous remark—a rose is a rose is a rose—she meant a rose is a rose from whichever perspective you can see it from, explaining Cubism to those who could not see a rose in the bizarre geometric mélange that Picasso assembled on the canvas. In seeing an image already dissembled, which made it hard to recognise what began where and how it ended, Stein put herself in the mind of the painter, and saw the rose through Picasso's eyes, saying: a rose is a rose is a rose. Upset over an argument with her once, Hemingway quipped: a rose is a rose is an onion.

Rue de Fleurus leads you back to Luxembourg Gardens, on the other side of which lie the busy boulevards St Michel and St Germain, with three famous cafés—Rotonde, Lipp's, and Les Deux Magots, with its quaint Chinese statues. But we live in a different time, and the conversations are more prosaic. At Les Deux Magots, I survived a rather loud discussion that went on and on between two businessmen from Oklahoma about real estate prices in London and Paris, or something like that.

I remember one of my more recent visits to Shakespeare and Co.—it was evening, and young writers were to read from their works before a small audience. The authors weren't known, but Whitman was excited about the evening. Paris attracts these wandering souls, he told me; he was their inn-keeper.

He celebrated imagination, comforted writers by giving them a place to sleep and space to think, to display their books, to let them read in the shop, even if sprawled on a couch, allowed them to stay overnight in the Tumbleweed Hotel above the shop—but they had to read one book every week.

A few summers ago, my son Ameya had joined a group of new writers reading from their work. Ameya was sixteen then; his short story was about cricket, and the other writers were European or American, and all much older. None of that mattered; this was Paris, it was open to everyone. And it was Whitman's turf: his doors remained open. Tramps, poets, adventurers, and penniless writers stayed with him—as did Miller, Nin, and William Saroyan, and as did my contemporaries and friends, Suketu Mehta and Jeet Thayil, at different times. You needn't be famous: when I sat in the study, writing my poems, one resident walked by—he was the former British vice-consul in Nice and Monaco, who was writing a history of Napoleon. Whitman didn't turn away anyone, for, who knew if the person turned away was an angel in disguise? And Whitman was the guardian angel.

On the windows outside the shop, there is a text written in white chalk, which reads like his manifesto, called Paris Wall Newspaper. Dated 1 January 2004, it says:

> Some people call me the Don Quixote of the Latin Quarter because my head is so far up in the clouds that I can imagine all of us are angels in paradise. And instead of being a bona fide bookseller I am more like a frustrated novelist. Store has rooms like chapters in a novel and the fact is Tolstoi and Doestoyevski are more real to me than my next door neighbours. And even stranger is the fact that even before I was born Doestoyevski wrote the story of my life in a book called The Idiot. And ever since reading it I have been searching for the heroine, a girl called Nastasia Filipovna. One hundred years ago my bookstore

was a wine shop hidden from the Seine by an annex of the Hotel Dieu Hospital which has since been demolished & replaced by a garden and further back in the year 1600 our whole building was a monastery called La Maison du Mustier. In medieval times each monastery had a Frère Lampier whose duty was to light the lamps at nightfall. I have been doing this for fifty years. Now it is my daughter's turn....

His daughter Sylvia has been illuminating Paris in her own way now—she has been running the shop for some time, reviving *The Paris Magazine* which Whitman had started as the poor man's *The Paris Review* in 1967, and launching a literary festival. The shop is in safe hands; angels in Paris needn't despair— there is home at the Tumbleweed Hotel.

'The spirit of Paris will survive,' I remember Whitman telling me from our first meeting. 'It allows new writers a place to think in, a space in which they can write. Paris is a lyrical city. The Seine is prettier than the Tiber (which flows through Rome), the Thames (of London) cannot equal it. There is no river so beautiful and unique. The parks and gardens give you a multitude of things to do. The cores of our cities are usually destroyed, but not in Paris ... families now have two and three cars, but I prefer to be in a city where you can live as a pedestrian.'

I like walking in George's Paris, following Ernest's footsteps.

THE LAST GOOD COUNTRY

We were in an open square and there was still some light left in the sky although it was nearly nine at night. Perhaps it was the same square where we had begun our wandering through the streets of Madrid earlier that afternoon, but by now we had consumed several bottles of Rioja, and there were nearly a dozen of us by now, at least half of whom we hadn't known until that afternoon, but it was the kind of evening when it no longer mattered where we were and who we were with, so long as we found a place that served food.

But it was still early for dinner in Madrid. Nobody ate at nine, even though you might feel hungry; nor at ten, when the sun was still bright and there were all those bars you had not yet visited, and the crowds on the streets looked as if they were just stepping out for the evening; nor at 11, for the night was still young; but maybe by midnight, when the air felt cool again, and your friends finally felt slightly hungry, the remnants of tapas consumed several hours earlier now a faint memory, and the young women around you, with their flimsy tops and tight skirts began wrapping light shawls around their shoulders acknowledging the chill, and almost immediately their boyfriends placed their comforting arms around them, holding them tight. It was time to go indoors, and that was the signal.

At that late hour, with its soft breeze, Madrid reminded you that it was a mountain town, with what Ernest Hemingway once described as the city with 'the high cloudless Spanish sky that makes the Italian sky seem sentimental and it has air that is actively pleasurable to breathe.'

Hemingway had written more about the war and bullfights in Spain than about bars in Paris, and yet it took me several years after my first trip to Paris to visit Spain. I had planned on meeting an old eccentric English tour guide, whose idea of a walk around Madrid following Hemingway's footsteps meant going from one bar to another, getting tipsier by the hour, with his stories getting less interesting, his speech slurring slightly. A cute Spanish woman, about half his age, who said she was his secretary and administrator, accompanied him, enjoying the drinks, but uninterested in the city or the writer. And yet, the sites he took me to had some historical resonance, and the footsteps I followed were indeed Papa's.

Many of Madrid's bars show the fading, grizzly image of Papa Hemingway enjoying a drink. You often wonder if Hemingway did anything other than frequenting bars in Madrid. Our first stop was at Taberna Chicote on the Gran Vía. It is an art-deco bar, and when it had opened in 1931, its professed aim was to promote "talk and opinion". We found the bar to be rather quiet, with a morose bartender serving us drinks reluctantly, as if we had woken him from a mid-afternoon siesta. General Franco's troops had bombed Gran Via often during the Spanish Civil War. The road was called Avenida de los Quince y Medio, or the Avenue of the Fifteen-and-a-Halves, after the 150 mm howitzer shells that devastated the area. But as a dour British shop would do during the Blitz in London a decade later, Taberna Chicote had refused to down its shutters despite the attacks and probably inspired those shopkeepers, and for that foolhardiness—or bravery—it earned Hemingway's eternal loyalty.

From Chicote, we went to Cerveceria Alemana, in Plaza Santa Ana, where, as in many parts of Europe, old men play chess with large black-and-white pieces in the shade of trees. The bar is charming, with a wooden exterior, and inside, there are clean tiles and marble tabletops, and on the walls you see oil paintings and photographs of bullfighters. Hemingway liked being in this part of the town, because bullfighters lived close by, and he was researching their lives to write *Death in the Afternoon*. He even lived nearby during his early visits, at Pensión Aguilar in Via San Jerónimo, because bullfighters lived there.

The Cerveceria's simple décor reminded me of Bombay's old Irani restaurants. The marble tabletops, the dark chairs, the still afternoons, the drinks served in small glasses, the unobtrusive waiters blending with the curtains: to me, this was the "clean, well-lighted place", where an older waiter, who has seen life, is willing to indulge you as you sat for one more drink, while the younger one, impatient, keen to close the bar and return to his girlfriend, would act like a latter-day bartender, trying to stop you from drinking more, as if he cared for your health. The mood was desolate and empty, which the sullen Spanish women sitting two tables across did little to relieve.

When it was time to eat, we walked towards El Sobrino de Botin, in Calle Cuchilleros, south of the Plaza Mayor. The restaurant is nearly two centuries old. This was where, it is said, the painter Francisco Goya had once been a dishwasher, and where the wood-fired oven roasts suckling pigs and lamb to perfection. Hemingway's 1926 novel *The Sun Also Rises* ends in this restaurant, as Jake Barnes invites Lady Brett Ashley for a meal sharing a bottle of Rioja. As with those coffee shops and bars in Paris, many people came to Botin just to photograph the restaurant from inside. Feeling left out, a restaurant next door has a plaque saying, with inverted snobbery, "Hemingway never ate here".

The mood in Spain that summer was peculiar. A conservative government was back in power, but the people were turning distinctly Left. Nobody wanted Spain to join the imminent war in Iraq, when the Prime Minister was keen to show his solidarity with the Americans. The Spanish divide was not new. Earlier that evening, we had seen the poet Federico García Lorca's statue in a square. Spaniards now perform his plays and read his poetry, but nobody seems to know where he was buried. Some from the Left were lobbying the authorities to dig what could be a mass grave from the Civil War, because they suspected Lorca's remains could be found buried there; others wanted to avoid reopening old wounds. A Spanish judge, Balthazar Garzon wanted to unearth past secrets. He had succeeded in grounding Chilean dictator Auguste Pinochet and forced him into an extended house arrest in the United Kingdom. Now he wanted to investigate crimes committed during the Franco era. But he was stripped of his powers because conservatives felt he was going too far and by so doing he had torn asunder the unspoken rules of the truce that paved the way for the return of democracy in Spain. Let sleeping dogs lie.

But ignoring the pain, and failing to reconcile with the past, can continue to affect any society. The Spanish Civil War was pivotal in defining the "us-and-them" debate that was to engulf Europe in the lead-up to Second World War. The savage manner in which the Nazis' Condor Legion of Von Richthofen and the Fascists' Aviazione Legionaria bombed and devastated the town of Guernica in April 1937 as part of Operation Rugen became the symbol of human suffering. The unforgettable large dark canvas that Pablo Picasso painted expressed his anguish, anger, and suffering, and he refused to let the painting be shown in Spain until democracy was restored. I had seen it at the Museum of Modern Art in New York many years ago when I was a student in America; Spain was now a democracy, and the painting had come home, as per Picasso's wishes.

And so we went to the Museo Nacional Centro de Arte Reina Sofía in downtown Madrid. Guernica is a bleak, grim painting with large figures—some human, some animal—writhing in agony, their mouths agape, and their eyes wide open. Its scale is numbing, and it succeeds in shocking you. You hear the faint, almost soundless scream from the figures. The United Nations has a tapestry of Guernica in the Security Council, reminding diplomats of the horrors of war they must prevent.

The museum does justice to Guernica—the painting has a room dedicated to it—and the mood is subdued. You feel awed by Picasso's vision and helpless at your inability to do anything about it. It inspires pacifist thoughts. But Hemingway's courage—grace under pressure—was of a different kind. He wasn't a pacifist. He liked the just war; some causes, and some lands, and some people, were worth fighting for, worth defending. Even an honourable defeat was preferable to a dishonourable retreat. Hemingway wanted the bad guys beaten; he wanted the good guys to win, get back home, and he wanted that soldier to come back to his girl and sweep her off her feet and plant a long kiss on her lips, as if in a Norman Rockwell painting, even if it was a momentary pleasure, even if what was to follow was miserable loneliness, of working in a steel plant or stacking shelves in a small town, after those few months of pure heroism where to win something, you had to destroy something else.

After the Great War, as the First World War was known before there was the Second World War, the Spanish Civil War in the 1930s symbolised the conflict between good and evil. There was Gen Franco, seeking to establish a Right-wing dictatorship by overthrowing a Left-leaning republic. To defend the republic, idealists came from many parts of the world. For them it was the great, heroic struggle of their age. It was the line the Fascists and Nazis were not supposed to cross. And they came to fight, and they fought valiantly, and there was honour in their courage and glory in their defeat. Supporting the beleaguered republic and defending its integrity was the right thing to do, because, as Hemingway put it, Spain was "the last good country".

The mountains that surround Madrid are called Sierra de Guadarrama. On the road to Segovia, north of the Puerto de Navacerrada, is the bridge Hemingway writes about in *For Whom the Bell Tolls.*

> 'Spain,' the woman of Pablo said bitterly. Then turned to Robert Jordan.
> 'Do they have people such as this in other countries?'
> 'There are no other countries like Spain,' Robert Jordan said politely.
> 'You are right,' Fernando said. 'There is no other country in the world like Spain.'
> 'Hast thou ever seen any other country?' the woman asked him.
> 'Nay,' said Fernando. 'Nor do I wish to.'
> And Jordan blew up the bridge.

By the time we reached the end of the street in another town where we'd find the bar I had been looking for, we had walked through several back alleys behind the opera house. Pakistanis ran little shops and cafés alongside the alleys, and one of them curiously called his shop a Tandoori House which oddly served pizzas.

After another left turn at the end of that alley, we came to a square that was barricaded because the ground was being surfaced, and as we had been warned, we saw several women wearing dresses that hugged so close to their bodies that it was a miracle they were able to move at all, and as they walked, the men alongside us, single or not, stopped doing whatever they were doing, and stared.

Bar Marsella was right there. And it was closed.

I hadn't come all the way to Barcelona to see this bar with its shutter down. My friend Melissa had come with me out of a sense of intrigue because she had heard I was looking for a rundown bar, and not Gaudi's architecture and other spots tourists make it a point to visit. Seeing my disappointment, she tried to cheer me up and told me to stand in front of the shuttered bar while she took my picture. As she asked me to smile, one of the charming ladies walking the streets said: 'Mister, it opens at 10 o'clock.'

I relaxed and smiled, and she winked. It felt like a Hemingway moment.

Melissa and I walked along the long avenue, all the way to the spot where there is a tall monument of Christopher Columbus, looking at his hands pointing towards the sea but unable to decide whether to go left or right. We went to the marina and saw the sailboats swaying in the wind, and passed a giant Roy Liechetnstein sculpture and settled down in a bar serving tapas and more wine. Later that night, we headed back to Marsella, hoping to raise a glass of absinthe to Papa.

A week later, from my home in London, I wrote to Jack Turner, asking him about the bar. Turner is writing a book on absinthe, and he wrote back: 'The bar is a mandatory stop for all admirers of Hemingway, absinthe, and callow American English majors abroad, impressed by the relevant passage in *For Whom the Bell Tolls*.' I wasn't American, nor an English major. Two out of three ain't bad.

By the time we reached the bar, the women outside were busy—they had found companions for the evening and they began disappearing into the blocks of flats near the bar. Marsella had an imposing ceiling but it looked yellowed, like fading newsprint, as if no one had washed it in the nearly two centuries of the bar's existence. The light was yellow too, looking brighter because of the chandelier that reflected and magnified its reach. Its yellow glow, and the green tinge of absinthe, gave the bar a muted, contemplative and nostalgic look, as though we had stepped into L'Absinthe, the Edgar Degas painting also known as A Sketch of a French Café, which had a woman and man sitting alongside each other. The man wore a hat and looked away; the woman looked down. A glass of absinthe was in front of her. In their non-communicativeness lay the angst and ennui of urban isolation.

The mirrors behind us were tall and faded, the woodwork looked solid and old. In its seedy air, it looked like the kind of bar where Hemingway would have found home, if only for his own melancholia to find a natural habitat.

One table had three men, saying little to one another; another had two women, sitting close to one other. The bar had a large floor, but it didn't seem as if any couple had ever danced there. This was where you went to sit, brood, and be alone. As the night lengthened, it became a bit more cheerful, as more people came to the café, and the bartender, who had looked morose, seemed to brighten a little.

I watched the waiter place a glass and a fork on my table. He put a sugar cube on the fork and gave me a bottle of sealed, chilled water, with a tiny hole in its cap, asking me to pour it over the cube until it dissolved. The sweetened water would drop on the spirit below, releasing the powers of the green fairy.

Absinthe was banned for some time in the last century. Made from herbs such as anise and fennel and wormwood, absinthe supposedly had magical powers that played with your mind. The French symbolists—Rimbaud, Verlaine, and Mallarme certainly, but to some extent even Baudelaire—credited absinthe with spurring their creativity and they grew to depend on it. In 1995 on a trip to the Mediterranean, I had discovered pastis, the "parental-guidance" equivalent of absinthe, and had often wondered what was so special about a drink that tasted like fennel juice. But I liked it enough to bring back a couple of bottles to my then home, in Singapore. Turner credits Hemingway for being 'almost single-handedly responsible for the American myth of absinthe, namely its supposedly hallucinogenic properties. He was gifted in this respect: what he did for bulls in Pamplona, and daiquiris in Cuba, he did for absinthe in Barcelona. It helped enormously that absinthe was underground, and so the real thing was no longer available. And it didn't hurt that the drink was so strong. It appealed to both the alcoholic and the sentimentalist in him.'

I sipped absinthe, and it began its work alongside the ambience of desolation. It was more potent than pastis. Melissa took a picture of me with my glass. I promptly uploaded it on my Facebook page. Within moments, my friends began responding and talking to me about absinthe and my being in Barcelona. My friend Susie, a novelist in London, promptly wrote:

Go on, have one more.

I will, for you, I wrote.

Then another one.

You want me back safe and sound, right? I asked.

She drew a smiley. Meanwhile another friend in Seattle, concerned about how much I might drink, reminded me what absinthe did to the French symbolists.

Hemingway would have challenged the entire bar and succeeded in outdrinking everyone—or, at least claimed to have done so in a finely crafted story, even if he might have actually sat there alone, like that old man in *A Clean, Well-Lighted Place* who had no one to talk with and had attempted suicide only a week earlier.

I had no cause for despair. A little electronic device had connected me with the friends I'd have wanted around my table, and, for a brief moment, we had created a conversation across continents that collapsed so many worlds into one, cheering me. Besides, Melissa smiled cheerfully as she sipped her wine taking my pictures.

We left the clean and pleasant bar. It was well-lighted, even if unpolished. From the outside, I couldn't be sure, but there were perhaps shadows of the leaves as well, under which an old man liked to sit alone, his loneliness understood by an older waiter. Café Marsella was clean and bright, as a café should be, and it gave space to the lonely. Melissa and I left that alley and walked to the wider public square which had its taverns and music and youth and laughter, for what was left of the night.

TRUE AT LAST LIGHT

The Swahili word for freedom is *uhuru* and, as is the case with postcolonial societies where most landmarks get named after a revolutionary cry (think of the number of things Malaysians have named *merdeka*, for example), many landmarks in Nairobi are called *Uhuru*. The hotel I stayed in was near the arterial Uhuru Road, and the first name of the politician wanted in the Hague to respond to charges for international crimes was Uhuru. But if *uhuru* meant independence, for many Kenyans it had nominal appeal. As I looked out of my window on the street on that hot summer day, almost every Kenyan man I saw walking in that sweltering heat was wearing a business suit, which was not necessarily ironed. Squares and parks were renamed, but the appearance of the buildings, and people's attire, remained the same, even if it was hot and stuffy.

One suburb whose name they hadn't changed was called Karen, named after Karen Blixen, the Danish author better known as Isak Dinesen, who lived for a while there, at "a farm in Africa, at the foot of Ngong Hills". I read about her in Ernest Hemingway's writings from Africa. He had praised her and I had read that at a time when I hadn't been to Africa, so I was curious to read her, read about her, and visit the places where she had lived. I had found the film about her life, drawn from her memoir, *Out of Africa* (1985) utterly romantic, and I wanted to walk in her garden and look at those hills. Sixteen years after I saw that film, I was there, walking through her colonial house and seeing the coffee farm behind the house.

The four-poster bed inside was small, and some of the machinery for roasting coffee beans, which plays such an important role in the film, was still there. But many other objects from the house had gone, replaced with surplus props from the film. The khaki trousers and jacket, displayed in a glass cabinet, weren't Ms Blixen's; they belonged to Meryl Streep, who acted as the Danish writer in the film, giving the museum a peculiarly postmodern touch.

I sat on a bench outside her room, not far from the tree near which Denys Finch-Hatton leaves the gramophone, as Finch-Hatton and Blixen listen to Mahler. On the horizon, I could see the beautiful Ngong Hills, whose arresting image frames the dramatic opening sentence in Blixen's memoir:

> I had a farm in Africa at the foot of Ngong Hills. The equator runs along these highlands, a hundred miles to the north, and the farm lay at an altitude of over six thousand feet. In the day time you felt that you had got high up, near to the sun but the early mornings and early evenings were limpid and restful, and the nights were cold.

The hills rise evenly, forming a ridge along the Great Rift Valley. Somewhere on its slopes is the grave of Finch-Hatton, who was, for some time, Blixen's lover. Blixen's house is a haven of an island in the turbulent sea of humanity that Nairobi has become. I wanted to be free of that tumult; I sought my own *uhuru*.

We were on another Uhuru Road, but the snarling traffic in front of us suggested that nobody was free to leave. There were craters and rocks all around, even on the road once we left the city, and people living on either side used the road as an extension of their village; we, the foreigners in a four-wheel drive, were the intruders. Some had laid out their crop of chilli on the road to dry, so that our vehicles would drive over it, presumably to crush them. Women in bright reds and yellows sold corn and chicken along the road. Boys ran with carrots and peas in plastic bags. A hawker had spread out an array of shining shoes. Another sold plastic buckets, and in a corner there was a billboard advertising an evangelical priest offering instant salvation. Below that board was a hair-dressing salon that promised to straighten your hair and lighten your skin.

The villages became fewer, the population sparser, and the valley opened out. From 7,000 feet above sea level, the valley below looked red, the soil fresh as though it had just been dug. The terrain was flat, with patches of trees and huts; herds of animals moved briskly, leaving behind a trail of dust, creating a blurred layer, like a photograph slightly out of focus. We stood silently staring at the vast stillness. This is where the earth parted once, creating two different plates. We were in the Rift Valley in Kenya, the centre of that vast, long stretch running across Africa, where everything began.

Even if the geographical importance of the Rift Valley is lost on those among us who aren't scientists, it commands attention because of its grandeur. It opens out dramatically, revealing its earthen colours. How powerful the force must have been when it was unleashed to bring these cliffs together, uniting the plates, with the valley staying and holding firm at its centre, its frayed surface like stitches that have mingled with the skin after binding a massive wound.

We resumed; further down the road we saw monkeys running across roads as though they owned the roads. They looked at us intently. If there were a piece of dead wood lying nearby, I'd have expected one of them to pick it up and fling it high, letting it soar, as though I was watching, in real time, the opening sequence of Stanley Kubrick's film, *2001: A Space Odyssey*. Only the monolith was missing.

The monkeys were there first; we were newcomers to this part of Africa. They owned the place; we were tenants. We come, take pictures; they are the landscape. We watch them, they live here.

Our first stop was to be a town called Kericho, at the edge of Mau forest, which has a square named after chai —for tea is grown in plenty in the highlands near this town. In Kericho, we woke up to the sounds of birds, the breeze shaking the curtains of our colonial guesthouse. With the conversation among birds as our constant companion, we walked along a clear path. At dusk, if you were lucky, you could spot an elephant; at night, the sky was clear and it was full of stars.

The weather was crisp when we left the tea garden, looking like miles of green carpet. A handful of men and women plucked leaves which would later get sorted, air would get blown through the leaves, they'd get ground, allowed to turn the right shade of brown and black, and after being processed further, to be tasted—and tested—and packed at the factory in Jamji. The tea garden was evenly laid out, not a single leaf out of place, and it rose and fell with the landscape, looking like waves caught still.

When we passed through the valley again, the sun was bright. As we descended into the valley, the sun disappeared behind the white clouds, but its harsh light managed to penetrate through the layers. It was afternoon and the thick haze cast a pall over the red earth, now looking yellow and brown, and the solitary trees, the remote huts and the Masai herdsmen looked grainy, like crayon drawings. The clarity of that dawn belonged to another time, when the air was cold and the light gentle.

Throughout our ride we were chasing a mirage, which glistened about a mile ahead of us. It would quake and tremble as the distance shrank. It would then disappear, only to emerge nearer the horizon, like quicksilver that enjoyed teasing us, shifting quickly as soon as we got any closer. Later, when the sun shifted its position, the hills changed colours. Now they were blue, at times grey, sometimes they'd darken, seeming black, and once they even looked like a white apparition, so faint, as haze settled firmly in the valley.

How green were those hills, and how red the valley, even as the film of haze covered much of the landscape.

We were heading towards Lake Naivasha. I was travelling with Hillary, an American environmentalist. I had known her from college and hadn't seen her for nearly a dozen years since. We met unexpectedly at a seminar in Nairobi and I suggested that the next day we should go and see flamingos, and she said yes.

We reached the forest lodge by the lake, where they were taking last orders for lunch. This being Kenya, I went for the section that might have local food. Appropriately enough, there was a lavish Gujarati vegetarian spread.

The sky was clear and blue as we sat out after lunch, and the air seemed filtered and clean. There were only a few scattered clouds and, with the breeze blowing from the lake, the heat became bearable. We followed our guide up a meandering trail scented by dry grass that got dense as we rose higher. Walking on that trail was hard work, and what seemed like mild weather suddenly felt hot. The ground was flat at the top of the hill and there were few trees. Our guide led us towards the edge of the cliff, pointing his hand down, smiling.

Curious, we walked towards the edge.

Below us lay the lake in its full glory, golden ripples reflecting the sun as the breeze caressed its surface. You could hear the gentle sound of the wind, going *whoosh*. And there, on the other side, was a pink flotilla—thousands upon thousands of flamingos. That pink blanket was oblivious of the rhinoceros that came alongside, drinking from a small pond. The birds stayed clustered together, their tall legs reflecting in the water, and with the mist layering the view with a thin film, it looked like a panoramic painting.

The flamingos walked gracefully, like ballerinas, picking bugs and fish from the lake. They bent low to drink some water, then raising their heads, giving us a startled look when we came too close, and then they scurried away from us, creating a delightful symmetry of ripples across the water.

We also saw Thomson's gazelle—spunky and cheerful, the gazelle with the body of a gymnast and with elegant horns which looked like someone had crafted intricate jewellery on her head. She moved swiftly, vanishing in the grass, until she emerged moments later, much further from where I had seen her disappear, with a puzzled look on her face.

The wind gushed in, pushing the water, shattering the reflection of the flamingos. As if on cue, the birds soared together, forming a divine arc, floating above the water, before settling on another part of the shore. No Martha Graham, no Merce Cunningham, could have choreographed such beauty. If there was a background score, it was in their minds.

I stood there still, in awe. Words were superfluous. This was freedom, *uhuru*.

On another visit a few years later, I was in a forest lodge with a few friends in a comfortable wooden chair in the veranda of the bar after dinner, aware only of the silence surrounding us. In an interview with *The Paris Review,* Dinesen spoke about what her grandmother told her about the meaning of silence:

> Where the story-teller is loyal, eternally and unswervingly loyal to the story, there, in the end, silence will speak. Where the story has been betrayed, silence is but emptiness. But we, the faithful, when we have spoken our last word, will hear the voice of silence. Who then tells a finer tale than any of us? Silence does. And where does one read a deeper tale than upon the most perfectly printed page of the

most precious book? Upon the blank page. When a royal, and gallant pen, in the moment of its highest inspiration, has written down its tale with the rarest ink of all—where, then, may one read a still deeper, sweeter, merrier, and more cruel tale than that? Upon the blank page.

No wonder, Hemingway thought the world of her. To capture the essence of meaning around us on a blank page in simple, clear and true words—that was a writer's calling.

They would come at night, but we hadn't known and they wouldn't tell us. Had we listened closely and talked less, we'd have heard the soft thuds and whisper-like rustle of the waterbucks and impalas as they jumped over the fence around our forest lodge, and squatted in the grounds of the lodge where we stayed (I checked the next night—I was alone that night outside the complex where I stayed, and I did hear, and witness, that silent takeover).

We stepped out of the bar, and saw them amble and settle in at their favourite spots—the hotel complex had kept muted lights on, and in the glow of the lodge's light, their luminous hair looked golden.

The waterbucks were there again at dawn. They tolerated us: they had seen us arrive the previous day, and looked at us with wry amusement, as some of us desperately tried to fix telephoto lenses on our cameras, and others requested their friends to take their pictures on their cellphones, fearing that the waterbucks would run away.

But the animals seemed to like being photographed, so they stayed; they sat quietly, continuing to look at us as our friends posed, conscious, some eyes facing the camera, others casting furtive glances at the waterbucks, lest they stealthily came anywhere near them. But the waterbucks sat impassive. They could outrun us.

The following morning we had woken up to the sounds of birds. Even though theirs was a vocabulary we could not understand, we knew it was a conversation, rapid and loud. It was just after 6:00 am, and the landscape was magical, true at first light, as Hemingway once wrote. At dawn, by the lake, the truth was simple, clear and pure.

Timothy was our guide, taking us to the shore of Lake Naivasha. On one side we saw a few giraffes, walking away from the lake, their necks swaying. Zebras ran towards the lake. The mild mist in the air, accentuated by the lake's presence, made it look as though we were stepping into the pages of the *National Geographic* magazine.

From the height of the watchtower, we saw the lake as it awoke—the still view of the calm water, the sound of the birds, and the light on its surface. Some hippos were already in the lake—partly submerged, they lay content, convinced about the utter inconsequentiality of our presence. A few birds sat on the hippos' hides, exchanging gossip.

Suddenly, we saw a spring hare race past us, as if in a great hurry, carrying an important message for his friends. A blacksmith plover circled us, chirping excitedly, as if warning us. *Shoosh*, Timothy said, asking us to be quiet.

Then he pointed out a tree, next to which I saw a massive rock. Besides the rock sat a hippopotamus, groaning. Timothy spoke in Swahili to two men passing by, who told him the hippo was hurt and in pain.

The hippo wanted to go back to the water, but was in no position to do so. I remembered what Timothy had warned us about before we started: never stand between the hippo and water. The wise option seemed to be to follow Timothy, step by step, and so we did.

The two men slowly went to the hippopotamus, hoping to convince him to move, even if slowly, back to the water, to be with his mates. I was with my friend Usha, who is a human rights lawyer, and she usually doesn't like forced evictions. But she accepted that this eviction was on compassionate grounds, so she let it pass. The giraffes and zebras went to the mist-covered lake, as if they were bored and had their fill of watching people from outside Kenya who had come to see them.

As we returned to the city, the animals we saw along the highway were domesticated. They followed their masters' orders—the sheep, head down, following the boy with the stick; the cows, marching quickly through the field, obeying the tall Masai. The triumph of human will over animal instincts was complete by the time we entered a Nairobi suburb. The animals were caged, or in enclosed areas, in a safe, child-friendly national park. The wild abandon of the valley had been tamed. The gulmohar shone from the branches; the jacaranda shaded the streets with its purple gaze; and there was laburnum itself, drooping like melting yellow necklaces.

The Ngong Hills marked the horizon, the five peaks clustered together, like a clenched fist, the knuckles visible.

The road to the mountain was long and flat and the land on both sides was dry. A sheet of greenery lay evenly on the hills in the distance. The sun was bright at that hour, and its light surrounded the hills where they touched the sky, and it looked as if the blue of the sky had begun to drip on the green hills.

The Masai men wore red and yellow *shuka* and they stood out in the grassland. One of them carried a stick on his shoulders, and a herd of goats and cattle walked slowly along the plain.

The sky was filled with clouds, which was not a good sign. We had set out when it was still dark and my driver Bakari had warned me about the clouds.

'Will it rain?'

'Not rain. But there are many clouds. They will hide the mountain,' he said, and then brought his hands close, as if shutting a window.

'That's all right,' I said. 'We can't force a mountain to do what it doesn't want to do.'

Bakari nodded.

You had to wait for the mountain to reveal its beauty. You cannot force the peak to unveil her face. You wait for the beauty to look at you; you do not rush truth. It comes out when it wants to; truth cannot be hurried.

We drove for two hours towards Tanzania's border with Kenya, and we saw her image at many places. Kili time— If you can't climb it, drink it, one billboard said, and I saw a few tourists at the bar, with bottles of the beer named after the mountain open in front of them, the men settled in comfortable chairs, their eyes squinting towards the peak. A tailor had named his shop after the peak. And there was a nightclub called Kilimanjaro.

My guide was called Goodluck, and I hoped that some of his name's charms would rub off on us, and that we would get to see the peak. On the forest trail, younger people walked ahead of us, briskly and firmly, as if they expected to meet someone at the mountain. They will reach the top, they will see the Great Rift Valley sprawled below—but will they see the peak's face?

We took a steep path going down, following the sound of running water. The slope was sharp, and we passed a village where the Chagga lived, their children waving at us, following us, running ahead of us, standing on rocks by the waterfall, smiling at us, hoping to get photographed. The waterfall was gentle and the flow of water was even and you could see a rainbow, and Bakari said that was a good sign.

Maybe we will get to see the peak, he said.

We walked further, reaching the base camp, where the more serious mountaineers began changing into warmer clothing and rearranging their rucksacks. It will take them three to four days to reach the top of Kilimanjaro, but will they see what Harry saw, in Hemingway's short story *The Snows of Kilimanjaro*: 'As wide as all the world, great, high, and unbelievably white in the sun ... the top of Kilimanjaro.'

The clouds continued to shield Kilimanjaro's face. Part of me wanted to challenge the mountain and sit and wait and train my lens and trick the clouds into thinking that nobody was looking so that the clouds would slip off a little and reveal the peak's beauty, and I would be waiting just for that moment, my eye fixed through the lens, my finger circling the shutter, ready to press. I will wait till the mountain gives up. The mountain was not an animal; it would not turn away, running away from me, leaving a cloud of dust. The mountain will always be there. But could I wait, and for how long?

And another part of me said—the mountain will always be there and there will be another day and another season and you will be back and the clouds will slip the veil, if not for me then for my sons, and I should know my limits and stop where the road ends and accept that the mountain was bigger, that I lived in its shadow and not the other way round, and I looked at Goodluck's face and he understood and he nodded. It was time to head back.

In *True At First Light*, the novel published posthumously, Hemingway had described the continent and its essence:

> In Africa a thing is true at first light and a lie by noon and you have no more respect for it than for the lovely, perfect weed fringed lake you see across the sun baked salt plain. You have walked across that plain in the morning and you know that no such lake is there.

We had travelled across another plain in the morning and we knew that there was a peak but in the afternoon when we went there it almost seemed as if it had never been there. We saw Kilimanjaro's images again—on billboards of beauty parlours, restaurants, shops, and bars, on posters and beer cans, on T-shirts and tablecloth. But she had continued to hide.

Now it was twilight and we were driving back. And there, suddenly, Bakari stopped the car and before he could say anything I knew why, and I looked out of the window, and there I saw, Kilimanjaro, her jaw-dropping beauty, absolutely true, beautiful and believable, true at last light.

I raised my camera, bringing it close to my eye, my finger on the shutter. In that split-second, an enormous cloud surrounded it once again, and she was gone.

THE MOOR'S LAST SIGH

The spot we were looking for was not marked on any map. No great man had been born there, nor had anyone famous died there. There was no mountain peak someone had scaled there either. We had driven an hour looking for it, and had a vague idea we were near the right place.

We had been looking for a site remembering a loss, which was known for something as ephemeral, transitory and fleeting, as a sigh. This was where a man had turned his back one last time to look at a fort which was once his, from which he had ruled a land which was now no longer his; he had lost it. And there, at that spot, overcome with grief, he had let out an audible exhalation, a breath, a sigh—of despair and sorrow.

The man who sighed was Boabdil, the last of the Nasrid sultans of Moorish Spain. The Moors had ruled large parts of southern Europe for centuries. The Umayyads had extended the early Islamic empire between the seventh and eighth centuries, and established the Caliphate of Córdoba, where they ruled till the eleventh century. Science and arts flourished in the time when Europe was still in the Dark Ages. They knew the positions of stars more accurately than the world had known earlier; the scholars of that time wrote tracts on philosophy and mathematics; people belonging to different religions lived largely at peace with one another, and libraries were revered. Córdoba became the centre for Jewish scholarship. The magical palace-city of Alhambra epitomised the period. With its beautiful gardens designed symmetrically, and the palace itself, with its intricate, geometric patterns carved on the walls and the neat Arabic calligraphy, Alhambra was a jewel.

But empires wane. By the late fifteenth century, Ferdinand and Isabella, who ruled Spain, wanted control over the entire Iberian Peninsula. In 1492, Catholics had surrounded Granada, forcing Boabdil to surrender and pushing the Moors into defensive positions. The Moors had to leave Alhambra; they surrendered. Christopher Columbus apparently saw the surrender—later that year, he would get the royal approval to find a sea route to India but reach America instead. Defeated, the Moors retreated, Boabdil settling in the mountains of Sierra Nevada, before their eventual disappearance from Europe.

Today, the Arabs who make their way to southern Spain do so to work. On the way from the coast to the Alpujarras valley, you see long stretches of greenhouses where Spanish farmers grow vegetables which Arab labourers pick.

Earlier that week, further away from the coast in the town of Lanjaron, we had explored an old, abandoned "Arab" castle (as the locals called it), facing the inspiring mountains, its isolation underscoring its desolation, as if symbolising defeat. An empire had ebbed and another one was rising. We were keen to be where the Moor let out that invisible sigh.

Here, Salman Rushdie describes the scene in his 1995 novel, *The Moor's Last Sigh*:

> He (Boabdil) departed into exile with his mother and retainers, bringing to a close the centuries of Moorish Spain; and reining in his horse upon the Hill of Tears he turned to look for one last time upon his loss, upon the palace and the fertile plains and all

the concluded glory of al-Andalus... at which sight the Sultan sighed... whereupon his mother, the terrifying Ayxa the Virtuous, sneered at his grief. "Well may you weep like a woman for what you could not defend like a man," she taunted him.

A few days later I was in Córdoba, the syncretic city from where the Catholics banished the Jews in 1492. Syncretism had been at the heart of Córdoba. As I walked through the old town I came across a statue honouring Maimonides, the twelfth-century Jewish philosopher, who was born in Córdoba, and whose home is now a well-kept museum. The homes in the area proudly display their menorahs, and inside the homes, I could see beautiful courtyards with water fountains, and resplendent flowers adorning the windows.

In Córdoba, eventually all roads led to the church. But to enter the church, I had to go inside a mosque. The street signs outside called it Mezquita, a mosque. But inside, you could not pray to Allah, and once you walked past the pillars and arches, in the distance, you could see Christ on a cross.

Mezquita *looked* like a mosque, with its hundreds of curved, horse-shoe shaped arches, symmetric patterns, muted colours, and the absence of icons or idols. But most of all, those pillars were unique—there were hundreds of them, in red and white, surrounding us from all sides. In the courtyard outside, orange trees stood. 'A piece of Eastern architecture with a Baroque cathedral stuck in the middle of it,' is how Salman Rushdie had described it in *The Moor's Last Sigh.*

In this unique structure, there was arithmetic precision behind the rows of pillars, with red and white stripes along the curve of the arches at precise intervals, so that when I walked slowly from one angle to another and saw the pillars, the stripes seemed to move at the same pace that I walked.

If I stood at one spot and then walked in a circle around that spot, and then looked around, I would see those red and white stripes moving continuously, and yet going nowhere, in an eternal animation, like in a drawing of M C Escher, the Dutch graphic artist, who imagined perpetual stairs and other never-ending mathematically challenging visual puzzles. The forest of pillars and the red-and-white striped arches that hemmed me inside seemed to go on till infinity.

The mosque was built on the remains of a Visigoth church, which in turn had displaced a pagan temple. Abd al-Rahman I had come to power in 756 AD, making Córdoba the capital of the Moorish caliphate. The Umayyads built the mosque over two centuries. In the years that followed, Córdoba gained fame as a city of intellect and civilisation, with poets writing love poems, astronomers tracking the skies, and the city's urban waste disposed off in pipes.

Eight centuries later, Christians conquered Moorish Spain. Charles V of the Habsburg dynasty did what conquerors like doing in their flag-planting zeal. He built his own monument at the site of the big mosque. He had several arches taken down, and built a cathedral inside the periphery of the erstwhile mosque. This church within a mosque is not a mosque any longer, but with hundreds of arches still standing, it continues to weave its magical illusions.

Once the Moors withdrew and Granada fell under Catholic control, most residents, including many Muslims, embraced Christianity. The few Muslims that still live in Córdoba have made peace with the existence of the church within the mosque. Most of them have no complaints, nor do they claim the mosque. But some of the more recent Spanish converts do object. Their group, called Junta Islámica, distributes leaflets in hotels and passes sheets to tourists, pointing out the *mihrab* and finely-honed mosaic tiles inside the mosque and the delicately-carved choir stalls, arguing how the mosque-church could represent the spirit of *convivencia*, or social harmony at a time when Europe is divided, the world more so.

Their plea: to be allowed inside to offer Muslim prayers. But the city's bishop has refused. Muslims from elsewhere, some inspired by Osama bin Laden's rhetoric (he wanted to reclaim this region that he called Al-Andalus, as Andalusia is known in Arabic), have attempted to pray collectively inside what they still consider a mosque, and then the guards come and evict them.

There is one god here, the one permitted to be worshipped. Demetrio Fernández González, the city's bishop, has already appealed to the town to refer to the structure as a church, and not a mosque, to avoid confusing visitors. In an article in ABC, a Right-leaning Spanish newspaper, he wrote: 'In the same way, it would be inappropriate to call the current mosque of Damascus the Basilica of St John or to expect that it could be both a place of Muslim and Christian worship,' referring to an Umayyad mosque in Syria which has been built above a church which reportedly had the remains of St John the Baptist.

But shopkeepers, motivated by tourist-dollars and not consumed by atavistic longings, react differently. Ask any shopkeeper where the church is and he's likely to ask: 'Which one?' Then you ask where Mezquita is, and instantly he points in the right direction.

Shakespeare asked in *Romeo and Juliet*: 'What's in a name? That which we call a rose by any other name would smell as sweet.' Perhaps; but the bishop is talking about something more serious—formidable faith, not a flower. Yet, what draws people to Mezquita is not the faith, but beauty—an overwhelming proportion of the 1.5 million visitors who visited it last year came to admire its architecture, and not to connect with the supernatural, of this or that faith.

Outside the mosque, the mood is convivial, not combative. There are stands selling Christian religious artefacts and photographs of the mosque and church. Besides the chilled soup gazpacho, the restaurants serve tapas made naturally from pork, and Rioja wine. Former Muslims who had converted to Christianity after the fall of Moorish Granada demonstrated their fealty to the new faith by consuming the tapas and Rioja eagerly.

Along the streets, one dark hotel stands ominously, facing Mezquita. There is a mannequin outside, in steel armour, looking like a crusader. That he is, the hotel reminds us; it is called El Conquistador, as the soldiers who defeated the Moors were known.

Some battles continue, even if only in people's minds.

I wanted to think of Granada in a happier time, and I left for one final look at Alhambra from that spot where Boabdil sighed, as he glimpsed the glory he had lost. It is a tiny patch of land, between two motorways. You cross the motorway at some personal risk, as there is no zebra crossing, nor a bridge or an underground walkway. Along the grass you find a weather-beaten milestone, where, in fading paint, the text says—Suspiro del Moro, or the Moor's Sigh.

It looks like any other milestone, except that it is older, needing a fresh coat of paint. Even the road sign indicating the spot is faded, unlike the blue-and-white billboards pointing towards Granada. The stone looks unattended, and its surface is chipped, the paint fading, and the site looks desolate. Cars and trucks rush by, scarcely aware of the spot. There is no sign informing visitors—if we can be grandly described as such— why someone had thought the spot was important enough to mark it by placing a stone there.

At the café in the modern building called Suspiro del Moro, which also runs a convention centre and has an active swimming pool in which children were frolicking, I ordered something called Suspiro del Moro—a portion of caramel custard which comes with vanilla and coffee ice cream and a fresh slice of pineapple. I thought of the ingredients—coffee beans, sugar itself, the pineapple, and the vanilla essence—and how they were introduced to Spain only after its conquests in the Americas, and the opening of new trade routes.

From that spot I looked towards Granada. A few stubborn trees block some of the view, but the hill stands out, and up on the hill, you can see the solid, invincible-looking fort, looking tiny, but at once pink and red, surveying the vast territory it commanded. Alhambra sat alone on the hill, which Rushdie called 'that monument to a lost possibility... like a testament to lost but sweetest love, to the love that endures beyond defeat, beyond annihilation, beyond despair.'

And which can be felt only fleetingly, like a sigh.

THE SEA, THE SEA

The snowline floated like a delicate arc in the sky. There was an entire mountain beneath, but it was invisible; the yellow mist that surrounded this Andean valley would not clear so easily, making that silvern sliver—the peak—look like an apparition, like the giant wings of a bird flying above Santiago. It remained above us, like a heavenly body, and the yellow mist made the city look golden, as I left with Carlos, the tall and amiable driver. He was dressed in an impeccable suit, and we were about to leave for Pablo Neruda's homes in Chile.

I first read Neruda's poems when I was at college in Bombay; our textbooks had Keats and Byron and Hopkins and Wordsworth. It was as if only dead white English poets wrote poems. (To be fair, they did include patriotic poems by Sarojini Naidu, which put generations of Indian students off reading Indian poets who wrote in English.) A couple of college professors understood this—and interestingly, they didn't teach us English—and they exposed us to European and Latin American writers. Neruda sounded exotic and at the same time accessible—his love poems, dripping with warm emotions, were just what this teenager wanted to read, while trying to write his own love poems meant for that special girl. Life intervened, all of us moved on, but re-reading Neruda inevitably made me slightly misty-eyed, taking me back to a younger, more innocent time.

And now I was in Santiago, teaching at a workshop, and I had a day to spare. So off we went, Carlos and I, and headed for Isla Negra, or the Black Island. It is a small fishing cove, and it lies on the edge of the Pacific on a rocky shore. We were gliding along the thin waist of Chile, which stretches itself along the American continent, slim like a ballerina in a figure-hugging leotard, balancing herself on her toes.

Isla Negra—black island, neither black, nor an island. As I was to discover later, in Chile, some things were not what they were called, and some things appeared to be what they were clearly not. Neruda had built his house on the waterfront. Robert Graves did indeed say: 'There's no money in poetry, but then there's no poetry in money, either.' Neruda clearly had both. He was a Marxist and a poet, and he could fill a stadium when he read his poetry. But he was also a diplomat, and he had money: enough to build several houses—just as he loved several women, and had several personas as well (his name was not Pablo, and his surname not Neruda—he was born Eliecer Neftali Reyes Basoalto—but then there is such a thing as poetic license—remember Isla Negra).

Neruda had that license. He designed that house to look like a ship, and he was its captain. As you entered his house, you saw intricately carved figureheads that were once on the prows of sailing ships. His was the captain's table. The view from the windows was of the sea, the wooden floor, the narrow passages where sailing memorabilia lay scattered, framed, placed everywhere. It was as though he was in a ship ready to sail somewhere, but it was not going anywhere, except where his mind wanted to wander. He once said that he is a sailor of the mouth; meaning, he liked to talk about sailing, but didn't want to be in the ocean, for he liked to see the waves, but probably didn't like the feeling of being tossed around, or the wetness of waves hitting his face, as they might have lashed his boat, or the helpless desolation when the waves came rolling in like clouds of darkness shrouding an unhappy evening.

The house at Isla Negra began with a stone tower, to which he kept adding and refining parts. He was an avid collector of stuff. Those boat prows, but also oddly-shaped bottles, carousel horses, stones, butterflies, carvings from different parts of the world, including India, even large bells which would strike to announce lunchtime. And above all, agate stones and sea-shells, so many of them.

For many young lovers, the home became a point of pilgrimage. The Chilean poet Marjorie Agosin writes about the place: 'In the summer, Isla Negra is inundated by vacationers seeking to escape the noise and smog of Santiago. During that care-free season, many young people fall in love for the first time, reciting Neruda's Twenty Love Poems and carving hearts into the trees.'

That book must lie in the hip-pocket of every young man in Chile out to woo the woman of his dreams. Consider this:

Leaning into the evening I throw my sad nets

Into your ocean eyes

There my loneliness stretches and burns in the tallest bonfire,

arms twisting like a drowning man's.

I cast red signals over your absent eyes

Which lap like the sea at the lighthouse shore.

How would she not notice? How would she not see what it was all about? How could she say no after this? (But they do, they often do.)

By winter, Isla Negra is a different place. That is the time when "a strange flowering is dressed by the rains and the green and yellow cold of the blues and the purples" appear, as Neruda wrote in his memoir, I Confess that I have Lived, remembering 'this smell of winter at the sea, a mixture of sweet herbs and salty sand, seaweed and thistle.'

In *Houses from the Past,* an essay about the places where he has lived, Neruda wrote: 'I am frightened by houses I have lived in. The arms of their compasses are opened wide, waiting: they want to swallow you and bury you in their rooms, in their memories.' Poets need comfort but they also need isolation. Isla Negra was far from Santiago, and his house was sufficiently secluded when he bought it. And yet, it was as if this house, washed by the ocean, was not distant enough from the big city. So he had built a cabin for himself, closer to the water, from where he could see the ocean, and sit on his desk, imagining drunken sailors and mermaids. Nubile nymphs appear often in his poetry, and they inspire him to write about their eyes, their enveloping, long tresses, their soft, comforting breasts, and their sweet kisses. The sea appears often, too: 'To whomever is not listening to the sea,' he promised in his poem, *Poet's Obligation,* to bring its sounds and waves:

And a vibration starts up, vague and insistent,

A great fragment of thunder sets in motion

The rumble of the planet and the foam,

The raucous rivers of the ocean flood...

To Neruda, his obligation as a poet was to carry the sounds, the freshness, and the salty air of the sea for all those who had to remain in offices and factories and prisons in distant cities, and who had asked him: 'How can I reach the sea?' He wanted to bring them freedom and the sea, the "starry echoes of the wave", and "the cry of sea-birds".

As I walked towards the sea, I saw large birds flapping their wings, chattering noisily. Further along lay a rocky cove, where penguins huddled, like waiters at a grand hotel before guests have arrived. The sharp sand flying in my face didn't seem to bother them.

Neruda's house is large, with quaint masks looking appropriately whimsical, and curvy glass bottles, appearing deliciously seductive. On the walls and ceilings of his bar he had scrawled the names of poets he would have liked to sit around him and share a drink: Guillaume Apollinaire, Nazim Hikmet and Walt Whitman. It was as if they were his constant companions.

Neruda knew his women and his ocean, his wines and his flowers, his vegetables and his mountains. Inspired by his poetry, Michael Radford's 1994 film, *Il Postino* imagines him in exile in Italy, where a temporary postman serves him. The film is a latter-day Cyrano de Bergerac, where the poet is amused by the postman's plight—the postman is in love with a beautiful woman, Beatrice, but lacks the skill to woo her, and so Neruda helps the postman, who is handsome but forever at a loss for words. Neruda writes lyrical love poems, with which the postman wins Beatrice's heart. The story is fictional, but his poetry resonates with images of the sea.

Neruda's politics was a different matter, for he was a political man. He was admired by many who viewed themselves as progressive. Neruda was close to the Chilean president, Salvador Allende and died soon after Allende's assassination. And Allende was replaced by the brutal regime of General Auguste Pinochet, whose specialty for torture included throwing Leftists from helicopters into the Pacific Ocean, to an icy death. Pinochet's rule was indeed evil, and Neruda was on the right side of history then; but he wasn't, when he spoke about Communism elsewhere in the world. He won the Nobel Prize for Literature, but another Nobel Laureate, the Polish-born Czeslaw Milosz, was to write about Neruda's politics thus:

> When he describes the misery of his people, I believe
> him and I respect his great heart. But when he paints
> the joyous, radiant life of people in the Soviet Union,
> I stop believing him. I am inclined to believe him as
> long as he speaks about what he knows: I what I
> know myself.

Indeed, when poets imagine and describe what does not exist, it works really well so long as they are in the realm of poetry, but when they say something factual, and which can be verified, and if those images clash with reality, as lived and understood by others, problems begin.

Later that afternoon, Carlos took me to Valparaíso, to Neruda's other home in Sebastiana, where he had built "an extravagant house, entirely of air", as Bernardo Reyes describes in his book, *Casas Neruda* (Houses of Neruda). Neruda was tired of living in Santiago and wanted to be closer to the sea. But he wanted the conveniences of a city and Valparaíso offered that. He wrote to a friend that he wanted a house so that he could write in peace—not too high, nor too low, with invisible neighbours he could not hear either; original but not uncomfortable, light but firm, not too big, not too small, far from everywhere except the stores. And cheap.

He did find such a house, and that house "grows and speaks, supported on its feet," as Reyes puts it. Describing the house, Neruda wrote: 'I built the house. First, I made it of air. Then, I raised the flag in the air and left it hanging from the sky, from the light and the darkness.' It is a tall house, and from its top floor, you get a magnificent view of this charming city set on forty-odd hills. There are labyrinthine alleys, cobble-stoned paths, and funicular cable cars. The mighty Pacific roars in the background, its sound penetrating through the wall-sized glass windows.

From his bed, Neruda woke up to see the sprawling landscape through those windows. His typewriter sat by his bedside; his pillows were smeared with his favourite green ink, for Neruda wrote by hand.

As I left the house, I saw his familiar silhouette on a bench. It was a life-size outline of Neruda with his flat cap, pensively looking at the sea. You could sit beside him on that bench, and when the sun was right behind you, someone could take your picture with the silhouette, creating the momentary illusion of you sitting with the poet, admiring the valley below and the ocean beyond, lost in thoughts.

'Look around,' Neruda had told Pinochet's soldiers who raided his home the day the general overthrew Allende's government. 'There's only one thing of danger for you here—poetry.'

On our way back, Carlos opened up. He asked me about India, the country that he once nearly visited, but ended up not going. He paused as he recounted that story. He used to have a girlfriend once who was passionate about the mysteries and mysticism of the east, and she wanted to explore India. He was too poor to join her; he thought he would wait for her. But life intervened, and they moved apart. But she was special; you could see it in his eyes as he talked about her, after all these years.

Then, as we drove near a vineyard, with the sky clear and blue, and yellow flowers bending in the mild breeze, he told me that he too wrote poems. And he showed me a fountain pen with green ink.

'I like Neruda. I want to write like him. I write my poems in green ink,' he said.

The green grass outside swayed, as if waving to us.

NO PLACE TO HIDE

The haiku is a deceptively simple form of poetry. Three lines made of seventeen syllables are divided in the pattern of 5-7-5, and they don't have to rhyme. What could be simpler? Sonnets have complicated patterns of rhythm. The ghazal appears easier, but its internal grammar is exacting, and only a few poets have managed to write ghazals successfully in western languages—Federico García Lorca and Agha Shahid Ali come to mind. Limericks are entertaining, but try injecting humour in the fifth line, after maintaining suspense over the first four. The haiku, in contrast, depends entirely on syllables and needs only words.

When I was a teenager, I attended the Open Classrooms at Sophia College in Bombay, where the poet Saleem Peeradina ran a course in creative writing. My instructor was a British writer called Julian Birkett. During our first session, he explained what the haiku could do and asked us to try our hand at writing one, giving us twenty minutes. There was silence in the class, with some students staring vacantly out of the window, hoping for inspiration to strike, even as a crow kept yelling and hecking us. Some scribbled a bit, and stared at their page. A few could be seen counting syllables. I plunged into the exercise with supreme confidence, and I think I wrote nine haikus in the allotted time—all of them were mawkish, sentimental love poems. That was inevitable; I was madly in love with a girl who didn't yet know how I felt about her at that time, and I wrote poems about her as a way to shed my timidity, so that I could "prepare the face to meet the face", even though she would ultimately turn around and say, that was not what I meant at all, not at all. But such is first love.

I was rather pleased with my efforts, until the time came for us to read from our work. A couple of my classmates had written striking haikus; several others hadn't been able to write anything. I proudly mentioned my nine haikus, and read them rather rapidly. Julian, who was later to like my prose and even some poems, shook his head rather vigorously. 'These are short sentences that you have broken up; these are only words. These aren't poems. Haikus are made of images. They happen when you reflect. You need to be calm. You don't have to be excited. You have to distill your experience through images, not words. These are only words.'

It's only words, as the Beatles sang. Although Julian put it across to me more gently than how I've recounted the story, I learned my lesson. Poetry needs passion, but also patience; it was not words alone; poetry happened when words were chosen for certain purposes, invoking a sharp image. The haiku required discipline, brevity, elegance, imagination, design, clarity, and delicacy. And a good haiku doesn't merely have impressions; sometimes it contains sharpness, even violence; and most times, it is visual and tactile.

At my home in London I have four woodcut prints by the Japanese artist Katsuyuki Nishijima. They are numbered, and they cost me a minor fortune when I bought them in Kyoto in 1995. They show the roofs of homes, drawn from odd angles. The roofs are black or dark grey and made of wood, the sidewalk spotlessly clean, and lanterns—red and yellow—glint from corners, giving the bleak, black-and-white imagery a life of its own. I look at them often, and think of them as visual haikus. Joel Tyler Headley has described the essence of Japanese architecture as 'the beauty of clean, fine grained natural wood and the fallacy of glass and paint.' Those prints take me back to Kyoto.

While Tokyo is the gateway to Japan, and the frenetic pace of life in that city is an experience to savour, to understand the Japan that lives beyond the bright lights of Ginza, you have to leave the babble of Roppongi, the crowds at Pachinko parlours, and the odd sight of grown men in dark suits, wearing 3-D glasses and playing video games after hours—like boys who haven't or won't grow up. There is something boyish about them—think of the male obsession with schoolgirls wearing white socks.

I took the *shinkansen,* as they call the bullet train, to Kyoto, and entered a different world.

Before his arrival in Kyoto, Nikos Kazantzakis wrote:

> I wonder what other joys await me in Kyoto, the widow royal city, where I will arrive tonight. Traveling is captivating hunting: you go out never guessing what bird will come along. Traveling is like wine: you drink and you can't imagine what visions will come to your mind. Surely while traveling you find all that you have within you. Without wanting to, from the innumerable impressions that overflow your eyes, you choose and select whatever corresponds more to the needs or curiosities of your soul. "Objective" truth exists only—and how insignificant it is!—in the photographic cameras and in the souls that see the world coldly, without emotion, that is, without deep contact. Those who suffer and love communicate through a mystical intercourse with

the landscape they see, the people they mingle with, and the incidents they select. Therefore, every perfect traveller always creates the country where he travels.

What would my journey be like?

I reached Kyoto during early spring, when snow still clung to the sidewalks, while cherry blossom trees had begun to unfurl their glorious foliage. Awakening from deep slumber that winter had imposed, the flowers look cheerful. As Matsuo Basho wistfully recalls in these two haikus:

Under the cherry blossoms

None

Are altogether strangers

And he revealed the beauty of the night:

Lingering a moment

The moon in a night sky

Beyond the blossoms

The tree, the flowers, the landscape: poets want to carry them in their afterlife, even as they accept their own impermanence. Issa wrote:

Long after my departure

In the old village

The cherries went on blooming.

Reflecting on that, I walked on a stone path, towards the single-storey building that was my hotel. The roof was black and its walls were white, and orange lanterns hung in the verandah.

They were placed at an even distance, right between two pillars, creating a picture-perfect view.

The mild spring weather was comforting, and the manager at my hotel told me that I should return in autumn if I really wanted to see the colours. In autumn, he said, the path I had just walked on would be difficult to find, with brilliant autumn leaves lying like a thick carpet on the stone steps, swallowing the path. Fujiwara no Toshiyuki has a beautiful poem about autumn:

The colour of dew

Is white alone

How can it be

That it can dye

The leaves of autumn

So many shades

Nature plays an important role in haikus, and Japanese poets often write about flowers. They describe them in striking, clean prose, and plead with them, as Saigyo once did:

Mountain cherries

Although it is the custom

To be tempted by the winds,

Wait for my visit

Before you fall

Or they capture them, as Kobayashi Issa sees them:

The spot

Where the spring sun sets:

Wisteria flowers

Here's Masaoka Shiki:

One fell

Then a second fell:

Camellias!

And Ogawa Haritsu:

Until they bloom

No one waits for them:

Azalea flowers

Azalea, wisteria, camellia, mountain cherry—each crystal clear, each vivid, each haiku written so that you can visualise the colours.The certainty of the return of those flowers a year later makes their impermanence bearable. The moment matters; that moment has to be captured and savoured. On the train journey back I remember sitting eagerly by the window, after having requested my co-passengers to let me know a few minutes before the fleeting moment when I'd be able to see Fuji Yama, the famous snow-capped mountain. The train was at one time the world's fastest and when the mountain came, and went, it indeed happened in the blink of an eye. I was told I wouldn't have the time to take my camera out and train the lens, and wisely, I didn't go about fidgeting, looking for the camera—I let my eye capture the image, where it stays, the mountain floating by.

Impermanent pleasures are like seasons; they disappear soon. But their brevity does not dilute the intense experience. Their intensity is captured in the concept of "the floating world," which flourished among artists and writers in the Edo Period. In the seventeenth century text *Ukiyo Monogatari* (Tales of the Floating World), Asai Ryoi defines the concept as:

> Living only for the moment, turning our full attention to the pleasures of the moon, the snow, the cherry blossoms and the maple leaves; singing songs, drinking wine, diverting ourselves in just floating,

floating; ... refusing to be disheartened, like a gourd floating along with the river current: this is what we call the floating world.

In Kyoto, I saw spotlessly clean homes where nothing, not even the tatami mat, was even slightly out of place. The city exuded perfection in the tapestry of its streets, the symmetry of the design, the artistry of the screens, and the poetry of the landscape: it was sublime. I went looking for the Golden Temple—for Kyoto has one—which a deranged monk had destroyed in a fire some years ago. It took the Nobel Laureate Mishima Yukio to reconstruct the story in *The Temple of the Golden Pavilion*, a novel where he described the temple at the centre of the lake, and its impact on the monk:

> Gradually the Golden Temple came to exist more deeply and more solidly within me. Each of its pillars, its Kato windows, its roof, the phoenix on top, floated clearly before my eyes, as though I could touch them with my hands. The minutest part of the temple was in perfect accord with the entire complex structure. It was like hearing a few notes of music and having the entire composition flow through one's mind: whichever part of the Golden Temple I might pick out, the entire building echoed within me.

Such personification and idolisation of an object can lead to passion, and passion, when uncontrolled, can have devastating consequences. Japan's imperial history shows what can happen when intense devotion to a cause knows no bounds. They call it divine, but it is madness. The root of the word, *kamikaze*, for the pilots of the Japanese air force who went on suicidal missions during Second World War is kami, or divine, and comes from *kami no kyoki*.

What divine madness gripped the monk, to want to destroy the temple? I don't know. But I couldn't help reflecting on another Golden Temple, whose sanctity was destroyed by another man driven insane by religion, which ended when the Indian army sent troops inside that temple in 1984, and shattered its walls with bullet marks, destroyed an insurgency and wounded a nation.

From Kyoto, I went to a town on Japan's west coast. High mountains formed an imposing wall on the horizon. Sunlight fell on the snow, which reflected it on the village, spreading a yellow glow, like sprinkled gold dust. Skiers snaked their way through steep slopes of the mountain, along the army of evergreen trees. The trees were laden with fluffy snow on their branches, which occasionally collapsed in a flurry of whiteness, when sharp winds shook the trees hard.

We were sitting in an open *onsen*, as the Japanese call their hot springs, our torsos feeling the autumnal chill, while warm, volcanic water invigorated the rest of our bodies. My legs floated in the water, taking painterly liquid shapes, as I perched myself along the wall, my arms holding me up.

We were in the hot springs of Niigata. It was morning; my friend Ushio was by my side, telling me about a complex mathematical problem he had been unable to solve the previous night. This hour at the springs, he was convinced, would help clear his mind, and he'd be able to fix the proof he was working on.

Does this water really have healing qualities, I asked. It has regenerative qualities, and it can lighten the load you are carrying, and help you look at things clearly, Ushio said.

Ushio had politely told me the etiquette of *onsen*: you shower before you enter; and yes, you wear nothing, not even swimming trunks, although you can carry a washcloth. And you don't stare at the men or women who are also in the water, no matter how attractive.

The idea, then, was to walk nonchalantly, as if you were fully clothed, and yet briskly. Walking quickly also helped because it was cold outside. It was an unreal experience—to walk through that path of stones through an even lawn, as we looked for a more secluded part of the pool, wearing nothing.

Ushio moved on his toes, and I kept pace with him. We had three more friends with us—colleagues of Ushio—two of them Japanese, and the third from a country in India's neighbourhood. He had lived in Japan for many years, but my subcontinental cousin used the washcloth to cover himself during our short walk. He said I could do the same, 'It is allowed,' he reassured, as he tried to cover himself modestly with that tiny white cloth. But I didn't; I wanted the freedom that came from conformity. I also remembered that old silly joke about five Cambridge men, punting naked in the river, when suddenly they heard the laughter of women from the bank. Worse, these were women they knew. Promptly, four of the men covered their private parts. One covered his face. And from behind the mask he said: 'Gentleman, I don't know about you, but women usually recognise me by my face.'

In Niigata, at the *onsen*, nobody knew me; I was happy to walk without any clothes on. Once in the open, in that cool, crisp mountain air, I felt there was nothing to hide, and indeed there was no place to hide.

Months later, I wondered why my subcontinental cousin had covered himself. He lived in Niigata; it was a small town, and his face was known. Taking off all clothes before entering the hot springs was an ancient custom here; everyone did it. The Japanese saw it as a form of bonding. Did he not want to bond?

For him, it was his sense of modesty. It prevented him from disrobing and revealing himself fully, a deeply ingrained sense of shame associated with the display of the body. That modesty is oddly selective. Many bristle at the idea of their own divinities painted in the nude (think of what India did to the painter Maqbul Fida Husain) but think nothing of the angels in the nude that they see in Western religious art. Many even fall at the feet of naked ascetics—some sadhus and digambara Jain munis being two examples. And then there are Khajuraho and Konark—temples that celebrate erotic art. But those ancients can do what they want, modern India rationalises. Modern Indians are—what's that word?—decent. But to what extent is that Indian morality? Or is it Victorian?

In any event, feeling the shock when you see a naked body is not a particularly subcontinental trait. Travelling in Europe with American friends several summers earlier in my college days, I had noted how stunned the Americans were when they saw European women going topless so nonchalantly on beaches and in parks. I have to admit, the first time I saw rows upon rows of people wearing as little as the weather permitted, I was taken aback, too. For my American friends it was the first such sight, and they kept taking pictures of the women, training their zoom lenses from a safe distance, lest their boyfriends come chasing after them; the women stared back angrily, some covering themselves with beach towels.

In Niigata that day, though, there were no cameras. The nudity was aseptic, almost as if in a hospital ward. Taking off your clothes became a functional act. If you tried to cover yourself, it would seem you were acting like those novice monks in that Zen story. It seems their Master had taught them never to look at a woman, let alone touch her. When the two novices and the Master reached a river they had to cross, they saw a beautiful woman who also wanted to go across, but she could not swim.

The Master carried her in his arms and brought her to the other side. The novices were shocked. Later at night, sensing their troubled minds, the Master asked them what was bothering them.

One of the novices said: 'Master, you carried a woman across the river....'

'And I left her on the other side. You are still carrying her in your mind,' he said.

In the land of Zen, that's what the hot springs taught us—to shed not just our clothes, but also our inhibitions. Then, slip into the water, let its warmth cleanse and rejuvenate you. And you sit there, admiring the snow-capped peaks.

I turned to Chiyo:

On fields and hills alike

Nothing moves:

A snowy morning

The following morning, indeed, nothing needed to move. It was still, calm. Later that evening, Ushio told me he had solved the problem troubling him. And he too smiled.

There was rare beauty in that ending, like the moment in the floating world—where you refuse to be disheartened, diverting yourself in floating—until inspiration strikes; a mathematical problem solved; my haiku is born.

The warmth of water

Breeze rushes; my skin shivers

Sunlight on the snow.

THE DELIGHT OF
THE UNKNOWN

I was in a ramshackle bus that bumped over craters, swinging vigorously at every turn, as we left the tiny airport at Sylhet in Bangladesh, for Srimongol. As we careened forward, the driver kept honking, announcing his imminent arrival, but the villagers ignored this twentieth century intrusion into their pastoral lives.

Our bus was filled not only with passengers, but with life itself. One *jhalmoori-wallah,* selling local snacks, continued doing his business while inside the bus, deftly mixing his *chana, mirchi,* and onions, while his radio blared a Mohammed Rafi song. A woman casually unbuttoned her blouse and breastfed an infant. Nobody noticed; nobody thought anything was unusual about that.

We reached Srimongol; at the roadside, the stalls sold soft drinks, masala shrimp and roasted peanuts. Yes, masala shrimp: they eat things differently in Sylhet, I was told later.

I hired a Land Rover to take me deeper, towards Lawachara National Park, a rainforest. We were still on a paved road, and in the ditches along the road I saw little violet flowers growing in careless abandon in the water. My driver told me the flowers were called *kochuripana*, or water hyacinths. They grew everywhere, without warning, and they formed a natural border between where the tarred twentieth century ended, and where the Satyajit Ray territory unfolded.

All around me I saw vast stretches of fields, shining as sunlight rested temporarily on the blades of the swaying crops. I saw little children running in the field; they could have been Apu and Durga. I saw tea garden labourers wearing conical hats which I thought were worn only in Vietnam. I saw women in red and green saris, sans blouses, who could be stepping out of *Ashani Sanket (Distant Thunder)*. And I saw a shining lake on the horizon.

Soon, we were in the rainforest. The trees grew dense; their leaves, bright and translucent, covered the foliage, vibrating lightly in the breeze, rustling softly, as if they were murmuring to one another, changing light and shapes as if in a kaleidoscope, as a gentle shaft of light penetrated the shrouded greenery. In my mind, I was already humming the theme of *Pather Panchali (Song of the Road)*.

We were climbing a steep, rocky hill now; the Land Rover could no longer ascend the path. So we got off and I walked, quietly taking photographs. The forest grew more dense—forget history, certain areas of this forest had not even experienced sunlight, you would think. I could smell the freshness of earth. I saw a spider tenaciously building a huge cobweb between the branches of a tree. It was an artist's delight, sunlight resting on its edges, making the web's outline gleam.

We had walked a few miles, and I heard a sound I hadn't expected, the sound of this century, penetrating the silence. It was the puffing of a railway engine. It was delightful because it was so unexpected; it was the pleasure of the unknown— *ochenar anondo*—as Bibhutibhushan Bandopadhyay called the chapter that described Apu's and Durga's discovery of the train dissecting the *kaashphool* (kans grass) field in *Pather Panchali*. But this was not a black-and-white world; I saw the clear red of the train compartments of the Chittagong Pahari Express making its way, disturbing the tranquillity only briefly, before leaving us in that spot of timelessness.

I saw a woman racing down the hill, nimbly carrying firewood. Perhaps she lived in one of the huts I saw on my way. Perhaps those children in the field were hers. And perhaps that labourer was her husband.

Later that night, at the forest rest house, while sipping tea made from freshly plucked leaves from the garden nearby, I wondered: the train must pass through the landscape often enough, perhaps even daily. Was the reality Ray captured so commonplace? Or did he elevate what seemed ubiquitous to an aesthetic height?

Bangladesh lured Indian filmmakers. Once the country was no longer Pakistan, Ritwik Ghatak went there in 1974 and made the film,*Titash Ekti Nadir Naam* (A River Called Titash) in the newly independent country. The border between India and Bangladesh established a boundary, but it did not really separate the people—you can't tear apart a language. And Ray and Rabindranath Tagore—despite Bangladesh's independence—continued to reappear, reassuring me of the ties that re-emerge when border lines cease to be battlefields.

On my second night, Nazrul Islam, the forest ranger in the area, invited me to his home, and prepared Horlicks for me. On his walls, I saw posters of Sridevi, Tagore, and Gen Ziaur Rahman. As if on cue, the lights went off, as they often do in this part of the world, and he lit a lantern. Then his wife arrived. Her name was Rashida. He asked her to sing for me, and after some hesitation, she sang a Tagore song. She insisted I eat fish and rice with them. That night, Nazrul walked with me, a bright candle in his hand, finding me a cycle rickshaw with little bells that tinkled. I reached a bus stop from where I'd go to Bhairab Bajar, and from the ferry point there, I would go south.

There are forests with more diverse wildlife in the world, and there are prettier lakes. Trains run through picturesque tea garden territory all the time. But that week, in Lawachara, near Srimongol, I saw a confluence of these images and, for that brief moment, stepped into the landscape glimpsed only in imagination. It was unexpected—I had gone to Bangladesh to write about its politics—instead I had a different delight— of something unexpected, unknown. *Ochenar anondo.*

A quarter century later I was again in Bangladesh, looking for the home where Tagore wrote his poetry. I reached Kuthibadi late one winter afternoon, when the sun was still bright but was slowly losing warmth, its light making the pale white walls of the house glow. Kuthibadi, which translates to "retreat", was Tagore's family home in Shilaidaha, near Kushtia, not far from the Indian border.

A well-kept garden lay on either side of the path leading to the house. Trees cast long shadows and the chirping of birds mingled with the laughter of children visiting the house. Orchards of mango, jackfruit and other trees stood nearby.

Kuthibadi is a terraced, three-storeyed bungalow made of bricks, timber and corrugated sheets. The house stands within an eleven-acre estate, and has over a dozen rooms. The open terraces on the ground floor and first floor are partly covered with a sloping roof of Raniganj tiles. Displayed inside the house are Tagore's portraits and letters, including those where he would fill the white space between words by making graceful, deft strokes in black ink. The doodles revealed elegant abstract patterns, creating a new aesthetic around the poems.

The land around the house was vast once: the poet's grandfather, Dwarkanath Tagore, had acquired the estate in 1807, and young Rabindranath often came here from Calcutta, as the city was then known. The tranquil landscape, the pastoral countryside, the timeless fields, and the flowing waters of the Padma moved him deeply. 'The holy place of my literary pursuits during my youth and middle age was the village of Shilaidaha, kissed by the waves of the Padma,' he would write later.

Inside a pond that is part of the estate, the boat *Padma* sat atop its own reflection, swaying gently. In his Twenties, Tagore would often go in a houseboat and spend days travelling on the mighty river. The poems he wrote there form an essential part of his literary canon. Fakrul Alam, the noted Tagore scholar at Dhaka University, told me: 'The English *Gitanjali* is based on eight different Bengali collections, though many of the poems in it are from the Bengali *Gitanjali*. Quite a few of the poems collected in the English *Gitanjali* were composed in Kushtia, but not all were.' Tagore translated the poems from Bengali into English in Kushtia and he revised them in 1912.

Tagore couldn't travel to receive the Nobel Prize in 1913, but he was able to go to Stockholm in 1921, and made what is now considered to be his Nobel Prize acceptance speech. He then recalled his time in Shilaidaha, the "obscure Bengal village" where he lived in a houseboat where:

> The wild ducks which came during the time of autumn from the Himalayan lakes were my only living companions and in that solitude I seem to have drunk in the open space like wine overflowing with sunshine and the murmur of the river used to speak to me and tell me the secrets of nature. And I passed my days in the solitude dreaming and giving shape to my dream in poems....

Tagore was wistful about the silence that helped him reflect and contemplate, and he doubted if Western poets and writers had the opportunity to spend their youth in such absolute seclusion.

In his famous poem, *The Golden Boat*, Tagore writes about the rumbling clouds and anticipates the teeming rain. He speaks of being sad and alone along the riverbank. The harvest has ended and the fierce river is swollen, its flood waters twisting and swirling everywhere. There he sees the boat, steering close to the shore.

I feel that she is someone I know.
The sails are filled wide, she gazes ahead,
Waves break helplessly against the boat each side.
I watch and feel I have seen her face before.

He then requests the boat to come to his shore and take away his golden paddy and himself, but, the boatman says:

No room, no room, the boat is too small…
Across the rain-sky clouds heave to and fro,
On the bare river-bank, I remain alone.
What I had has gone: the golden boat took it all.

I sat near the pond, looking at the reflection of trees in the water. Sunlight pierced through the leaves, lighting up the faces of the men who sat by the pond, with a harmonium and tabla, singing Rabindra Sangeet. The song's melody was soothing and its lilt gentle, and the singers expected nothing except a nod of appreciation as we sat a while longer listening to their music. The evening light was pale; the boats sat on the water, swaying lightly; the men sang; the music spread wide across the landscape; and it started to darken.

Later that evening, we went to the banks of the Padma. Boys from Shilaidaha village were playing cricket using a large tree as their wicket. The land by the river was even and sandy. I walked towards the river. At the jetty, fishermen unloaded their day's catch and lifted the load on their heads, walking the last mile as they had done for centuries.

The sun dipped lower on the horizon, the scene became blurry. The departing boat became a silhouette. I saw it leave the shore, making its way, slowly, towards another town. The boatman was singing, *haiya ho*. The sun was now pink, looking as though it was going to melt. As the sky reddened, the river dazzled, as if someone had lit a fire and millions of little lamps had come alive, twinkling like stars.

The boat made its way through the water, disturbing the still surface of the river. I looked at the sun, now a mere molten fragment of its former self, rapidly disintegrating on the horizon. The temperature dropped, the long-suppressed wind emerged, scattering leaves on the ground. I could not see the boatman any more. But I could hear the faint song he was singing.

And I thought:

On that bare river-bank I stood alone.
The time I had had now gone.
The golden boat took it all.

THE QUIET PATH OF POETS

With its toy-like telecommunication tower poised as though it is a rocket about to take off, Shanghai has the look and feel of a familiar landscape: Disneyland, drawn by a young artist imagining a futuristic city, but unable to think of original images. Shanghai's skyline looks like the copy of a copy of a copy. Shanghai tries to outdo Singapore, just as Singapore wants to outdo Hong Kong, and Hong Kong wants to be pre-eminent, and has a skyline more inspiring than New York's. But even as New York has lost one of its iconic landmarks, the World Trade Center's twin towers, and even as the Bank of China Tower and the Jardine House in Hong Kong give the city its distinct edge, and even as Singapore has added an entire set of skyscrapers which did not exist a dozen years ago when I lived there, Shanghai's skyscrapers are remarkable because they are so indistinguishable from one another. It must irritate the party bosses in China that in spite of all the buildings, taller than in Manhattan, more hi-tech than in Singapore, and younger than in Hong Kong, most people want to walk by the Bund, and admire the stately grandeur of old Shanghai, or Puxi. There stand those buildings constructed by the colonial powers and enterprising businessmen like the Sassoons, now transformed into boutiques and hotels and shops and restaurants, looking entirely at peace with themselves, even as across the river, in Pudong, in the new Shanghai, the buildings yearn to grow taller, higher, and louder.

In a city that has erased its past with greater disdain than Singapore did, old nomenclatures cling to certain places out of a sense of loyalty. Nothing seems French about the French Quarter, for example, with its shops selling marinated barbecued meats. Here, waiters set afire the asparagus on my plate, which we dutifully photograph, and later we walk around the old town, hoping to catch a glimpse of Shanghai's past. And nothing seems very Chinese about the large mall, which could easily have been in any large Asian city.

In this commercial capital of the copycat nation, nothing seemed authentic either. A hawker offered me a Montblanc pen that looked exactly like the Montblanc pen in the shop behind him, where it was sold for a hundred times more. And nothing seemed ancient in a city where each building was a skyscraper taller than the one next to it, and shone like it had just been unwrapped. Nothing seemed modern too, in a city where on weekends in a public park hundreds of men and women talked animatedly, exchanging photographs of their sons and daughters, arranging their marriages the way their parents had arranged theirs, and their parents theirs, and so on, uninterrupted, generation after generation. Despite the apparent spontaneity of those conversations, the moves were rehearsed, the dialogue planned, a bit like the city itself, where the centrepiece at the museum of planning was a miniaturised model of the metropolis, as though everything, including this sudden growth, was exactly as the Party intended and the city had planned.

The parents in the park were particularly animated. When I asked our cab driver what they were doing, he pretended not to know. What's inscrutable about China must remain inscrutable to the outsider, it seemed. But I was with my friend Tina, who runs a literary festival in Shanghai, and while she is a Tamil-speaking woman of Sri Lankan origin born in Singapore, she speaks Shanghainese with the aplomb of a local. And she knew the interior landscapes of Shanghai, and told me to get off the cab and start walking with her, to help me unravel the mysteries of the city.

Oddly enough, if you wanted to see old Shanghai, the kind of houses J G Ballard wrote about in his 1984 novel *Empire of the Sun*, the best you can do is to see the film Steven Spielberg made so lovingly. In Shanghai itself, the next-best option was to visit the museum of urban planning, where you left the room which had the model of miniaturised Shanghai, and went to a large hall, with its oil paintings and photographs of homes of old Shanghai. The city resisted uniformity—it was among the last to fall to the Communists, and it provided many intellectuals to the country. Shanghai looked east, but it was China's face to the west. And it is in those large canvases that you saw the charm of the colonial era, with gardens and foliage implying a permanence which empires believe they possess, until the revolutionaries arrive and raze everything to the ground. Interestingly enough, the Party failed to see the aesthetic of the paintings. There was no catalogue I could buy with those images—it is almost as though the Party was still embarrassed about the time when foreign traders dominated China, even though China has grown today because it has embraced foreign trade again and become the factory of the world.

And there is pride in that accomplishment. When we went to the other side of the same hall, there was a different exhibition, of images that modern China was proud of. The large photographs displayed were not those of children exercising in unison, but of Shanghai's port, with its ships and hectic construction activity, looking mechanical and prosaic. There are probably bureaucrats who are prouder of those photographs of modernity, unlike the canvases I had just seen, which show the stillness of the old. Those images of an industrial, modern China were remarkably featureless.

Tina has lived in Shanghai for over a decade now, and takes delight by startling the locals by speaking in bursts of perfect Shanghainese. Having grown up in multilingual Singapore, her ease with other languages and culture is not surprising, and she is one of the key organisers of Shanghai's literary festival which is run by her and her colleagues. The festival is of primary interest for the expatriate community and the smattering of Chinese who like literature published in English.

Tina has promised to take me to a special place—Siming village, named after a bank now forgotten. The village itself is set away from the bustling thoroughfare that marks the border of what used to be the French Quarter. As my Singaporean friend Han Shih reminded me, at one time, Sikhs and Vietnamese guarded these streets—the Sikhs guarding the English concession, and the Vietnamese, the French. The street had identical two-storeyed shikumen houses with brick walls of a muddy hue that was unsure if it wanted to be brown or red. The street was spotlessly clean, and we saw a father taking his son out for a stroll. The father ambled; the son was riding an electric scooter, which the father manipulated with a remote controller, occasionally startling the son by changing his course and speed. The father was always in charge, while giving the child the illusion of being in charge of the toys that the father's prosperity had brought. It was a metaphor for modern China.

Neighbours sitting outside their homes, in chairs, exchanging news of the day, stared at the father and son—and us—as Tina led me to a wall with a plaque full of Chinese names—of actors and academics—written in elegant calligraphy. She wanted me to see one specific name, which stood out because it was engraved in English. It was Rabindranath Tagore. And things fell into the pattern Tina had planned, and her wonderful

Shanghai surprise made sense. I was delighted to receive such a priceless gift from her.

I was in Shanghai in the year of Tagore's 150th anniversary, and it coincided with the centenary of Sun Yat-Sen's republic, in this most independent-minded city of China. And she had taken me to the lane where Tagore often stayed at the home of his friend, the poet Xu Zhimo, who lived with his wife in house No. 923 (alas, now gone, to make way for that thoroughfare).

As we walked down the street, we saw more plaques, with words written in Chinese, some with graceful drawings on the side—many were Tagore's poems; others, verses by Chinese poets, some of the verses inspired by Tagore. It was a silent passage away from the noise and babble of Shanghai, taking me to an older, quieter time when this city of commerce valued a bearded poet from a distant land.

Contemporary Chinese poets often say they are inspired by Tagore—it is a useful starting point for a conversation with an Indian, since China has left India behind on so many other economic and social indicators. I remembered meeting a young Chinese poet, Shu Ting, at Vagarth, the World Poetry Festival at Bharat Bhavan in Bhopal in early 1989. She attracted much attention, and she was friendly and polite. After she finished reading her poems, a Hindi poet asked her about her favourite poet. Without any hesitation, she named Tagore. The Indian audience was delighted; given the way China selected its authors to represent the country at international festivals, it was impossible to know if indeed Tagore was her favourite poet or had she been tutored to say so. Had the festival been in Boston, would she have named Robert Frost? If in Santiago, Pablo Neruda?

Shu Ting had learned the hard way how challenging the Party can have consequences. During the Cultural Revolution, as a teenager she was forced to work in factories. There have been many exceptional accounts of what Mao's rule did to

China during the Revolution—the real and the cultural one. Nien Cheng's *Life and Death in Shanghai* marvellously recreates the day-by-day debilitation of a great city; the Indian poet Jeet Thayil, in a superb story-within-a-story in his novel, *Narcopolis*, recreates the paranoid mood of the Cultural Revolution, when you could trust nobody.

To survive, Shu Ting may have had to compromise, and she was allowed to write. She became part of the "Misty Poets" movement, which comprised poets who used euphemism, allegory, and metaphors from nature to make restrained criticism of authorities, while being constantly aware of boundaries, during that brief interlude between the Beijing Spring of 1979, as Deng Xiaoping asserted his authority after the confusion following Mao's death, the fall of Hua Guofeng and the arrest of the Gang of Four—Chiang Ching, Yao Wen Yuan, Chang Chung Chiao, and Wang Hung Wen. Deng had yet to visit Shenzhen and express admiration for what he saw there; entrepreneurs in Guangdong didn't yet know that the mountains were high, and the emperor was indeed far away. And Deng hadn't yet said he didn't mind what the colour of the cat was, so long as she could catch mice—all those aphorisms were signals for private businesses to grow, but to do so by crossing the river by feeling the stones, and not by plunging headlong, as Mao did in the Yangtze on 16 July 1966.

The Beijing Spring lasted a decade, because in 1989, months after Shu Ting returned to China, students had taken over Tiananmen Square. Instead of listening to them, as Zhao Ziyang suggested, the Chinese authority sent tanks—the image of that lone man walking to a tank, asking the soldiers to return, stays embedded in our mind; we will never know what happened to that man. Many of the Misty Poets left China at that time. Shu Ting still lives there. Does she still like Tagore? The Tagore who wrote about that heaven of freedom where the mind is without fear and the head is held high? Is China anywhere near such a heaven?

Tagore visited China in 1924, aiming to understand its ancient civilisation. At that time, both Tagore and China were preoccupied with different concerns. Tagore had opposed the Opium War—he had even expressed anguish over the complicity of the Indian merchant class, which had thrived trading opium. He was hurt by Japanese aggression as well—a militant, militaristic Japan did not fit well with the image of Japan he had in his mind, of a peaceful, cultured nation.

Tagore was sympathetic to China's vulnerability. He liked aspects of Chinese culture so much, that at his university, Visva-Bharati, he had set up the first Indian centre seeking to understand Chinese thought. Tagore liked Western liberalism, but its colonial power disillusioned him. He was shocked by the violence of First World War, which was still fresh on his mind. He treasured a letter from Susan, the mother of the poet Wilfred Owen, who had died in the war, in which she had written to him how much Tagore had meant to Owen.

And there were fresh wounds closer home. The Jallianwalla Bagh massacre of 1919 had pained Tagore; he had returned his knighthood. He became increasingly skeptical of the idea of the nation-state, and of vehement nationalism—think of the circumspect Nikhil, in contrast to the gung-ho Sandeep, in *Ghare-Baire*, his remarkable novel about nascent nationalism in Bengal.

China had cheered when Tagore received the Nobel Prize in 1913, but in 1924 it was a different country. The revolution that overthrew Puyi—the "last emperor" in Martin Scorsese's film—in 1911, was still fresh. The 1919 Treaty of Versailles at the end of First World War had handed over Shandong to Japan, which was reviving nationalism in China. And on 4 May that year, students revolted against that treaty.

In China, Tagore spoke of the country's past and ancient traditions, but China's younger, radical intellectuals had little time for those traditions and less for spiritual thoughts, which they associated with the establishment that they sought to replace. Those ideas had kept China fossilised, a subject nation. Such cultural battle lines were drawn in China when Tagore arrived. So when Tagore praised traditions, he disappointed some radicals. Left-leaning writers challenged Tagore's idea of venerating the past.

Tagore had met the dethroned and unlamented Puyi, but did not meet Dr Sun Yat-Sen when he was in Guangzhou, which sent the wrong signals to the nationalists. The Chinese writer Shen Yambing (who used the pen name Mao Dun) wrote in the journal *Juewu* in 1924:

> We respect [Tagore] because he is pure in heart. We respect him because he feels for the oppressed and the underdogs. We respect him because he is on the side of the peasants ... But we do not welcome the Tagore who loudly sings the praise of Oriental civilization, nor do we welcome the Tagore who creates a paradise of poetry that has made our youth intoxicated and self-complacent.

But there were some who venerated him. Liang Qichao gave Tagore a Chinese name, Zhu Zhendan, and Tagore wrote a poem:

> *Once I went to the land of China,*
> *Those whom I had not met*
> *Put the mark of friendship on my forehead*
> *Calling me their own.*

In a GDP-obsessed India, China may seem like a model, but might it not be the case that if Tagore were to see China today, he'd want it to be more like India, where the mind is without fear? With all its flaws, India did not have a Cultural Revolution that sent a teenager like Shu Ting to work in a factory, nor a Great Leap Forward that caused starvation deaths. Amartya Sen has himself written about how China dealt with the famine in the 1960s, and how the crisis worsened primarily because of the lack of fundamental freedoms. And Tagore would have sung with the peaceful students at Tiananmen Square, with his head held high. Those students hated old virtues, just as the ones that Tagore met in 1924. The older generation was critical of Tagore's universalist message, seeing in his words an escapist naturalism. But for the students in Tiananmen, the poem *Where the Mind is Without Fear* could as well have been an anthem.

Later that evening Tina took me to the Bund, with its colonial buildings lit up and transformed from banks and trading posts to art galleries and restaurants, upscale shops and hotels. Pudong sought our attention, like a permanent expo pavilion on display. The buildings were lit, the breeze cool, and I saw hundreds of families, lovers, and friends along the Bund walking without a defined destination.

But this is China; there are rules. Even celebrations must end on time. And almost like that father turning off the remote controlling device earlier that evening, the lights went out, stopping lovers mid-kiss and reminding families to go home and sleep soundly.

After I returned to London, Tina sent me a postcard: it showed the sketch of the compound in which Tagore had lived—it was the same spot where the modern hotel where I had stayed now stood, oblivious of that past. There was a large mural inside that hotel, of Zheng He, the eunuch admiral who left China in the fifteenth century to trade with the world. He came to Southeast Asia, bringing Chinese influence and presence to the Malay Peninsula and archipelago. Zheng He is known in certain parts as Cheng Ho, and I have seen him venerated like divinity.

At that hotel, the admiral became an object of art on the wall. The world had now come to trade with China, oblivious of the admiral's journeys centuries ago. And the hotel was built on a plot where a wise Indian poet lived, admiring this land at a time when its traditions had not been overhauled, its spiritual thinking hadn't turned temporal, and its rulers didn't send warriors to mow down students.

CHASING A DREAM IN A PARK

You can tell it is summer in New York by the bright light that invades your hotel room early in the morning. The light is an in-your-face kind of light, and very New York. There, the city is already out-and-about, can't you see, and what are you doing, wasting your precious hours huddled under a blanket, it seems to say. (New York hotels have excellent air-conditioning, which means you can ignore the temperature outside which may reach the high-90s.)

In other cities on a warm summer day, you want to sleep longer. But New York does not allow indulgence; each moment is precious, and you have none to lose. You look down the street from your 25th-floor window, and cars are already crawling along those linear streets. The day began long before you woke up, because, silly, the night had never ended. The city is on the move—you want to get down and join the crowd, otherwise it will leave you behind.

I have been going to New York since 1983, and it remains my favourite city. There are two types of people in the world—those who like a real city and those who like a city that attempts to be one. I prefer Bombay over Delhi, Saigon over Hanoi, and Hong Kong over Singapore for that reason, and that's why I pick New York over Washington.

New York has its landmarks, but they don't instantly symbolise the city, as the Eiffel Tower means Paris, the Big Ben means London, or the Leaning Tower stands for Pisa. The Statue of Liberty is technically in New Jersey; the twin towers of the World Trade Center eclipsed the Empire State Building. The twin towers were functional, not elegant, looking like tall, slim pin-striped cigarette lighters standing next to one another. There is the Rockefeller Center, but its charms have less to do with how it looks, and more with what it does to you. No matter how often you pass by the Rockefeller Center in winter, it is impossible not to pause and look at the large Christmas tree, and the dozens of people skating in that ice rink, your face showered by a flurry of light snow, strong winds slicing you as you walk between skyscrapers, the music, the schmaltz. The Chrysler Building has character, rising like a well-sharpened pencil, and there, downtown, Flatiron Building looks like a slice of cake. But none stands for the whole city, which is fine. Maybe New York's icon, then, is the collection of skyscrapers, which look like the city's cardiogram. The city becomes a part of your being, and as you walk along the Brooklyn waterfront and look at Manhattan, if you close your eyes briefly, you can imagine the grey silhouette of the scene from Woody Allen's *Manhattan*, George Gershwin's rousing *Rhapsody in Blue* playing in your mind.

Other cities may have more landmarks, but New York is blasé about that. It is too self-absorbed to notice what matters elsewhere. As Saul Steinberg commemorated in the famous cover of *The New Yorker* in 1976, the view from the 9th Avenue is clear: the dense city gets sparse beyond the Hudson River, turning less detailed beyond Jersey, with China, Russia, and Japan looking like distant salt pans.

New York's infectious energy makes you a New Yorker within days of your arrival, and you begin believing the mythology of Steinberg's cartoon, that New York alone matters, and that it can ignore the world, because it is a world on its own. The world is too large a subject—how about one's own life? In my case, when I walk through the streets of New York, I do feel as if I am walking through parts of my life. If I were to slice my life in neat five-year intervals, I'd find someone I'm related to, someone I've played with at school, someone I've studied with, someone I've worked with, someone I've loved, someone I've shared laughter and tears with, living in the city and its outer boroughs—at least Brooklyn and Queens. I see Nalini Malani's art again at Soho; I see Jehangir Sabavala's canvases near Flatiron Building; I rediscover Zubin Mehta at the Lincoln Center; I go with a cousin I haven't met in decades to listen to a Sri Lankan-American novelist read from her work. It is like my life is laid out on that map, and by meeting that friend, I'm able to step into different times of my past, reliving the pains and pleasures, and seeing my life in one long continuum. New York offers that intimacy—I've unexpectedly run into an uncle near Wall Street when I'm headed for dinner with Sumitra Shah, my mother's closest friend from her college days. I've had drinks with someone I reported from Indonesia with and stayed overnight at the home of my college room-mate, before leaving the next morning for a walk in the Central Park with a friend I started out working with in journalism. These individuals may not know another, but they form my universe, and where else, but in New York, can I find these diverse strands of my life come together?

There, in Queens, lived an aunt who carried me when I was an infant; in Brooklyn lives another aunt at whose house in Bombay I'd go for dinner when my mother would be travelling on work; over in Brooklyn is the one who inspired my first poems; at Madison Avenue is a creative director who edited the college magazine where I wrote; Wall Street is full of classmates I went to business school with; in the UN Building I find a colleague who admonished me like an older sister, making sure I didn't eat too much cake; in the fashion district is a young photographer whose father was my colleague in Singapore in my early Thirties; the office of *The Wall Street Journal* has colleagues with whom I reported out of Asia; on campuses in this city are lawyers with whom I organised human rights campaigns; and elsewhere, there are writers, journalists, bankers, academics, and poets with whom I've shared experiences at various points in life. It is like the city has shadowed me—or New York is such a global city that anyone in the world can reacquaint himself with remnants of his past in this city. And both my sons, for now, are living in New York, making it home.

Each of us brings one's own memories to New York. Each of us also brings dreams and aspirations. The early joggers are already pounding the street. The man selling bagels has set up his stall. The newsvendor is ready with his supply of newspapers, chilled bottles of water, and granola bars for sale. The Congolese man in dreadlocks has spread the carpet on which he has arranged the masks and beads and necklaces that he hopes to sell today. Women in business suits carry coffee from Starbucks and the smell of caffeine wafts from those stores. These are formidable women—you don't want to get in their way as they march to their next meeting. I remember emerging from a subway station some years ago, and saw a man hesitantly asking one such woman directions to the Empire State Building, and without looking at him, and continuing to walk, the woman said: 'Do I look like an information booth?'

Many people will arrive today in New York, hoping to fulfill their dreams. The mother who has arrived from Punjab will look for her son-in-law waiting to pick her up in the arrivals area of JFK Airport, hoping that the child his wife (and her daughter) is expecting is a boy, a good, Made-in-America boy.

The Chinese father will turn on the lights of his dry cleaning service, dreaming of his daughter graduating some day from Harvard Medical School. The excited young man from Indiana will have stepped out of the bus at the Greyhound terminal and will rush to midtown Manhattan, staring expectantly at the office of *The New Yorker,* the portfolio of his clippings in his duffel bag. The young woman in that aerobics class you can see on the second floor of the gym across the Central Park will aspire for hers to be the face on that advertising billboard. The trader will be racing up the escalator at Wall Street to buy the stocks about which he has received a hot tip, and watch the market follow, so that he can strike it rich and retire, leave the rat race, and return to the Mid-West. And at Grand Central station, trains will disgorge thousands of men and women, some stepping into the city for the first time, their resumes in their briefcases, consulting their maps, calculating the time it would take to reach that office for that interview, hoping for that job, to make it here, in this city, to get that ticket for life, to have a Manhattan address.

In his 1949 essay, *Here is New York,* E B White divided the city into three categories: the city of the one born here, the one who commutes (whom the island's natives now call the "B&T" crowd, for bridge-and-tunnel, the vestibules that connect the city with the rest of the continent), and of the person who came here in quest of something. And it is the energy of the third that keeps pulling the city along. That's why New York does not tire, and nor do you tire of the city, and New York rejuvenates itself constantly. An elevated railway line becomes a pedestrian garden. An underground sewage tunnel becomes a walkers' paradise. A door without signs is a new speakeasy. The meat-packing district becomes the home of art galleries. Grand Central station reclaims its glory, with the ceiling of its concourse filled with constellations and astronomical signs, as if making sure you know your place in the universe—at its centre, never alone, never lost. If you've forgotten the name of the person you are to meet and where and when, right there is the clock, where people wait anxiously, at the stroke of 12, hoping to keep the appointment they've made.

It is a languid summer day, and I am to meet a friend at Central Park. The holiday mood is everywhere: I see women off from work or on holiday in frilly dresses showing their bare shoulders, some in tank tops and tiny shorts fraying at the edges. They compete for attention with the row of flowers that divide Park Avenue. New Yorkers don't give either a second look; everyone is in a rush, so what if it is summer and half the offices are empty. But those who aren't from New York ogle: this is the feast for their eyes that their culture denies them. You can tell that that tourist, whose protruding zoom lens settles uncannily on scantily attired women in Central Park and the way he clicks, mentally undressing them, that he comes from a land where women are not to be seen "like that" in public.

I enter Central Park. The greenery does its magic, lowering the temperature instantly. I walk past the lake. The Dakota Building where Lennon was shot towers over us. To understand the park, you have to understand the subway map of New York. Lay it flat on the ground and look closely, and you will find that the island of Manhattan looks a bit like the Statue of Liberty herself, with her right hand pointing skyward, the toes curled at the bottom, as if she is pirouetting on the Hudson. The subway lines roam through her body like veins, the energy of the people rushing through those veins become her lifeblood, and the green lung at the centre, the Central Park.

I have met many business-minded friends who look aghast at this vast expanse of emptiness, ruing the lost opportunities that vacant space represents: in a city such as Hong Kong, it would have already been converted into a mass of identical high-rise apartments, standing shoulder-to-shoulder, with bustling malls and noisy restaurants. Once, someone did estimate the Park's commercial value: about half a trillion dollars. That's what sets the investors apart from the poets. There may be money in the Central Park. But there is poetry—a lot of it.

It is the constant mid-point of this town which is, at its core, unabashedly sentimental. It came about because Americans wanted to teach snooty Europeans a lesson. Europeans, from the Old World, thought Americans lacked class and character, and were obsessively money-minded; New Yorkers wanted to prove that they, too, possessed a sense of public spirit and could appreciate finer things, even if it meant earmarking a vast stretch of extremely valuable land, ostensibly for no commercial purpose. The city took over 843 acres of land, covering two-and-a-half miles from the 59th Street to 106th Street (later extended to 110th Street), and half a mile from Fifth Avenue to Eighth Avenue. In terms of area, that makes it bigger than two of the tiniest nations—Monaco and Vatican—and the park today draws more visitors a year than the Grand Canyon does.

I once lived for about a year in an old brownstone not far from the Park with my friend Patrick. We had just graduated from the business school at Dartmouth. Patrick had started work as an investment banker; I was exploring options, including writing. We lived where Columbus and Broadway intersect. I introduced Patrick to curries and biryani that I made; he introduced me to sushi by the corner, and the delicious taste of maple syrup from Vermont, where he had a farm and where we celebrated Thanksgiving (and where I cooked a curry, and Patrick claims his older relatives took days to recover from my spices. Trust me, he'd have made a good fiction writer).

It was a quiet neighbourhood, where the local theatre showed art house classics, retrospectives of Francois Truffaut and what were at that time new releases like Satyajit Ray's *Ghare Baire*. The Park was a short walk away, and once you entered that expanse, you felt invigorated. The trees muffled the perpetual whirl of the traffic on Central Park West; the quieter hum merely reminded you of the tremendous amount of energy of the city surrounding you.

I have gone to the Park in all its seasons, but it seemed at its most spectacular in winter. Tall skyscrapers along its edges cast a benign shadow on the park. The trees were bereft of leaves, dark and skeletal, their limbs covered by layers of fresh snow. Wind would jostle the trees often, and the snow would get disturbed, sprinkling you with flurries, occasionally chunks falling on you gently, disintegrating on your hat. At times, a huge load of snow might fall, hitting the ground with a giant thud. The sky would always be brilliant and blue, the weather crisp and clean, and the lake made of ice upon which people skated. Where did the ducks go during winter? Holden Caulfield wanted to know that in *The Catcher in the Rye*; nobody answered that question, because they were all grownups and they thought Holden was acting silly.

In spring, the snow would melt and the first leaves would sprout, hinting at the promise of love. You saw it in people's clothing, which changed from blue and grey and black to pink and red and violet and maroon. But the air was still chilly, and it wasn't yet time to put away those jackets. I remember the Park one afternoon in early spring in 2005, when sunlight shimmered on its frozen pond, as if it was aflame, and an orange glow was cast on the path, as if autumn had descended prematurely in New York. The Dadaist artists Jean-Claude and Christo had installed their public work—fluttering saffron gates which circled the contours of the park with twenty-three miles of tall, sturdy gates. Its impact was so powerful that I saw many strollers wearing something orange, as if they wanted the colours to rub off on their skins, as if the colour were a lucky charm. The wind lifted the cloth, and the gates billowed, assuming graceful, identical shapes, as if responding to some intricate choreography.

Saffron and orange are our colours—from Asia—and here, New York was appropriating them. Children in the West may think of Halloween when they see orange; the Dutch royal house may think it owns the colour, and a budget airline may have thought it now owned it. But for us from India and elsewhere in Asia, orange colours our food, our robes, our temples, and our moods. It is one of the predominant colours we grow up with. It surrounds our lives, punctuating birth, marriage, even death. The colour is omnipresent in our spices—saffron, of course, but also the mixture of turmeric with red chillies, creating an orange illusion. The Chinese give even-numbered oranges to young ones at the time of the Lunar New Year, together with *hong bao*, the envelope with gifts, the phonetic sound of the word for the fruit orange, meaning wealth.

The Gates opened one February morning in 2005, the same weekend that Hindus celebrated Vasant Panchami, or the fifth day of spring, the season the classic Sanskrit poet Kalidasa called *rituraja*, the king of seasons. And the flower that personified spring's arrival is called *kesudo*, which produces the orange dye that is among the many with which people smear one another to celebrate Holi forty days later, marking the official rite of spring in much of northern and western India. From my earliest days of childhood in Bombay I recall picking up *kesudo* fallen on the ground from trees, and rubbing it on my palm, turning it orange.

The Gates could have been Rajput warriors then, riding on horses to take on the enemy, donning *kesariya* (orange-coloured clothes), engaged in do-or-die battles to save the kingdom's honour. The spectacular sight of hundreds of fluttering gates could have only come out of Akira Kurosawa. *The Gates* also took me to Hong Kong, where even today, a Chinese *sampan* occasionally emerges in the busy harbour, its orange sails translucent, surrounded by skyscrapers, a lost villager in a metropolis he cannot fathom. And as I climbed atop a giant rock and saw a meandering orange trail emerge, I could only think of a line of Buddhist monks going to their *vihara* through a forest in the Mekong Delta.

The Gates inspired several people that afternoon to blend in with the landscape. I saw one man wearing orange sneakers, another wearing an orange jacket, and no, he wasn't an emergency worker. A woman with a blissful look in her eyes, holding hands with a man, had covered her neck with a sequined, silken orange *chunni*, the Indian scarf, the *chunni* reflecting sunlight as she walked. And a little girl racing down the path was wearing orange mittens.

This brief spark of autumnal grace in the otherwise bleak, winter-struck park brought Asia's warmth to New York.

The Park turned its most colourful in autumn, when the green leaves started turning first into glorious yellow, later golden, then russet and brown, before succumbing to the icy winds of winter. I recall taking a long walk through the Park one autumn afternoon, finding two disciples of the Hare Krishna sect bothering an old man. It was only when I got closer that I saw the camera, and noticed that the old man was Woody Allen, filming a scene in what became *Hannah and Her Sisters*, perhaps his wittiest film. Allen knew how to capture the Park lovingly. In film after film, his characters would take a walk through the Park, come there to repair themselves and to reflect, like many New Yorkers do. In all, the Park features in fourteen of his films.

One July evening I walked through the Park with my friend Bharati, with the sun still bright and panting joggers' hoofs providing a quiet rhythm. Even though the temperature outside was in the 80s, and the atmosphere heavy and muggy, once we entered the Park, a gentle breeze comforted us, and the Park lifted us from the quotidian to the sublime. The willows drooped on the lake, and the water gleamed, reflecting the skyline. Horse carriages passed us by.

On our way out, we paused by the carousel and ate ice cream. I had read about the carousel in *The Catcher in the Rye* before I had seen it. It was originally built in 1871, when a ride cost ten cents (later reduced to five). It was burnt down in 1950, and now a more robust carousel has replaced the old one. The early carousel was literally powered by a mule and a blind horse, which walked in a circle beneath the ride. Later, the carousel was powered by steam and now, by electricity. It now has fifty-eight hand-carved, brightly painted horses and two chariots on a turntable that measures fifty feet in diameter. A new mechanical organ with eighty-six keys, two drums, a tambourine and cymbals play the music.

The carousel has an important place in my journeys seeking out places that inspired great literature. It features in *The Catcher in the Rye,* the coming-of-age, must-read novel of my generation. Shashi Aunty, as I call my mother's friend, Sumitra Shah, had given me J D Salinger's later books—*Nine Stories* and *Franny and Zoey*—when I was thirteen. Those books led me to look for *The Catcher in the Rye,* which I bought from a pavement stall in Bombay a year later for the princely sum of ten rupees. On my first visit to New York, when I was twenty-one, I wanted to see that carousel. I have seen it often since then, from the corner of my eye on subsequent visits, reassuring me that the city might keep changing, some things won't.

That evening, we saw the carousel, with happy children sitting on those ponies, chasing some elusive dream, going round and round, cheerful and merry, along the brass ring. Everyone had a dream to chase in New York. I looked at the grownups, standing along the railing, some waving at their children, some taking photographs, a few on their cell phones, talking agitatedly, pacing away from the carousel and its music. The carousel is full of kitsch, but in the critical scene at the end of *The Catcher in the Rye,* Holden Caulfield discovers his own private pleasure, when he sees his sister, Phoebe, happy. It reminds him of his own joyful times; he remembers his own dream, of being a catcher in the rye:

> Anyway, I keep picturing all these little kids playing some game in this big field of rye and all. Thousands of little kids, and nobody's around—nobody big, I mean—except me. And I'm standing on the edge of some crazy cliff. What I have to do, I have to catch everybody if they start to go over the cliff—I mean if they're running and they don't look where they're going I have to come out from somewhere and catch them. That's all I'd do all day. I'd just be the catcher in the rye and all. I know it's crazy, but that's the only thing I'd really like to be. I know it's crazy.

Holden Caulfield is the Peter Pan, the guardian, trying to keep them safe in a more innocent time. And he decides that that role is not for him; that children must learn to fall so that they can get up again and walk again; that you cannot avoid growing up.

I have fallen, as does everyone, from that innocent carousel, our encapsulated childhood. In life there are many falls. I have lifted myself, with more than a little help from my friends. But some day I want to go back even if in winter and find out where the ducks go when the lagoon freezes in Central Park.

LOSS

&

REMEMBRANCE

FOUR SEASONS IN VERMONT

I have seen that lonely tree in all four seasons over many years now. During summer, its crisp leaves flutter like little green flags. Sunlight rests briefly on its leaves, the leaves deflect the light downwards, and the light, unusually bright and blinding, hits my eyes as I sit on the rocking chair, taking in the view of the rolling farmland below. Diagonally across, almost at the edge where the woods begin, is a shimmering pond. Hillary, a friend of the family I'm staying with, emerges from the water and waves at us, asking us to join, as she dries herself. But it is a lazy afternoon, and I prefer sitting on the porch, the thick pile of the Sunday edition of *The New York Times* luring me, even as my hosts tease me, saying I should take a dip. But the papers win; Hillary smiles as she walks in our direction, waving her hair such that drops of water fall on us, and she laughs.

In autumn, the foliage turns spectacular, like a painter's wild palette, the colours dazzling your eyes with beauty. Those colours seem to change almost every hour, and where the woods begin, you can see the trees come alive in their gorgeous splendour, as if the forest is aflame. In its autumnal glow, the landscape shines: trees on the other side of the pond sit on their reflection, revealing a symmetry that you never want to see disturbed. Then, one November afternoon, wind sweeps by, scattering the leaves. Soon, those branches will be barren. In that twilight between the fall of the leaves and the onset of snow, the trees will look old and skeletal. They will call it the stick season.

It is winter now. The landscape turns stark, sharp, white, clean as laundered sheets, as an improbable amount of snow rests on the branches. The tree's bark is dark; it is the only outline you can identify in a sea of whiteness. Wind comes unannounced, unsettles the branches, sending the snow flurrying across. When a large amount of snow falls on the bench below, it sounds like a cloudburst. The sky struggles to stay bright and blue. In a few hours, it gets dark, bringing with it the penetrating chill of the brief December day. You can see the moon in the afternoon—and its blue glow rests on the white land beneath, and the lights of the truck shining on the snow-covered road, and in the beams of those lights, you see snowflakes continuing to fall lightly. And the stars, so many of them! Robert Frost, who lived in these parts, wrote about fireflies in the garden attempting to mirror the stars:

How countlessly they congregate

O'er our tumultuous snow,

Which flows in shapes as tall as trees

When wintry winds do blow!—

The stars, the snow, and the tracks of light of the truck move slowly along the hill. I could picture the driver listening to National Public Radio, for Vermont is that kind of place. Burlington, which has twice in recent decades elected a socialist mayor, is not far from here. There is a communal spirit, and yet everyone is an individual—the place understands where the individual wants to slip away from the society, and respects his choice to do so, as he relishes the joys and pleasures of solitude.

Frost is the laureate of this region. He derived inspiration from the snow and the cottages, the foliage and the rivers, the wind and the stars. He'd get cheered by the birch trees "loaded with ice a sunny winter's morning." There is a tactile quality to some of the poems—the swimming buck pushes the "crumpled" water, the wagon's wheels "slice" the fresh April mire, and he could make you feel what caressing a sharp axe felt like. He also wrote about picking apples and the roads to be taken, or not. The individual was at the centre, but the neighbour never very far. 'We keep the wall between us as we go,' he wrote about his neighbour beyond the hill, not to keep him away, but because his field was full of pine trees, and Frost's own, an apple orchard, and Frost did not want his apple trees 'to get across and eat the cones under his pines.' His neighbour replies, 'Good fences make good neighbors.' The individual in a vast landscape, with a neighbour who could be a friend a short distance away, but never intruding, never eavesdropping, appreciating space and privacy. That's quintessential Vermont, and quintessential Frost.

Frost wasn't from Vermont; he made Vermont his home. He was born in California and moved to Massachusetts after his father died. He read poetry early when he grew up in Lawrence, and in 1892, went to Dartmouth College in New Hampshire. He opted out, taking up a range of jobs including working in a mill. But he started writing poetry published in New York. He also spent time at Harvard, but could not continue because of ill health. He then became a poultry farmer in New Hampshire, even moving to England, before returning to America to teach at Amherst College in Massachusetts. He finally made his home in Vermont and set up the Bread Loaf School of English at Middlebury College, inspiring young writers. Vermont became his inspiration.

Frost's poetry wasn't all heart and no head. He told young poets that they must include the mind and their emotions in their writing. 'Too many poets delude themselves by thinking the mind is dangerous and must be left out. Well, the mind is dangerous and must be left in.' His fame grew; he went on to be invited to read a poem at the Inauguration of John F Kennedy (he read the poem, *The Gift Outright*) in 1961. He died two years later. His gravestone reads: "I had a lover's quarrel with the world."

In *Dust of Snow* he writes about a day that hasn't gone well for the poet. He is walking along a path, when a crow shakes down snow on him from a hemlock tree. The dust of snow sprinkles on him, instantly changing his mood, the combination of solidity, wetness, and cold tingling his skin cheers him, saving "some part of a day I had rued". What could have been mild annoyance becomes a moment of pure pleasure.

Meanwhile the hemlock tree stands alone, its bare branches layered with snow. And when you feel those dark nights won't end, and you fear that winter has gobbled up the sun forever, the first buds sprout, the leaves wake up, as if shaking off slumber, and they emerge from the same branches, like little palms outstretched, reassuring us of sunlight, of life, its loves, and of birth. That hard snow will melt.

Frost captured the nuance of this place, and with the gift of his elemental verse, he revealed its unending cycle and its rhythm, built on the idea that nature is by your side, your silent ally. Respect its power, harness it where you can, flow with it where you can't. Some things that happen are too big and complicated to make sense of immediately. But when everything seems to be getting scattered, that unbending tree, the land, and the stars remind you of certainties, if only you know where to look, and when:

But nothing ever happens, no harm is done.

We may as well go patiently on with our life,

And look elsewhere than to stars and moon and sun

For the shocks and changes we need to keep us sane.

It is true the longest drought will end in rain,...

Still it wouldn't reward the watcher to stay awake

In hopes of seeing the calm of heaven break

On his particular time and personal sight.

That calm seems certain safe to last tonight.

I have lived this cycle and been part of its rhythm at this particular farm in Vermont over the past quarter century. The farm belongs to my friend Patrick's family and over these years, that warm family has made me part of their lives. That farm resonates with many memories: fishing in the lake one morning and returning home without catching anything; swimming in that pond one balmy afternoon with no Sunday papers to distract me, but the water is so cold, the dip into the water becomes almost a religious experience—something to be endured because some day it might get rewarded; walking through a canopy of bright yellow leaves shading us from the sun, and when we try to look at the sky, we see the translucent leaves all bright, and if you are close enough, you can see the lines on the leaves, glowing like streaks of lightning. On another day, we ride on that old tractor to the town, visiting the market. We buy maple syrup from the farmer next door. We take the family dogs for a long walk one afternoon. And one Thanksgiving, I cook probably the first-ever curry at a farm in that part of New England, as the fireplace crackles.

The bonds I have formed there are deep; the feeling of being with loved ones real. That home reassures.

Henry David Thoreau too went to one such location about 150 miles southeast of here—at a pond in Walden. Explaining his decision to go to the pond, he said: 'I went to the woods because I wished to live deliberately, to front only the essential facts of life, and see if I could not learn what it had to teach, and not, when I came to die, discover that I had not lived.' He gathered his thoughts, publishing a book in 1854, and among the many he inspired was a young Indian in South Africa called Mohandas Gandhi.

The hills and brooks and trees here didn't offer the key to solve all problems; the quietude offered space to reflect. Patrick's farm grants the space to explore the self within. I had needed that. I needed to understand pain and let the agony filled within me leave me gently, so that I'd emerge with wounds and scars but with less pain, what analysts call "processing" pain and agony. But I also needed to recollect moments of happiness, to clear the clouds in the mind, to give shape to ideas that simply cannot emerge out of the tedium of the quotidian. For it was in woods like these, somewhere along the path of a tree quite like the one I saw near the farm, beyond a cottage by a stream, that Frost had chanced upon two roads that diverged. And he took the one less travelled by, and that made all the difference.

It was Frost's decision to do so—nobody told him. Had he walked on the straight and narrow path, nobody would have objected. He was responsible for his choice, and prepared to face the consequences. He wanted that freedom, and this landscape offered him that freedom.

For two decades, Patrick had a neighbour who was famous and reclusive, who did not like visitors. When we drove by the tall trees that formed the border of his property, Patrick would tell me—there, that's someone you'd like to meet, but who wouldn't see you. Alexander Solzhenitsyn lived there during his exile from the Soviet Union, before returning to post-Soviet Russia. He craved privacy, and the town offered him that privacy. That is the essence of New England. Kate, a dear friend I have known for a long time and who has a house by a lake further to the north, told me once: here, your neighbours leave you alone because they respect you, but they will help if you ask; and the unwritten code was that you didn't ask for help—you cast your lone furrow and waved at the neighbours in good cheer. They were always there, with their maple syrup and apples, their hand-crafted furniture and farm produce.

They understood Solzhenitsyn's need to stay apart and aloof—he did not interfere with the lives of the town, nor did he participate in its lively local democracy. Town hall meetings in small New England towns are the heartbeats of American democracy. Norman Rockwell captures it well in an inspiring painting of a man rising to speak at a meeting. Rockwell called it his homage to the right to speak. Solzhenitsyn was denied that freedom in the Soviet Union. In America, he could use it. He chose not to; the town knew its famous resident, but let him be.

Walk along those snowy woods and it was easy to see why Solzhenitsyn lived there—and not in larger American cities where other émigré writers made their home, like Boston with its universities, New York with its adrenaline rush, San Francisco and its laid-back beat culture, or Washington and its air of self-importance. Northern New England is cold and harsh, and its landscape is laden with snow for nearly six months of the year. In winter the sun sets early, and the weather is bone-chillingly cold. Living there, while not exactly a struggle with nature, requires you to respect forces larger than yourself. The birch bends here, Frost reminds us in another poem, not when the boys swing from the trees, but when it faces the force of the ice storm—a force bigger than itself.

Neighbours respect rugged individuals because they are rugged individuals, too. Nobody watches over you, nobody pries into your affairs. There is a community, but it does not force conformity. Good fences make good neighbours, as Frost's neighbour had told him.

Solzhenitsyn must have liked that. For over a decade, his life was not his anymore. He had once criticised Stalin as "the old bastard in Moscow with a moustache" and was later sent to jail. He had written about the Soviet system sucking individuality out of people by using the metaphor of a sewage disposal system, through which the unwanted were no longer counted; they were shunned, and shunted in *The Gulag Archipelago*. The Gulag was harsh. The Soviets sent millions through that disposal system. The "good one day" in the life of Ivan Denisovich was when there was no punishment, and nothing bad happened to anyone.

To revive his spirit, to discover himself, and to assert his identity, Solzhenitsyn needed a place where he could be himself, live by his rules. And he found that in this remote part of America. He did not embrace his neighbours. But the view from his window was no longer bleak. The sun rose. The sky was blue. The leaves changed colours. The birds sang. He could smell the fresh wood being chopped and hear the horse shake the harness bell. And he could take a dip in that icy lake if he so wished.

That stretch of the road, connecting Ludlow, Proctorsville, and Cavendish in Vermont, became my personal lifeline. The white churches, their bells, the clear lakes, the green meadows, the red paint on the barns, the creaking noise of the barn door left ajar, the heady smell of cinnamon-flavoured apple cider, and the hushed sound of the squall rushing through the leaves, was a sensory choir that often played in my mind. I wanted to feel that again, to come to grips with myself. And that lifeline was there when I needed it. It also breathed love—for life, people, and humanity.

This was in 2007, during the summer, after a life-altering tragedy. My wife Karuna had died a few months earlier. With my sons, I wanted to make sense of what had happened; I needed a place to come to terms with our loss. And Patrick opened his farm to me again. We went there, picking up pieces, in the hope of tying the knots again and create a sense of continuity which had shattered so abruptly. We had the warm company of Patrick and Kristen and their sons (their daughter would come later). We went to cottages on Lake Rescue, splashing water and getting soaked. Nearly a quarter century earlier, Patrick, his twin brother Tim, and I had rowed in a boat. Now, our children played there, while we cooked.

We needed that space—where we could be ourselves, learning again how to take tentative steps. Pat and Kristen—and Tim and Liz—were never far. We could be alone, and we were never lonely.

Patrick took us to the porch again, and showed us the vistas. He loved Frost. He knew I liked his poetry, but he loved it, lived it. In 1986 when I left America after college, uncertain if I would return to the West, he gifted me the 1949 edition of Frost's collected poems, placing tiny tick marks next to the poems that meant a lot to him and which he wanted me to read first. It was a pure gift, a gift outright. He passed his love of Frost to me. I could picture him saying:

I'm going out to clean the pasture spring;

I'll only stop to rake the leaves away

(And wait to watch the water clear, I may):

I shan't be gone long—You come too.

I'm going out to fetch the little calf

That's standing by the mother.

It's so young,

It totters when she licks it with her tongue.

I shan't be gone long—You come too.

He extended his hand, and I clasped it. He took me to the barn, he drove me around on his tractor, he gave me the keys to his car and to the door of the home, and he ate what I cooked and lit the fire that kept us warm. This outwardly anonymous patch of New England became important for our healing.

After you are healed, you walk. And so we did. And Pat and Kristen smiled and cheered us. Frost's memorable lines, found on the desk of Jawaharlal Nehru when he died, came to my mind:

The woods are lovely, dark and deep

But I have promises to keep

And miles to go before I sleep

And miles to go before I sleep.

John Lennon and Paul McCartney had put it differently: the long and winding road never disappears. The colours of the sky change; the leaves fall; snow casts a blanket over the farm. But the tree stands firm, helping you navigate, and find your road. And we see that road—it meanders, but it always leads to your door, wherever you are.

THE BLUE
PERIOD

How do you describe the Mediterranean? Blue—that's the easy word. More ornate words don't quite capture it. Sapphire seems too shiny, like the glittering jewel a starlet might wear at Cannes, to capture the attention of the paparazzi during the dull moments of the film festival. Azure sounds pretentious, as though it has been pulled out of the bottom of a well-worn copy of the Thesaurus, used for effect, as if to hide the commonplace language surrounding it in a bad poem. Ultramarine has the metallic feel of cobalt, suggesting a solidity and hardness, which the liquid sea lacks. Cerulean sounds like you are describing an age in history. And turquoise is a word best left for brochures of travel agencies selling honeymoon packages.

Blue would do; it is simple and effective. The final open vowel gives the word a sense of infinity and continuity, like the sea stretching into the horizon, like the waves washing the shore, the water clear, and the light always shining. I like the way Mediterranean sounds too. There is a musical ring to that word. Think of Amal telling Charulata in Rabindranath Tagore's short story, *Nashtaneer* (The Broken Nest): 'Mediterranean, *jeno tanpurar jhonkar'* (Mediterranean, like running your fingers over the strings of a tanpura). Mediterranean's water has that certain luminosity, which envelopes that sea. The blue has richness and depth of Alpine lakes. Everything looks sharper and starker, and however good your camera might be, and however many pixels it can capture, the image on your screen looks artificial, lacking the vibrancy, the brilliance, and the buoyancy of the sea.

I had come to the Mediterranean the first time in 1994: I was in Nice to write about a banking conference. The town was an odd location to host the annual meeting of Asia's biggest banks. France was a member of the Asian Development Bank, and at least on paper, its decision to host the meeting didn't seem out of place to anyone except the bankers from small islands in the Pacific, who noted, correctly, that the amount of money spent on the conference could have been used instead to wipe out the debt of those islands. But the bankers meeting in Nice had other priorities—by night, they went to the casino in Monte Carlo; by day, they slept through the proceedings. A photograph I cherish from that time is of a row of Japanese bankers, in deep sleep, sitting in the front row, as another banker gave another forgettable speech. The smarter ones left the convention centre altogether, walking by the waterfront, training their binoculars on the hundreds of women who lay on the beach, most of them topless, their backs shining in the sun, but some obliging them by lying flat, looking at the sky.

Karuna had come with me on this trip. One evening, we went to the home of a wealthy Indian tycoon who lived overseas—we sat in his garden, up on the hill, from where we could see the town below, the beach, and the water, as enchanting French women in white shirts and short black skirts served us puris, peas pulao, papads, kadhi, and dal, a vegetarian feast in that most unexpected setting. He had invited me by mistake. He was extending his invitation cards to members of an Indian banking delegation. I was standing there, waiting to interview a banker. He thought I was a banker too and invited me. I told him who I was—not a banker, and only a journalist. He had the grace to say it would be an honour if I came.

The next day, while I interviewed the bankers, Karuna went off to see the home where Henri Matisse had lived. Later that evening, she got excited as she described how Matisse moved from painting to craft. As he grew older, Matisse had come to realise he was losing control of his fingers and movements, and so he switched from painting to cutting abstract patterns from colourful sheets of paper, creating shapes that initially defied meaning, until he started placing them in a pattern, sticking them, so that while they still looked abstract, they revealed elegant human forms.

The colour he had chosen was blue.

Later that week, after the bankers had gone home, we went to Antibes, a town further down the coast, where we went to the home where Pablo Picasso lived. This was the quieter part of the Riviera, away from the glamour of Cannes and the glitter of St Tropez, where the rich would bring their yachts during summer, and parties would go on till dawn. Writers and painters lived in Antibes, seeking inspiration from the changing colours of the sky. The mild breeze made the heat bearable, and the colours from Picasso's windows were vivid—there was clarity in that light.

We explored much of the Picasso country in the week that followed. The time Picasso spent in Antibes was a joyous one—there was a new love in his life—Françoise Gilot, who was nearly forty years younger than him—and the Second World War had just ended. Picasso and Gilot lived in a villa during the summer of 1946, and the Chateâu Grimaldi was a local museum nearby, to which Picasso was to give many of his paintings. The museum's curator offered Picasso a room with large walls, which became his studio, and Picasso entered a flamboyant, creative phase, splashing colours on everything he saw around him. I recall the cheerful painting, *La Joie de*

Vivre, which shows a curvaceous nude dancing happily, prancing goats surrounding her.

Karuna loved that painting, and many more, and she'd get close to the paintings, her hand moving gracefully, following the curves of the artist's brushstrokes, as if she was trying to learn how Picasso moved his hands.

Further along was the promenade where you could walk along a winding strip facing the sea. We wanted to come again.

It took me many years before I was back in these parts. In August 2009, I returned to the Mediterranean with my sons. I was continuing an unfinished journey, showing my sons the region I had once seen with Karuna, who was now no longer with us. I wanted to see one more time the art that had once made her happy. And I wanted my sons to see that art, and that landscape, and walk by that sea. She had liked Matisse and Picasso. We would go to the places that inspired Matisse and Picasso.

This time, we stayed with friends in a town called Collioure, where just over a century ago, Andre Derain, Raoul Dufy, and Matisse had experimented with wild colours and launched the short-lived movement called Fauvism. The street we lived on was named after Dufy, and along the town's waterfront, flanked by bars and restaurants, you could see reproductions of Fauvist paintings on the wall. It was less than a movement, but more than a fad, chronologically sandwiched between Impressionism and Cubism. If firm brushstrokes and the changing quality of light capturing the mood of the moment characterised Impressionism, broken and reassembled objects seen from multiple viewpoints was the hallmark of Cubism. From geography to geometry—and in between, a riot of colours.

Fauve means wild beasts, and the critics who gave it that name did so because they were struck by the way the colours leapt at the viewers. As we walked along the Collioure waterfront and saw those images on the walls, yellow, orange, and shining white jumped at us.

There were terraced fields around us, neat and symmetrical—but they grew grapes, not rice. Nearly half of France's table wine came from here. Some beaches had stones, others had sand. We saw children building castles, tossing stones in the water. As the sun gently descended, we saw lovers lost in long kisses. The sky blushed pink. The wind caressed us, and you saw the lights coming alive in people's homes, almost reluctantly, surrendering in recognition of the fading twilight. We walked to the edge of the land, the colours of the buildings pale, light blue and pink and cream and yellow and orange. Right at the end stood a stark, dark crucifix.

It was late, but the sky retained its blue hue. Matisse had said once, 'No sky in all of France is more blue than that of Collioure.' Was it the sky reflecting the water? Or was it the water mirroring the sky? How was I to know?

Looking at the sharp colours, I tried to imagine what prompted Matisse to use colours so vividly. Months later, I came across the excellent detective work of Damian Elwes, a British painter whose many works include specialised tributes to great artists, where he imagines the physical space the artist inhabits and recreates the setting in which the artist operated to create a new painting, where you see the artist's habitat, his inspirations, and clues to his work.

Elwes wanted to find the studio where Matisse worked in 1905, to see the place where Fauvism was born. He had one clue—in 1905, Matisse had taken a photograph of the port of Collioure from the window of his studio. He had also painted a canvas, called *Open Window: Collioure* that year. But that image did not match what the photograph showed. Matisse had replaced the tree and the port by ivy and a row of boats. 'Perhaps Matisse was inventing imagery just as he was surely exaggerating the colour,' Elwes wrote.

Elwes walked around the waterfront, but none of the locals had any idea about the location of Matisse's 1905 studio. They only seemed to know about the house in the port that he had rented in later years. Identifying the studio from where Matisse painted the Collioure waterfront wasn't easy—for the waterfront has many homes, all looking identical, all facing the water and the lighthouse. The cross was visible from some windows and the mountains on the other side from other windows.

Armed with his photograph and research, Elwes narrowed the possibilities and then consulted the old men playing boules on the beach. 'Together we decided from which building Matisse's photographs had been taken,' he said. Elwes further said:

> There was a tiny real estate office on the ground floor. I asked them if they owned the floor above. They did. We climbed the stairs and entered a dark office. Sadly it had recently been redecorated. The walls were bright yellow and the floor was now covered in shiny tiles. However, as we opened the heavy, shuttered doors, and examined the unusual window above them, I realized that this was the very studio where Matisse had invented Fauvism. The little tree had grown and there was now a large restaurant where there had been a few tables and chairs. The balcony had been replaced but there were screw holes in the wall exactly where the original balcony would have been. There were two identical windows. This finally explained the difference between Matisse's painting and his photograph.

Elwes showed Matisse's photographs to the real estate agent and she agreed that they were taken in her office. While Elwes sketched, he suggested that she restore the walls and floor and put an easel in the corner for the tourists who would love to see this. Speaking to *The Independent* newspaper, Elwes explained:

> I try to capture a moment of inspiration, to explore where creativity comes from, to make things dream-like. I feel as though I am painting someone's mind and soul as much as their physical surroundings. The way an artist places his things tells you as much about him as his painting does—these people were so visual that even the negative space—between objects—has been thought about, so what I'm doing is painting thousands of still lives laid out for me by the most creative minds of the last century. As a painter, it's joyful to discover frame after frame; it just amazes me that no one else has done it.

Later that week, we drove to Barcelona, across the border in Spain. Our destination was another Picasso Museum—an imposing structure with Picasso's works painted in or about Barcelona. As we walked through the dark rooms, we saw his pre-Cubist art—the Blue Period. Here, the colour was real, but it was also the metaphor for the state of his mind. Picasso's mood was somber in those years. He had lost a friend recently, who had taken his life. What he painted was blue or bluish-green; his subjects were beggars and prostitutes. The joy we saw in Antibes was decades away. The overwhelming colour was blue—but a stern blue, often lifeless and bleak, as if drawing life from the energy of his subjects. The sort of sad blue Krzysztof Kieślowski lets his film get tinged with, in *Trois Coleurs: Bleu*.

Picasso's human forms were recognisable at first glance in those days. Cubism was still years away; you did not have to peel through layers of the cubist iconography and view the canvas from different angles to see what he had seen, and wanted us to see.

We reached the last room, where the museum had kept its new acquisitions. These were paintings that had nothing to do with Barcelona. As I entered the room, along the long wall I could see about half a dozen canvases, looking somewhat identical. It was getting dark outside, but the room suddenly beamed with good cheer. These were paintings from the Mediterranean.

As we saw these landscapes, we were suddenly taken to his homes on the Riviera, and we saw what he saw from his windows in Cannes. One painting stood out: you could see the white and grey pigeons on the side, and you could almost hear their fluttering wings. The luscious green leaves of the trees seemed palpable, as you felt the tactile energy with which Picasso's brushstrokes had painted those trees. The earthy brown of the wood was rich. And beyond, there was the yellow sand and the deep blue sea, with frothy waves—and the sparkle of the Mediterranean.

My sons recognised that painting immediately. It is the one that Karuna had chosen for our home in 1994, when we were looking through the posters in Antibes to take a bit of that sunshine with us to Singapore, where we lived then. It was called *Cannes A.M.*, with his signature in blue. We had bought it instantly, and in the years that followed, it continued to bring some of Nice's sunshine to our home, calming us during the days of blinding light during the hot months in Singapore, and later, even during London's bleakest autumns and dark winters.

I saw my sons staring at that canvas; it made me feel as though she had been walking with us on this trip, even while we walked through the museum, as if she had never left us.

ACROSS THE HILLS AND TOWARDS THE LAKE

I had roamed in these hills a quarter century ago. I was young then; I had just finished college in America. I didn't yet know what lay ahead for me, and I had made no plans about what to do next. My generous college had given me a fellowship that had brought me to this sparkling city, Geneva, surrounded by mountains and facing a lake.

I walked almost daily by the lakeside—it is difficult not to, if you are in Geneva. I'd marvel at the spurt of Jet d'Eau, the fountain of water that sprang from the lake. People would run along the stone path by its side, getting splashed by the water. You could see the colours of the rainbow emerge, and the sails of hundreds of boats flutter. The boats with sails taken off the masts would clatter, like noisy kids tapping their desks in a classroom without adult supervision. One evening I had even seen Dilip Kumar walking by the lake, smiling obligingly as eager Indian tourists photographed him, the landscape behind him a tidier and tinier version of the hills and dales in which he once walked, singing *Suhana safar aur yeh mausam haseen* in Bimal Roy's film, *Madhumati*.

At night, the city glittered, vivid colours cast on the fountain, making it look like a swaying, technicolour sailboat; the lights of the buildings along the lake were bright, reflecting in the water, and it looked like diamonds were scattered on the lake's surface.

Milan Kundera described this lakefront in *The Unbearable Lightness of Being* as 'a city of fountains large and small, of parks where music once rang out from the bandstands. Even the university is hidden among trees.' Its peculiar punctuality, asymmetry and uniformity prompt some, like Kundera's character Franz, to think of Geneva as a "metropolis of boredom". But during the summer I spent there, the city looked gorgeous. I had few responsibilities and fewer worries those days, and during weekends, I'd use the lake as my compass, exploring the land by its side. There was Nyon, where an ancient ruin of Greek columns emerged on a hill, looking like the remains of stumps in a cricket match after a fast bowler had knocked one down. Further along was Lausanne, the home of the International Olympic Committee. At the museum there, I saw Jesse Owens's shoes and Dhyan Chand's hockey stick. Beyond was Vevey, where I stood by Charlie Chaplin's statue—he made Vevey his home in the autumn of his life, and I remember walking up the hills of Vevey, looking down a farm, where not a soul was in sight except a black cat, and that cat stared at me, intently, as I looked at the shed from which she emerged. And then I reached Montreux.

I had heard that Vladimir Nabokov had breathed his last in this town, and made the luxurious hotel, Montreux Palace, his home. Once I read more about it, I realised that he had spent nearly two decades in that hotel, in Le Cygne wing, and he had died there. His wife Vera continued to live there after his passing. He liked the hills beyond Montreux, where he could go looking for butterflies, his lifelong passion. He would take the train to Rochers de Naye or Dent de Jaman, and lose himself in the hills.

The blue of the lake below reminded him of the Mediterranean Sea. It was the warmest town in the Swiss Riviera, with the mountains protecting the town from the cold winds. The spectacular lake, seen from the balconies of the hotel, has a comforting effect. While writing *Nabokov: the American Years*, Brian Boyd unearthed an index card of a manuscript, which showed how Montreux's light seeped into the novel, *Pale Fire*:

> How much happier the wide awake indolents, the monarchs among men, the rich monstrous brains that can derive intense enjoyment and exquisite heartbreak from the balustrade of a terrace at nightfall, from the lights and the lake below, from the distance mountain shape melting into the dark apricot of the afterglow, from the black conifers outlined against the pale-ink of the zenith, and from the ruby and emerald flounces of the water along the silent, sad, forbidden shoreline. Oh my sweet Boscobel!

Montreux Palace looks like a wedding cake, with its ornate exterior and stately rooms. The hotel resurfaces in his novel, *Ada*, at the time of Van and Ada's ultimate reunion. It is an imposing hotel, and it has the feel of a place where European royalty arriving discreetly for illicit liaisons, Russian oligarchs concluding complex financial deals, Sheikhs from the Middle East meeting their bankers, chaste vegetarian Jain diamond merchants from Palanpur not trusting the croissants and going to their rooms to eat home-made *theplas* quietly, and James Bond keeping track of everyone, might feel at home. I wanted to visit the room where Nabokov had his evening drink, and see the window by which he sat, and I wanted to look at the lake the way he looked at it. I wanted to see what he saw.

But that wasn't easy. In Paris, cafés such as Le Dome, Lipp, La Closrie de Lilas, La Coupole and Les Deux Magots have plaques by the seats where Hemingway, Fitzgerald, Jean-Paul Sartre and Simone de Beauvoir would talk and solve the world's problems while smoking cigarettes and drinking pastis. There are no such plaques at Montreux Palace. But he was comfortable there, and he liked the life of luxury that he could afford. He treated the staff well.

I went to the reception and asked about Nabokov's rooms. The receptionist brought out a large register, looking for names. I thought he had misunderstood what I meant. My French was poor then as now, and so I switched to English, and explained that Nabokov had once stayed in the hotel, and could he tell me if he had a favourite place where he sat. He looked at me, looked at the register, looked again at me, and told me, while shutting the register with a thud that suggested finality: 'Mr Nabokov? Is not here. He has checked out.' The receptionist was young; he probably had no idea about Nabokov; he belonged to the generation that was inspired by the town's hero Freddie Mercury, whose statue graces the pier, his arm held high, and the refrain, "We will, we will, rock you!" reverberated in my mind. Finding Nabokov's window was a task I failed.

I made more journeys over the weekends, taking the ferry, visiting picture postcard villages with their manicured gardens, their clocks made of flowers without scent, and nude statues surging towards the water, frozen in mid-air as they were about to dive. And I'd get off and step into one of the cafés by the water, where waiters in black bow ties and gold-rimmed glasses would appear miraculously, bringing crisp croissants and coffee, whose steam would carry its fragrance across the street. Like Mr Wheeler in Hemingway's story, *Homage to Switzerland*, I was alone, but unlike him, not lonely, and I didn't flirt with the waitresses.

Then I'd walk along the lanes taking me to the trails that would ring the mountains, and I would follow the scent of the trees, pausing occasionally to look beneath. I didn't sing like Dilip Kumar in *Madhumati*, and I didn't always find that cat again.

What I saw was landscape as nature had intended. If there were gods, this is what they saw and how they saw the earth beneath, the green meadows, the snowcapped mountains and clear skies, and the deep blue lake. It seemed so perfect—palpable and momentary, making me feel it would always be like this—heavenly, cloudless, without tumult. Occasionally my friend Javed would join me, as would other friends he knew from Oxford who had come to visit him, and we'd go to places like Byron's rock and to bars and order Swiss white wine, because Hemingway claimed that's what James Joyce liked to drink. Sometimes my American friends would come, and we'd go on treks in those hills, our backpacks light, like the burdens on our young shoulders. In those days, we had our lives in front of us; our resolves, our plans lay ahead. We had seen the sun that warmed, the moon that mellowed, the stars that we thought would guide us, all the time. Life was going to be good; things would be all right. Bliss was it in that dawn, and we were young.

I often carried my Walkman, but instead of listening to the sounds by myself, I'd turn on the speaker, and with Vivaldi's *Four Seasons* or Ravi Shankar's *Megh Malhar* as my calling card, I'd make friends with kindred souls—from New Zealand, from Denmark—exchanging addresses at youth hostels at night, hoping that one day we might meet again. It hasn't happened yet, but I haven't given up hope.

The lake's calm waters dissolved differences, maybe even irreconcilable ones, or such was the hope of some of the organisations which operated out of villas by the lake. Many years later, I'd often visit one such villa, which brings together the most intractable and violent enemies, and gets them to talk, to stop the devastation that war brings. Peace talks, it seems, could happen only in Geneva. A cartoon in

The New Yorker once showed a grumpy couple, sitting in two separate sofas, at a slight angle to one another, looking away from one another. And one tells the other—"Lets go to Geneva for talks."

Almost two decades later, a little older, I came to these hills again; this time with my family. Neither Karuna, nor my sons had seen the Alps or the Jura yet, and I wanted them to discover the world I had seen once. This time, we did not travel by the ferry. We rented a car, and we'd drive along the lake, stopping to meet friends, reigniting old relationships, sharing memories, admiring how the infants we had known were now teenagers. We'd go to small towns, eating fondue at some places, looking for *chocolatieres* in other villages. There were few landmarks—how can you name the spot where you saw the cloud covering a peak, or where you first saw the swans fluttering their wings? But Mont Blanc was there—it obliged with its wistful smile in the evening, looking pink, as if blushing.

I wanted to spread my arms, seize those moments, and scatter them around my family, surrounding them with some of the happiest moments of that summer, part of the spring of my life. I wanted to share with them that innocent enthusiasm which youth brings; I wanted my sons to experience it before they became older. And I wanted that calm sun to shine on us, that cool breeze to give us the push in our onward journey.

But then darkness came, as it often does when least expected, shattering our lives.

While saying his goodbye to his mother at Karuna's funeral, my son Udayan, not yet seventeen, said:

> The distant rumble of heavy rolling and ominous black clouds came accompanied by terrible and violent bolts of lightning. The waves of clouds

flowing over the small schoolhouse moved quickly. Perhaps this would pass soon. The lingering calm was now irritating, no longer was the imminent downpour of concern, it was the waiting that was the worst. Predictably, but no less savagely, the rain clouds erupted, breaking open in the most fearsome and menacing manner. For five minutes, nothing but enormous drops of rain could be seen... the rain was pure and unique, and for those precious moments, nothing else existed. Just rain, thundering down.... It was rain that they hoped never to see again. Awesome and frightening, like God's fury. It did not last long, but had a profound impact on the lives of everyone there.

That rain forced all of us to grow older. It stole our smiles and dimmed our vigour as my sons and I learned to negotiate the path that lay ahead of us, but now, on our own, without her.

In September 2010, we were there again, my younger son Ameya and I, alone, one more time, marking the week that changed our lives. Udayan, who wrote those words, was also alone but in America, studying, soon to reach the age when I had left India the first time.

We had all had to grow up faster.

That weekend, around Geneva, a friend and his daughter drove us through small towns that formed the border between France and Switzerland. We stopped on a perch above Nyon and saw Mont Blanc waving at us, as if to tell us that it would be fine. Beyond that blue haze we could see the fountain in Geneva resurgent again, spurting gaily. The meadows spread out below us, and the blue lake reflected the sun countless times, making it look as though someone had placed thousands of memorial lamps on the lake.

Later that day, when it was morning in America, I talked to Udayan on the phone, and we talked about what we would do tomorrow and tomorrow and tomorrow and then the day after, and we continued to look towards what lay ahead. By living, we were reaffirming ourselves. The next morning, we went with a friend and her dog for a long walk by the lake. We bought cheese. We drank good wine. We broke bread at the dining table, sharing it among friends. We sat by the lake.

We knew we weren't alone. We had our friends. We had the sky and the lake and the hills which had once inspired; and now reassured us.

The sun would shine again—it already did. We had to shed that cloud of grief and let its warmth invigorate us—so that we'd all be in our Twenties again.

TWO SEASONS IN STOCKHOLM

Friends had alerted me that the sun never sets in Stockholm during the summer months. The sun disappears during the long winter, depriving the city of sunlight for months, and then it showers the harbour with all the light in the world. And that light is meant to buoy the mood in a society that believes depression is as common as cold.

I was there in late June, on the day of the Solstice, and the sky was clear, filled with clouds which were fluffy, like a mattress in which you could sink, and the boats in the harbour rose and fell gaily, as if coming alive after six months of hibernation, their sails fluttering in the breeze. I could not see the sun, but the sky was so bright you needed sunglasses. Sunlight reflected through the glass of white wine that sat on my table.

It was nearly 7:00 pm, and I left the bar and walked with some friends to the boat which was going to take us around the Stockholm archipelago. We would sip more chilled wine and look at other pleasure boats, before returning to our waterfront hotel.

The hours passed; the light showed no sign of ebbing. The light penetrated through the layers of clouds, and its reflection on the water looked like someone had sprinkled liquid silver on its shuddering surface. What passes for Stockholm's skyline was now a sharp silhouette and the temperature had fallen suddenly. The scene became sharper, reminding me of images deeply imprinted in my memory: of stark light and dark shadows that Sven Nykvist captured so effortlessly, each frame a work of art, in the cinema of Ingmar Bergman. I had looked for Bergman's house in Stockholm, but the tourist office said there was no such thing, nor a museum; to understand Bergman, I had to walk through Stockholm, and let the Swedish mood seep through my consciousness.

As the light began to fade, the mood on our boat changed, conversations becoming softer. You could hear the sound of the engine, the clinking of the glasses, and not much else. The glasses on the table sparkled; the cutlery looked solid and cold; the food on the plate looked more like an item of adornment and not something to be cut and swallowed. It was sumptuous, like the feast laid out in *Fanny and Alexander*. Our table was cheerful, and my joyous companions were getting lost in making plans about the rest of the summer and surprised regret at half the year having gone by.

I was with people I knew, and yet I felt alone. I wanted the boat to take us back to the pier; I wanted to get back to my room.

An hour later in the room, I found it impossible to sleep: the light was too bright. Several years ago, an Indian diplomat in Amman, who had been posted in Stockholm, had told me that during the summer, he would wear the sleeping mask airlines gave him, and even so, he felt he could not sleep. The hotel had draped each large window with thick curtains, but they were so thick that they plunged my room into complete darkness, like on a winter night. And yet, when I looked through the curtains even a little, a piercing shaft of sunlight rushed through the crevice, blinding me. I saw the odd cyclist riding home, and a column of Volvos silently following him as if going to a funeral, unable to overtake the cyclist on that narrow road. The traffic was sparse. There was still light in the sky, but the view was desolate and bare.

I noticed it was 11:00 pm. The road was quiet; the only sound you could hear was the cheerful banter of patrons at the bar. I went down to join them, but they were deep in a conversation about a rock group I hadn't heard of, and my friends had gone to their bedrooms.

The clouds had parted. It was nearly 2:00 am, but there was some light in the sky, and I was still awake.

So I stepped out and crossed the road. There were no cars, and the traffic light kept blinking amber. I walked towards the edge of the pier. There was no one around. The water was still. The sky was now cloudless, and on the horizon, you could see a thin sliver of orange glow, the sun trying hard to stay afloat, as if clinging to the edge by its fingertips, refusing to go to sleep. In that faint light, listening to the soft murmur of the water, I sat on a bench, and watched sunlight finally fade away.

I had first heard the Swedish poet Tomas Transtromer at the World Poetry Festival in Bhopal in the late 1980s, when he said, in his dour voice, how he had been writing one poem all his life. I sat alone on that summer night at that pier in Stockholm, and reflected on Transtromer's words about sleep, its deprivation, dreams which may be like nightmares, and the plunge which could take you from one kind of sleep to another—death.

Awakening is a parachute jump from the dream.
Freed from the choking vortex, the diver
sinks towards the green map of morning.
Things magnify. He sees, from the fluttering lark's
position, huge tree-root systems
like branchings of subterranean chandeliers. Above ground,
in tropical flood, earth's greenery
stands with lifted arms, as if listening
to the beat of invisible pistons. And he

sinks towards summer, is lowered
into its dazzling crater, lowered
between fissures of moist green eons
trembling under the sun's turbine. Then halts
the downward dive through time's eyeblink, the wingspread
becomes an osprey's glide over streaming water.
Bronze Age trumpets:
their outlaw tune
hangs motionless over the void.

In the day's first hours consciousness can own the world
like a hand enclosing a sun-warm stone.
The skydiver stands under the tree.
With the plunge through death's vortex
will light's great chute spread over his head?

These were disorienting thoughts. I had known happier sunsets, when cities came alive. Here, the sun was supposed to make us feel warmer and bring people out from their homes. But everyone was safely at home in their comforting beds, in the arms of someone they loved, possibly dreaming the same dreams. I sat alone by that pier, as if, like Max von Sydow I was waiting for death to turn up and continue that game of chess in Bergman's 1957 film, *The Seventh Seal*.

Only a few hours earlier I had been part of a group of friends and yet, at the end of our cruise, everyone had parted to go their separate ways, and I was alone. They did not mean to leave me behind, but they had their own conversations, and they left me alone. I wondered if loneliness got more acute here because others respected your desire to be alone, and whether that made those who wanted to cry out for help plunge into that depth of despair: one more step along the pier, and you could walk into the harbour.

This sunset had been telling me that something had ended.

I felt as if I was a minor character in a Bergman film, where a place without people makes the harrowing beauty more haunting. Contrasts—of light and shadow—get emphasised, and time and its passage play such an important role that those natural phenomena become characters themselves. Think of the titles of Bergman's films: *The Virgin Spring* (1960), *Smiles on a Summer Night* (1955), *Autumn Sonata* (1978) and *Winter Light* (1962)—all four seasons covered, all indicating a different mood.

Of all these seasons, summer featured often in his cinema: *Summer Interlude* (1951) and *Summer with Monika* (1953) were other films he had made. One of his first films I had seen was *Summer with Monika*, in which a nineteen-year-old boy meets a seventeen-year-old girl. They fall in love, and go on their family boat to an island to spend an idyllic summer. She gets pregnant, and they decide to grow up and become adults; they try setting up their house in the city, but it is no longer summer. Reality intrudes, and they part. But that summer on that island, and young love, created a stereotype about Sweden, when romance was possible when the sun never set. Roger McGough, one of the poets of the Mersey Sound in Britain of the 1960s, wrote a memorable series of poems, called *Summer with Monika*. Here, he wrote about the poignancy and fragility of young love, full of promise, but rudely interrupted by reality:

They say the sun shone now and again

But it was generally cloudy

With far too much rain

...

They say it was an average

Ordinary

Moderate

Run of the mill

Common or garden

Summer

...but it wasn't

For I locked a yellow door

And I threw away the key

And I spent summer with Monika

And Monika spent summer with me

The poet and his Monika made friends with the weather as the sun sprawled all over the place. The wind ran its fingers through their hair. The moon kept them company. They built sandcastles and went on walks, sunbathing lazily; they danced and they twisted around the bed.

But it didn't really matter

Because we made love songs with our bodies

I became the words

And she put me to music

For we had love and each other

And the moon for company

When I spent summer with Monika

And

Monika

Spent summer

with me

And so it is with summer and its myths in the land with little sunlight which it celebrates when it gets light, to hold on to it, aware that this too shall pass. When it is supposed to get dark, you see light, and there is life around you. And people still end their lives, even though the light tries to remind of what's possible—the freshness of the leaves, the warmth of the homes, and the sparkle of its clear water.

The other time I was in this city, it was winter. It would get dark so early you were lucky if you saw even a bit of sunlight as bleakness and greyness enveloped the archipelago. One evening I was in Gamla Stan, as Stockholm's old town is known. I walked with my boots deep in snow, each step an effort. The snow was fresh and light, and flurries hit our faces as we entered a Palestinian café for some shawarma and pita. The mood in that café was cheerful; the owner was warm. The snow was lighter than dust, and it fell silently as we came out. Icicles formed on the roofs of shop windows, gleaming, revealing the golden colour of streetlights. We went to a café by the harbour where my sons had hot chocolate with marshmallows.

The following day, I had gone walking in a forest encircling a lake. I was with my sons and some close friends. It was a barren landscape. The trees looked skeletal. The sky was dull, and it was impossible to imagine colour. It was like we had stepped into the sets of a 1950s Bergman film.

We walked along the slushy periphery of the lake, its surface flat and frozen. There was a primeval feel that afternoon. We passed other people walking along the trail, their faces nodding slowly, looking grave. They wouldn't exchange words with us, and we didn't talk among ourselves either. It was getting dark; the only sound was of our feet sinking into the snow and emerging, with metronomic regularity.

It wasn't an easy time. Karuna had left us barely a month earlier. We had come to heal our wounds and seek the comfort of our friends. They had opened their home to us, and walked with us along the slippery surface besides the lake. They wanted us to take firm footsteps and regain our balance and our rhythm. They wanted to be there, two steps behind us, ready with their hand, should we slip. They wanted us to walk through that forest, look at the harsh landscape, and there, close to the elements, in freezing cold, remind ourselves that the sun will rise again, that even on a very dark night, there will be the moon to guide us.

There were moments I no longer wished to walk. I wanted to stand by the lake, and stay there, frozen, like the lake's surface, and mingle, becoming part of that landscape. But my friends would nudge me, and we would walk once again, the light flurry of snow gently caressing our cheeks. That caress kept me alert. The bleakness was still overpowering: white snow on the ground, bare trees, looking dark, grey sky, and frozen lake. No birds, no flowers.

And there I saw the leaf. It grew out of the bark of a tree. It was easy to miss it; the snowfall continued to cast a pall over things at some distance. And the leaf mattered because it was so unexpected. It clung to the bark, the gust of the wind trying hard to dislodge it, but instead, the leaf kept dancing, as if waving its hand, calling out for attention.

It was bright yellow, and it fluttered lightly, bending with the wind, but not losing its firm hold of the bark. It was shaped like a heart, and it throbbed. It brought a smile to our faces.

One summer a few years later, the sunshine at midnight had seemed false. I had mistaken a flickering candle for a new dawn; its dwindling flame was dragging me towards that pier. But then another time, another winter, on the coldest night of the year, on a field filled with snow, I saw that tree, and that golden leaf clinging to it, shining, looking so true, feeling so real. There would be a new dawn.

IF ON A
SUMMER'S NIGHT
A TRAVELLER....

The unwary visitor from distant shores who wishes to enter the fair town of Venezia would be well-advised to note that this is a town that floats, and like other large organisms that float, it is not always in control of its movements. It can surge as though pigeons from a public square are carrying the city, as they soar into the blue sky. And on those gloomy nights it can sink into the deepest abyss, as if caught in a dark swamp, with a boatman's oars parting waters, his desperate swoosh suggesting gasps for life. Like anything that floats, the city needs to be anchored to reality, even if on one night, men and women wear masks pretending to be what they are not, imagining lives they cannot lead, playing out their fantasies. On most days, it is resplendent with colours, the winter mist muting the brightness, the summer sunlight making it glow, its turrets and gargoyles leaping to life.

The town is on water, but the easiest way to arrive is by air. Once on ground, the traveller will find that going to the city we know as Venice is not a simple matter. Whichever way he attempts to get there, he will discover that he will have to slow down, adjusting to the rhythm of Venezia, as if descending not just in velocity, but also decibels—from the deafening speed of the aircraft to the roar of a taxi, to the ritual chugging of a train, and finally, to a quiet boat, which must let its engine die as it reaches the city. Once there, he will see Venezia reveal herself in her glory, as the large buildings and palaces will emerge from the mist, unveiling themselves.

The visitor may think it would have been swifter to swim through those small canals. But the boatman rules out that impetuosity—he shows there are no swimmers. He pretends as if he is retching; the wise visitor should heed the warning of the boatman to the shooter in Ernest Hemingway's *Across the River and Into the Trees*: that the water is not safe enough to drink.

As the chastened visitor looks carefully where the stone meets the water, as the buildings' walls meet the canal, he will find thick growth of moss, with luxuriant seaweeds clinging to the edges like chains, and the building's feet look like a prisoner's, dark green as though diseased, its stone crumbling like an ancient parchment. The narrow waterways may remind the visitor of Bangkok, and sometimes the city's stench matches the stench of Asia, but he knows he is not in tropical Asia; it is too cold for that. And were he to look around, those art nouveau buildings that flank the waterway where it expands, reaching the city centre, he may suddenly feel that the plaza is lifted from Brussels, and the canal themselves remind him of Amsterdam. The light is different here, this is Italy, and each canal branches in a direction of its choosing, and the city is built around the languorous turns of the canal, unlike in the Dutch town where the symmetry of the canals looks imposed from above; its concentric circles suggesting the hands of a cartographer, or a master planner, taming the waters, directing them to flow, suiting the city's aesthetic sense.

The narrator in Italo Calvino's *Invisible Cities* describes the city to the emperor as the place measured not only by numbers but by their relationships to events from the city's past:

> [The] height of a lamppost and the distance from the ground of a hanged usurper's swaying feet; the line strung from the lamppost to the railing opposite and the festoons that decorate the course of the queen's nuptial procession; the height of that railing and the leap of the adulterer who climbed over it at dawn; the tilt of a guttering and a cat's progress along it as he slips into the same window; the firing range of a gunboat which has suddenly appeared beyond the cape and the bomb that destroys the guttering; the rips in the fish net and the three old men seated on the dock mending nets and telling each other for the hundredth time the story of the gunboat of the usurper, who some say was the queen's illegitimate son, abandoned in his swaddling clothes there on the dock.

The visitor can let his eyes wander instead, imbibing the joys the city has to offer—bridges that stand precariously over the water, connecting buildings and alleys, looking forlorn; the shaft of sunlight that pierces the gap between two ancient buildings; the crowds waiting to board the slow-moving vaporettos, while smaller boats zigzag past, unnerving the lovers in that gondola, waiting to kiss under the Bridge of Sighs, the gondola gleaming like well-polished furniture; and the gondoliers themselves, flaunting their well-sculpted torsos beneath tight T-shirts with black-and-white stripes.

Their reflection becomes an apparition. With each thrust of the oar, the reflection disintegrates into millions of images, shaking the illusion, becoming a Turner landscape, inspiring Geoff Dyer to describe it thus in *Jeff in Venice, Death in Varanasi*:

Light dissolving into itself, water and light, melting
into each other, colour becoming light, sunlight going
down in flames, over the water.... The water, liquid
and aquatic, an agent of dilution and dissolution, but
the main effect of the water ... to make the buildings
seem, by contrast, extremely tangible.

As the visitor walks near the Grand Canal and comes across
Rialto Bridge, he is in a global bazaar, with tourists from every
nationality surrounding him. He cannot find any Venetians,
and for a moment he thinks the entire city is on display; it
is without locals, except the people who run its boats, sell
postcards and ice cream, and collect money at the museums.
The city has its residents, but they stay hidden, in quiet houses
which you can reach only if you can remember odd landmarks
like the trattoria below the house with red flowers, whose
owner always complains about the butcher, and then take the
second turning after the blue door. Venetians hide themselves
from the public spectacle of decaying grandeur: they live in
quiet lanes away from the paths tourists take. Dyer sees them
as unchanging as the city itself:

This wasn't a town where, over time, generations had
been born, lived, and died. No, there was the same
set of characters that had always been, a constant
and unchanging population that had simply changed
their clothes according to the epoch they were living
through. Each individual remained at a particular
occupation and age till the end of time.

Venice gives that odd sense of permanence: it gives Jeff the
impression that Venice 'might be the only place standing after
a nuclear strike Turnered the rest of the world into a blazing
melt of water and scorched air.'
	It is noisy on the bridge, and the visitor can hear every
language spoken on the planet, but he reminds himself

that's not something new, for Venice has for centuries been a trading port, its ships sailing to fabled lands, bringing back silks, precious stones, and spices. One moment the visitor imagines Bassanio and Antonio trading with other merchants; another moment he pictures himself getting wet in the spray of water lashing him and other diners sitting by the water, as James Bond races through the canal on a motorboat, chasing a villain. And as he looks wistfully at the setting sun, he recalls Dirk Bogarde, the pained lover, setting out in a boat looking for that beautiful boy who has inspired an unusual outpouring of emotions, with Mahler's Fifth serenading in the background, in Luchino Visconti's film based on Thomas Mann's *Death in Venice*.

Venice becomes the global circus of wandering souls who seek authenticity but confront kitsch. The visitor meets that man on the Rialto Bridge selling cruises along the Adriatic, wearing a colourful Italian costume, until he starts speaking, and his halting Italian has Bengali lilt, and he is from Bangladesh, and his face lights up when the visitor speaks to him in Bangla.

This is not the first time the visitor has met Bangladeshis in Italy. Several years earlier, on the hottest day of the year, he was walking along the Roman Column in Rome, towards the Vatican, with an exhausted army of tourists in shorts and T-shirts, their skin peeling off in the heat. He was with a woman from Palestine who spoke eight different languages, but not Bangla, and they were thirsty, with the sun flooding the city with its mid-day heat, melting asphalt, chocolates, and resolve. And they saw a stall at the Vatican, with its dome rising, a long queue of visitors waiting for their turn, which had bottles of ice cold water for sale. The man behind the counter wore a skullcap and had a flowing beard.

The visitor asked him if he was an Indian, but the old man smiled and said he was from Bangladesh. The visitor was curious, wondering how a devout Muslim had found this little perch, selling water to Catholics and others waiting to get inside Christianity's holiest place. The old man told him a tale going back to 1971, when West Pakistani soldiers landed in their country's eastern wing, and began killing Bengalis because they had voted for a politician the generals did not like. The old man, then young, escaped through to India crossing the border, and ended up in the far north of Sweden where a refugee agency brought him. It was November and it was cold, with the day so short that sunlight disappeared in the blink of an eye, and the night was so long you would think it would never end. The man had no contact with his family, and the kind folks with pale skin, blue eyes, and golden hair, who gave him shelter, tried to keep him warm giving him vodka which he would not touch, and tried to get him to eat salmon and herring, but he wanted his *ilish* and *tengra* cooked with turmeric in mustard oil, with onions and ginger and salt and chilli, and he thought he could not survive the kindness of that cold land. So instead of contriving to smile, he rose and said: I will go south.

'Too cold, *dada*,' the old man says, 'So we came to Italy. Here, weather very nice,' he adds, and when it gets warm, this brown man in a flowing white beard gives ice cold water to the very pale, blue eyed, golden haired folks who cannot bear the heat.

The visitor walks among the multitude with his sons, both teenagers, and they walk past shops with outrageously priced garish masks (which people think Venetians wear—but Venetians wear a different mask, of impassiveness, as they blithely walk past foreigners, ignoring them). It is evening now, and they share an outlandishly priced bottle of wine with a friend at Piazza San Marco, where nattily-dressed musicians play familiar tunes like *Bolero* and *The Blue Danube*, now famous for Hollywood films—*10* and *2001: A Space Odyssey*—that used them as background score, *Bolero's* crescendo turning sexual, and not Maurice Ravel's martial tune, and *The Blue Danube* filling the space, not the ball when Johann Strauss intended it to be played.

The next afternoon, he strolls through the city, looking at the floating cherubs defying gravity, as winged angels hasten to clasp and embrace them, while ornate horses prance around gold-tipped domes. Those domes remind him of another time, in another trading city, not far from here, Firenze, or Florence, where he had been once with his enchantress. He felt dwarfed beneath the imposing circumference of Brunelleschi's Dome at Santa Maria del Fiore. Later that week he stood on a hill, following the river Arno, the ancient bridge Ponte Vecchio connecting the halves of the city, and beyond that, the dome rose through the mist, like a breast glimpsed accidentally, revealed unintentionally when an achingly beautiful woman rushed past, absent-mindedly, to be in the arms of her lover. Another afternoon, he stood before Botticelli's Venus, her milky nakedness frozen on the canvas, and told his son—look at the whiteness: isn't it like … marble?

No; the bored pre-teen replied. She looks like she is made of cement.

He sighs at those memories and enters Venetian churches, feeling small beneath the imposing ceilings and stained glass windows, at the Scuola Grande di San Rocco, seeking comfort from the mid-day sun looking at Tintoretto, but he has seen them all—the muscular men, the willowy women, the defeated evil, the triumphant good, and he is no Woody Allen and there is no Julia Roberts walking with him anymore, and overwhelmed by those divine images, he chooses earthly delights. He wants to savour love of another kind, a whimsical love, a charming love, an in-your-face love, which Peggy Guggenheim celebrates in her elegant villa, a love for the here and now, for modernity, for our times: Picasso and Chagall, Braque and Pollock, Dali and Mondrian, Kandinsky and Miro. Peggy Guggenheim has thumbed her nose at the Renaissance, at the baroque classicism in the churches and museums surrounding her villa, and defiantly celebrated the present in a city that valourises its past, shaking Venetian hierarchy, unravelling the intricacy, disturbing the expected—the straight lines, the circles, the spires and the arches that give this city its certitude, replacing it with the bohemian burst of creativity of this time, in a villa so unobtrusive, clean and white, that when seen from a boat, it looks like a sterile retirement home from the outside. But once you enter, it is a different world. It is like stepping out of the waltz and entering into a hall for tap dancing on a wooden surface.

The next night, at a wedding, a friend who has kept the visitor company leads him to his first, tentative steps of waltz. He has forgotten how to hold a woman delicately in his arc; his enchantress had died a few years ago. And that's when he understands the divine electricity of that dance, even though the music accompanying them is not *The Blue Danube*. It is desperately late in the night, the stars visible in the clear sky, and no one is in the mood to go home. The music in his mind is melancholy, and his steps falter, even though his dancing companion flatters him, telling him he has grace when he knows he has none left; that he looks wonderful when he knows he doesn't; and in dancing with him, she is showing her kindness.

Earlier in the evening, as the bride arrives on that island off Venice, it rains lightly, and the horse carriage in which she came takes the children for a ride, while the guests sip Bellini and Prosecco. The bonhomie proves too much for the visitor; he ambles off, drawn to the sunset, which looks so comforting, so calm, so majestic, and yet, in its waning power, it looks so fragile, like life itself. The city itself becomes a silhouette, the branches of a tree lurch into the frame, curving with serpentine fluidity. The light now yellow and pink: the sun no longer able to surround him with warmth, it brightens what's left of the evening, so that as he walks towards his sons, he won't stumble.

That light stays with him for the entire night. He carries it in his heart as he walks back at dawn, with his delighted and exhausted companions. He feels he is in a trance, the mood is light, the birds flap their wings, and he pauses on a small bridge, with the canals branching off in different directions like the lines on his palm, and, somewhere, in distance, he sees the sun rise.

It is tomorrow, a new dawn.

Did the city calm him, or did his calmness get reflected in the city?

Calvino read the city as the place whose past is contained:

> Like the lines of a hand, written in the corners of the streets, the gratings of the windows, the banisters of the steps, the antennae of the lightning rods, the poles of the flags, every segment marked in turn with scratches, indentations, scrolls.

And Venice gives him his gift, his understanding, and inspiration; it has reconnected his tormented present and uncertain future with a stable, imagined past; he will become what he was, as he faces the future. He feels strangely calm and contended, somehow convinced that tomorrows can only get better.

AT THE EDGE OF THE CLIFF

We were warned it would get windy as we got closer to the cliff. As we walked away from the last telephone booth and the pub by its side, the landscape was clean and sparse. There was no one around; the grass, only two inches high, shivered like a child caught unawares by the squall on a sunny day. There were forlorn cars parked along the footpath, with one car prominently displaying a sign saying it belonged to the local Samaritans.

The last pub, the last phone booth, the Samaritans. Something didn't seem right with this spot.

The desolation weighed you down, as you walked into the wind, and after a few minutes in that open field, I felt as if I didn't have ears anymore.

We walked towards the edge. There were signs warning us not only of the sheer depth—535 ft—of the cliff at Beachy Head, but also a sobering note, that the wind could sweep people away if they were not careful and walked too close to the edge. Picture yourself: a lonely cliff, green swaying grass, blustery wind, and the vast expanse of blue sea below, the waves crashing on the rocky beach. The setting for the beginning of a mysterious film—or, where all roads appear to meet; where you reach the horizon and find another horizon in front of you, just as far; or, the point where you thought something ended is actually the beginning of another long journey.

The Samaritans were there for a reason: over the years, this breathtaking spot has also become Britain's favourite suicide point, if such places can be called favourite. Some twenty people on an average take their lives here annually, although, in recent years, the numbers have started to fall, partly because the alert bartenders at the pub are now trained to lookout for those losing hope; those who ask for a special drink made in a particular way and drink it with great care, lingering over the drink. Then there is that telephone booth, where messages of hope are written, sort-of like one last plea before the one who wants to jump might pause, read, reflect, and turn back, to the warmth of that pub. The booth also prominently posts helplines, and there is the Samaritans' patrol, all waiting to stop the one from taking one step too far.

Once you reach the edge of Beachy Head, the view from that point is, in fact, ennobling. As you survey the sheer width of the sea, the limitless sky, the clarity of the light, and rhythm and roar of the undulating waves hitting the cliff, all looking identical, all looking remarkably gentle from the height, it feels as if you are watching a celestial ballet. There are seven cliffs, unsurprisingly called Seven Sisters. They stand, facing the sea, symmetrical, and when sunlight falls on them at an angle, they gleam, acquiring a painterly quality that is best captured in water colours, because the colours are pale and misty, with light mist making the view look hazy. It has a tidy look, but it is also bleak.

The sisters are at the point where the rolling land of South Downs meets the unruly sea. It is the kind of landscape an artist would have painted to show a place where land ends, and moving beyond requires negotiation with another element— the sea. These peaks are old: they were created over time, when old rivers flowed through the downs, slicing through valleys, disintegrating near the wall of chalk that makes the British Isles visible in a haunting way on a full moon night.

To call them peaks depends on your perspective. For a boy from a small town on the coast, these heights are immense, and the peaks are tall and jaw-droppingly scary. But if you have seen the Himalaya, the peaks are puny: Haven Brow, the highest, rises to 253 feet, less than a thousand times the height of Mt Everest. And yet, this one stands out, for it faces the sea; Everest, after all, stands among other tall peaks, higher than others, but it is a bit like spotting the head of the tallest basketball player in a group photograph of those men. The other peaks are called Short Brow, Rough Brow, Brass Point, Flagstaff Point, Baily's Brow, and Went Hill Brow. Call them seven peaks or seven dwarfs, they form a spectacular image.

These cliffs—from Dover and Brighton, all the way up to East Anglia—are formidable and insurmountable, providing a natural defence for England. Imposing castles and moats come to mind. And for those Englishmen who think their home is their castle, the English Channel is the moat, keeping the people who speak foreign languages at bay. (When there was fog in the English Channel, an English tabloid, appropriately and perhaps apocryphally headlined the story—Fog in the Channel: Continent cut off.) Much as cosmopolitan Britons might like to see themselves as Europeans, the Channel very deliberately keeps the island of fish and chips with vinegar, boiled cabbage, and potatoes, quite distinctly apart from the continent, lest it get contaminated with sun-ripened tomatoes, olives, spices, creams, and other foods meant to be enjoyed and not endured.

This is a desolate place with bleak landscape; the skies are grey here, the mood low. It is always raining, and it is cold. That makes its men phlegmatic and women dour; it gives them resilience—and where everyone does his duty, including fighting back invaders. One mustn't grumble. When it lets outsiders in, it absorbs them, but only reluctantly.

It is from such places on the periphery, like Beachy Head, that you get a clear view of the horizon, linking this quiet place with the rumble and roar of the Second World War. As I walk along the edge of the cliff, I see signs from that time: the Royal Air Force had a forward relay station here to improve radio communications with aircrafts. In 1942, the station picked up signals from television transmissions from the Eiffel Tower, from which the Germans used to telecast programmes for the local German elite. But like many places that are footnotes in history, nothing of tremendous significance was gathered from those intercepts.

Not far from Eastbourne are the white cliffs in Dover, which has been the first sight of England for people sailing from Europe from the Bronze Age to Julius Caesar all the way up to modern times. The troops that were evacuated from Dunkirk during the Second World War could feel they were safe again when they saw those cliffs. When Luftwaffe, the German Air Force, began pounding the land during the Battle of Britain, the cliffs, looking impregnable, came to symbolise a nation's determination to ward off attack. The American poet Alice Duer Miller was moved to write a novel in verse in 1940, which began:

I have loved England, dearly and deeply,

Since that first morning, shining and pure,

The white cliffs of Dover I saw rising steeply

Out of the sea that once made her secure.

❧

That war was far from our minds when we struggled to reach the rim at Beachy Head. You needed nerves of steel to go on towards the edge—the wind was vicious; instead, we turned left, enchanted by the mist which made the town of Eastbourne gleam, like a pointillist canvas. I tried to remember where I had heard the town's name first—and then it dawned, the tennis tournament for women in the warm-up before Wimbledon.

Eastbourne has the look and feel of British seaside resorts, with beaches full of pebbles, and some secrets hidden in the otherwise quiet town. A common feature of these resorts are the saucy postcards, which look innocent at first glance, but carry a hidden meaning, for a laugh. In the poem *Sunny Prestatyn*, Philip Larkin writes:

> *Laughed the girl on the poster,*
>
> *Kneeling up on the sand*
>
> *In tautened white satin.*
>
> *Behind her, a hunk of coast, a*
>
> *Hotel with palms*
>
> *Seemed to expand from her thighs and*
>
> *Spread breast-lifting arms.*

It being a Larkin poem, its ending is dark. Donald McGill was one such artist who made such postcards. He is buried here. His postcards themselves were naughty, full of low humour, double entendre, and apparent vulgarity, where the men had red noses, were middle-aged, with a nice spread around their middle; their wives had bottoms that George Orwell likened to Hottentots, but they were always the wives, and fully-clothed. It is the innocent things they said to one another, or what their children told them, that could mean something completely different in the same language read another way. Orwell defended McGill's humour vigorously. In McGill's characters, he saw how excitement in a marriage wears off after twenty-five—the body might look lithe and willing, but the drama and charm were disappearing. That's when taunts get traded, and traits once deemed cute and as virtuous now seem like annoying habits. In a culture where no one complains loudly, and stoicism is prized, what's left unsaid festers. And, who knows, when it reaches a point where it can't be contained anymore, the person leaves the town and makes that long, lonely trek up the hill, to Beachy Head.

McGill's cards, through their crude humour, made light of the circumstances, but they were banned at many seaside resorts, and McGill was even tried in 1954. Those rules changed in "nineteen sixty-three," as Larkin put it in another memorable poem, *Annus Mirabilis*:

> Sexual intercourse began
>
> In nineteen sixty-three
>
> (which was rather late for me) –
>
> Between the end of the "Chatterley" ban
>
> And the Beatles' first LP.

When they tried McGill, it was not for the images, which were not obscene, nor for his words, which were innocent, but for the potential thought behind the card. Orwell was dead by then, but he'd have seen the trial for what it was—prosecution for a thought crime. Donald McGill would have been the hero for whom Orwell would have gone out to bat again.

Orwell studied in these parts—the school where he went is called St Crispian's, and it is below Beachy Head. A plaque commemorates the site now. While his name appears—along with Cecil Beaton's and Cyril Connolly's—as among the school's famous pupils, Orwell himself had an unhappy time at the school. Class played its role: Orwell was from a poor background and the school had boys who came from aristocratic, wealthy families. St Crispian's headmaster and his wife make an appearance, not entirely flattering, in *The Road to Wigan Pier*, and he also wrote a chilling essay, called *Such, Such Were the Joys*, which painted such a dismal picture of his school years that it was only published after the death of the headmaster's wife, to avoid a lawsuit, even though Orwell himself had been dead for some time. When some readers complained that his description of torture in the novel *Nineteen Eighty-Four* was too similar to public school bullying, Orwell replied: 'The only English parallel for the nightmare of totalitarianism was the experience of the misfit boy in an English boarding school.'

Other writers who lived in this area had a happier time. Charles Dodgson, better known as Lewis Carroll, spent the last twenty summers of his life here, visiting from Oxford, writing about Euclid, and the novel, *Sylvie and Bruno*. Virginia Woolf, a writer who famously took her life, made a home in these parts, and Charles Dickens too came to Eastbourne. And yet another famous resident was Count László de Almásy, who inspired Ondaatje and was protagonist in the novel, *The English Patient*. The count studied here too, became a member of the Eastbourne Flying Club, getting his pilot's license.

My mother had an idealised image of Britain. She died in 2004. She had never been to Britain in her life till the year before her passing, when she spent part of the summer with us. She did not want to stay overnight away from home, so we would drive to places, starting early, taking her to places with wilderness, for she liked the charms of natural beauty, and not the stories of kings and queens who inhabited castles, but the home in which Shakespeare lived. As a tourist guide in Bombay, she had shown people enough places and described the literal histories behind them; she wanted to go to places which were nameless, which could be anywhere, and so we took her to the Cotswolds, to the heaths, the dales, and to the downs.

We went to some of the cliffs together. There were joys in walking through the English countryside: a pretty landscape, a heart-stopping cliff, the sound of the waves, and rolling downs. She liked the less visible parts of the landmark—not the white cliffs from the channel, but the dancing grass at the top; not the view of a castle, but the view from it. We lingered over the sight of the undulating green carpet surrounding us on all sides.

In the years since, I have travelled through the Downs often, on my way to Eastbourne, where my friend John lives. One winter afternoon, my sons and I joined his family for lunch at a pub in a village called Alfriston, which is about half way between Eastbourne and Lewes.

The stretch of land between those two towns is the Bloomsbury country. Virginia Woolf would leave from her home for a walk across the river from Rodmell to see her sister Vanessa Bell at Charleston Farmhouse. The house saw many visitors, including the author Lytton Strachey and the economist John Maynard Keynes. It is a pretty walk, with the channel on one side and miles of verdant carpet on the other side. Woolf would end her life by drowning into the River Ouse one day in 1941. The landscape is inspiring; it is impossible to think of what led Woolf to take the ultimate step. As I kept walking beyond the river valley and go higher, the expanse of the Downs filled me with awe.

We had walked barefoot part of the way; the wet grass beneath our feet tingled our skin, and the Downs looked like a green sea, the grass swaying gently. It was late spring, and by my mother's standards, the weather was cold. She took her steps slowly as we made our way to the top of a gently-sloped hill and looked around. The grass shivered a little each time the wind swept through. The pond below, with the mist rising and the soft sunlight resting on it, shook lightly. You did not need a soft-focus camera to capture that beauty; it left a deep imprint in the mind's eye. It looked like a painting.

There is a church nearby, in Berwick, where the murals are painted by Duncan Grant, who was part of the Bloomsbury set. Another artist who captured the Sussex Downs beautifully was Eric Ravilious—it seemed as if he had a discovered a way to let the light stream in from the sun and illuminate his canvas. His paintings of the cliffs capture their whiteness, reflecting the sun's moods and I sometimes can't help but wonder whether the source of the light was the sun or the cliffs.

Later that afternoon we entered Dover and drove to the cliffs, which stand imposing, looking almost impossible to surmount, like the ramparts of a fort. The cliffs continue to inspire poets, but it is a different England now, a babble of tongues, a rainbow of colours, and a place where the pub in the remotest part might serve pad thai or chicken tikka masala. Indeed, in his 2007 collection, *Look We Have Coming To Dover*, Daljit Nagra wrote of being assaulted by "yobbish rain and wind" along "the vast crumble of scummed cliffs," only to conclude:

> We raise our charged glasses over unparasol'd tables
> East, babbling our lingoes, flecked by the chalk of Britannia!

In 2012, the National Trust managed to buy the last part of the cliffs which had remained in private hands, to make sure that that part of England remains pristine. The poet laureate Carol Ann Duffy wrote a specially-commissioned poem about the cliffs:

> Worth their salt, England's white cliffs;
> a glittering breastplate
> Caesar saw from his ship;
> the sea's gift to the land,

where samphire-pickers hung from
their long ropes,
gathering, under a gull-glad sky,
in Shakespeare's mind's eye;
astonishing
in Arnold's glimmering verse;
marvellous geology, geography;
to time, deference; war, defence;
first view or last of here, home,
in painting, poem, play, in song;
something fair and strong implied in
chalk,
what we might wish ourselves.

When we reached the cliffs the light had turned pale, and the cliffs looked quaintly yellow. It had been a clear day, and far away, beyond the water, we could see France.

I still remember my mother's face, grinning happily as she saw the cliffs, the channel, and the continent that lay across. She was happy that afternoon and that was all that mattered.

I thought of that day when I was at Beachy Head, when the wet air carried with it a peculiar freshness that my mother would have liked. I was alone; my mother had gone, and so had Karuna. The scene was beautiful, but they weren't there to share the joy with.

Not all experiences are happy, and nor are all lives. But experiences shape us. Like waves, experiences lash at us; like the cliff, we stand stubborn against the erosions, taking blows.

But things change. On a hot summer afternoon on a Sunday, after a walk through the picturesque emerald carpet of the Downs, you reach a restaurant at Birling Gap, with its enclosed pebble beach. You stare at the sea and the rocks, which have swallowed many lives. And you sit out, under a parasol, a long lunch in the company of friends, with bottles of wine getting emptied.

THE SCREAM AT THE EDGE OF THE WORLD

Winter comes early near the Arctic Circle, like a guest turning up unannounced and allowed in reluctantly because of the sheer force of his presence. The unwelcome guest then occupies the only comfortable couch in the room, interfering in every conversation, refusing to take hints that he should leave, peppering your vocabulary with over a dozen nuanced meanings of snow. The Arctic winter is not for the weak. The mountain of snow and frozen lakes forces life indoors. The season expects obedience and spares no one.

The towns become quieter, looking so windswept and clean and white they might as well be bleached—white as the Norse God Baldur's brow. People love to boast about the proximity of the North Pole from here. They finish their meal with cloudberry, a fruit that only Norwegians think is sweet. (In the morning, they will spread dollops of cloudberry jam on their blackened, sour bread that is so hard you don't need to toast it.)

The landscape is breathtaking, but it has a peculiar severity, and on the waterfront, it has an end-of-the-world feeling, with vast slabs of rock jutting into the ocean, and swirls of thick mist rising, bringing a fine dust of snow. The sun looks sickly and, infirm, goes to bed early.

It was on such a night, over a hundred years ago, that the town Ålesund burned after a bakery caught fire. Once the fire started, it spread rapidly, devouring over eight hundred buildings. And what a fire it was: it lasted some sixteen hours, and some ten thousand people lost their homes. But it wasn't quite *ragnarok*, or the end of the world, as the Norse myths call the end of time. Indeed, remarkably, only one life was lost, that of an old woman who returned to her burning home to pick up her purse.

What followed was extraordinary, as Denmark, Sweden, France and Germany rushed to help, assisting this town of practical fishing communities. The people made their living catching cod, eaten with salt, and known as kleppfisk, and the minke whale. The town decided to rebuild the city centre with minimal fuss but maximum grace, and the result was a town with distinct character.

Ålesund had burned easily because it was made of wood. In rebuilding it, they chose stone over wood. At that time, the prevailing movement in architecture was Art Nouveau, or what the Germans call Jugendstil. Art Nouveau architects made bold, stark statements, using extravagant colours and design, adding elaborate ornamentation on the corners of buildings, creating an exuberant, celebratory feeling. Art Nouveau buildings have slender curves and their lines flow rhythmically. Here, Norway let its hair down, losing some of its resolute seriousness, succumbing to the seductive charms of design, with cherubic angels and voluptuous women emerging from the corners of buildings.

On the Norwegian coast where every whaling town looks like the sibling of the whaling town next to it, Ålesund stands apart. Its architecture is spectacular, but without appearing grotesque. It looks incongruous on the Norwegian coast—these buildings belong elsewhere—a Parisian boulevard or a German thoroughfare, with its ornamental buildings made of sturdy stonework and overwrought filigree.

Many of Ålesund's old warehouses and shops have now been converted into hotels and restaurants. Windows are narrow and roofs remain steep. The walls outside have subdued colours. Some ambitious and elegant turrets rival curvaceous spires, and some gargoyles jut out like intruders, adding to the twists and turns spinning and swirling around what would normally be Scandinavian straight lines.

Ålesund's buildings also have imposing gables and playfully decorative motifs, dressing up the functional structures, as if each building was a work of art. Other towns have a museum that preserves its unique past; here, its streets were the museum. And they add whimsy and humour to the town, in a fairy tale way.

Ålesund also has majestic fjords. I had reached there when some of the snow had started to melt, and there was sunshine with mild winds and occasional showers. With their churches with steeples, quaint streetlights, picturesque lakes, blue mountains, cloudless skies, cool water, and lush green trees, Scandinavian towns have a distinct character. Their capitals have trams and high-rise buildings, but smaller towns have a charming anonymity, the good cheer visible on the red-faced fishermen in brightly coloured parkas.

As I walked through Ålesund, its beauty revealed itself in unusual ways, through the gorgeous views of the waterfront from between buildings and the pristine sights of fjords once you went away from the town. We were determined to take to the water, so with Kristin, a friend I knew from London, I decided to go to the waterfront. It was too windy to kayak, Kristin told me, so we took a ferry towards Geirangerfjord, a heart-stoppingly uplifting jet of water that slices through land, dwarfed by snow-capped mountains that routinely gush forth, becoming glaciers over time. We sailed gently towards the fjord, with the towns becoming smaller, and homes near neat orchards.

With the sky darkening, we turned back and saw lights in those homes. It looked as if we were surrounded by stars on the hills, guiding us back to Ålesund, the air rich with the smell of freshly cut grass in the fields. I knew I was unlikely to ever return to these parts, which made the moment all the more special.

On another visit to Norway, some years later, I headed for a fjord outside Oslo with a group of friends. It was early autumn: icy Arctic winds hadn't yet brought the winter chill to the town. The warmth of summer was fading, and sunlight rested on the water surrounding the city. You could see a long trail of people walking up the gently sloped entrance to the national opera house; it was evening.

We were going to a restaurant that sat at the edge of the water, beyond the limits of Oslo. Large clouds had taken over the sky, hanging over us like a billowing shroud. The clouds were soft and looked like layers upon layers of fluffy, cuddly toys, dark blue and grey. The water, which sparkled in the afternoon, now looked solemn.

On the horizon, with the sea quivering gently, the clouds pressed in, as though tucking us in bed, as if we were going to get sealed in the comforting embrace of the night, while sunlight escaped through a tiny crevice between sea and darkness, still shining brilliantly, making the water look like liquid silver. The sunset wasn't golden, pink or red; the light was bright and white. It had clarity and starkness that I had not seen anywhere else. It seemed to penetrate the clouds, pushing them aside, and the clouds moved back meekly, making way for the sun, stretching the twilight hour.

Oslo's autumnal skies are special. The days are clear and crisp blue. The sky turns a warm pink, before becoming red, like the leaves of the trees that populate the hills surrounding the city. But at some point, the light stops following any preordained sequence, and becomes the palette of a painter with an overactive imagination. As a teenager would say, it is a scream.

The lurid sky that Edvard Munch painted in 1893 in his painting, *The Scream,* which has come to symbolise our age of anxiety, showcased a spectacular twilight in autumn. The light was sharp, but carried a sense of something extraordinary about to happen and like the human figure in the front, with its hands covering the ears, it was meant to freeze us. The light reminded me of Edna St Vincent Millay's poem:

My candle burns at both ends;

It will not last the night;

But ah, my foes, and oh, my friends—

It gives a lovely light.

The poem can be read in different ways—the insane awareness of impending finality and our utter helplessness; the sense that life is ending and the desire to live it up; the joy of living that life fully and celebrating what remains, the fireworks before the embers die. The poem is about the fleeting nature of mesmerising and yet terrifying light, leading to a range of emotions—excitement, ecstasy, fascination, fear, and the apprehension of an end. St Vincent Millay celebrates it; Munch reveals his fear.

Munch was struck by the sunset that he immortalised in *The Scream.* Describing the painting, he wrote:

I was walking along the road with two friends—then the sun set—all at once the sky became blood red—

and I felt overcome with melancholy. I stood still and leaned against the railing, dead tired—clouds like blood and tongues like fire hung above the blue-black fjord and the city. My friends went on, and I stood alone, trembling with anxiety. I felt a great, unending scream piercing through nature.

According to the Norse myth, in the beginning was the realm of fire, known as Muspell, the realm of ice, cold and fog, known as Niflheim, and the empty void, known as Ginnungagap. Muspell could melt anything it touched, and the friction between fire and ice created our universe. Völuspá, the classical Norwegian poem by the poet Edda, describes the fire:

It sates itself on the life-blood

of fated men,

paints red the powers' homes

with crimson gore.

Black become the sun's beams

in the summers that follow,

weathers all treacherous.

Was that the fire of Ålesund that Munch painted?

In fact, Munch painted many versions of that sky, recollected from memory. At the Munch Museum in Oslo, you can see various renderings of The Scream. Munch has been described as a naturalist, and the artist took care to separate himself from Impressionists (the dominant movement of the time). He insisted he wasn't an Impressionist, saying: 'They paint what they see, I paint what I saw,' emphasising the role of recreating memory. Impressionists, on the other hand, always attempted to capture the moment. The English poet William Wordsworth wrote in his introduction to Lyrical Ballads in 1802: 'Poetry is the spontaneous overflow of powerful feelings: it takes its origin from emotion recollected in tranquility.' Recollection was the key. In the turbulent sky that Munch saw, there was nothing tranquil, but he recollected it later—and the image was driving him to desperation.

Munch's painting shows a cliff on the left, a path with a railing descending beyond the cliff, and, in the fjord beyond, an island with a hill. To what extent was he painting what he saw as against what he imagined? And what, indeed, did he see? A few years ago, three American academics from Texas—physicists Don Olson and Russell Doescher, and English professor Marilynn Olson—retraced Munch's steps and identified a hill called Ekeberg, where Munch probably saw that fire of Muspell. The landscape had not changed much. But they saw something else that was revealing. They made the discovery as they looked towards the southwest, where Munch's sky had caught fire: It was not a vision from hell, as Munch probably imagined—there was a more prosaic explanation from the scientists. They guess that Munch saw the afterglow of the eruption of the volcano Krakatoa in Indonesia. (It sounds implausible, considering that the eruption had taken place ten years earlier; but the scientists analysed the statistical data and concluded that after transformative volcanic eruptions, afterglows can occur years later.)

They had reached the hill with some help from the art historian at the Munch Museum in Oslo. They were able to find the road with railings similar to the ones where Munch rested—tired, anxious, melancholic, and lonely, left behind by his friends.

Being left behind is a terrible feeling. Norway is a beautiful country, with magnificent vistas of land, mountains, and the sea. You can see miles of land on all sides around you and yet not see a single human being—only spellbinding landscapes. It is easy to lose oneself in that space; it is easier to feel lonely.

I had gone with friends to that fjord outside the city. But my friends hadn't left me, even as I felt alone on that darkening island that evening. They were somewhere around the corner, busy talking. When we sat down to eat, I could hear the clink of their glasses, the tinkling of their cutlery, and the pouring of water, even as my mind wandered, away from those conversations to the glimmers of light on the hills on the other side of the water. As I walked back with them, I could hear the soft sounds of their conversation ahead of me, I wasn't alone. I looked towards the line of lights on the other side of the water, while the clouds had regained their strength, and pressed in, smothering the source of the light in the sky.

You could sense fleeting desperation in that dwindling light. It seemed as if it was gasping, but there was pride in those gasps. The boundaries of the clouds looked singed, as though they had caught fire; the light discovering tiny openings and recesses as it spread out, like the fragile branches of a dying tree, like the fingers of a slipping hand trying to grasp the edge of the cliff, even as it slipped the surly bonds of earth. It was a triumphant, last burst, burning at both ends, knowing it would not last the night. The wind howled.

There were no human sounds now; the water was placid. Others had moved on, and I had been left behind. I walked faster, leaving Munch to his quiet desperation and melancholia.

At the corner of the trail, near the railings, I saw that my friends were waiting for me. They always do.

MY TRAVELS END AT GOLDEN GATE,

NOW YOU CAN SLEEP, FOR IT IS LATE

1.1

At sundown of the first day

Of a new year, a new decade:

The water sparkles, green as jade

The waves now lash the rocks and spray

These tiny drops my eyes can't see.

My boys run down while leaving me

Staring at the mighty ocean,
Churning like a magic potion.
The continent has reached its limit,
And I have lost my sense of time
And space, an era, my youth's prime:
Ten years have gone in just a minute.
The light will fade, the sun will set,
The Vietnamese kids are placing bets.

1.2

Cards and notes and coins and stones
Are laid on a desk: a still life.
In the boy's pocket there's a knife
That he has used, and broken bones.
My signal faint, my battery weak.
His head is low, and eyes intent.
I stand beside him like a gent -
I need some help I try to speak.
I hesitate but I've got to ask
His help to find a wi-fi spot.
The afternoon was very hot
The sun had taken off its mask.
I cough, move close and tug his coat
I see a deep scar on his throat.

1.3

"What is it, man? Can't you see?"
He does not want to talk at all
"I'd like your phone to make a call"
"There's a payphone, go, I'm busy."
The ocean is now quite choppy.
I leave; walk to that candy shop
They offer me an extra pop
I buy their freshly brewed coffee
The woman at the till is nice;
She spent the sixties in India
"Just looking for myself, my dear"
She found the food too full of spice.
She makes her ice cream with mangoes
And wears a cute stone on her nose.

1.4

The café waitress stares and thinks
That being Indians we won't tip
Nor order much and share the sips
Of Coke and water, large-sized drinks
That we will buy for eight of us
And sit for long, nor order food
But we drink wine, the company's good

And eat big burgers without fuss.
Tomorrow's lunch at sushi bar
For this is California
We settle back in Jiten's car
With kids, men and mama mia.
They also do teriyaki
My son will wear his new khaki.

1.5

But to me it is now quite certain
I've gotten ahead of this tale
Of days with friends in Silicon vale,
In the shadow of those tall mountains
Of Ansel Adams at High Sierra:
Where moon rose early by the lake
Click, there was no second take.
In distant stars he saw a tiara.
The beach is now shrouded in mist:
It hides so well, says that woman
Reading a sight-seeing list,
Knotting and untying her bun
Her boyfriend has a new Nikon
She poses like an old icon.

1.6

The viewfinder will let her see
How she looked in snaps he took
How she frowns, just see her look!
She turns away and comes to me.
She asks if I will take a shot
Of them together for their friends
To look happy, whether or not
They'll be together as journey ends.
She smiles but then she squints her eyes
She asks her Bob to come and stand
With her; he does, he's her boyfriend
He doesn't know she's told him lies.
For me it's just a little job
To snap her smile. And with her Bob.

1.7

We part, they walk, their hands clasped tight
I'm not sure if their mood is right
I hope they won't begin to fight
Later; it won't be a pretty sight.
I can hear her sob, whine and scowl
"This is hot" and "that is cold"
"That's not new" and "that's so old"

He nods and walks and grunts and growls
Life is short but they argue
Over movies, clothes, money, and food
Anything can spoil their mood
They can't agree on their preferred brew.
They'll go like this, on and on
Till one decides to leave, move on

1.8

Does she see those flying birds?
Sunlight resting on the grass?
Does she even know how crass
She sounds, with all those angry words?
But what of him, just standing by
Like a therapist, listening
The sea is frothy and glistening
He looks away, she starts to cry.
The weather is now turning foul
I pick up pace, and then move past
Them. I know their love won't last
A week at most, I sense; the wind howls.
She'll meditate to find Nirvana
He'll meet a man – this is California.

1.9

I am glad that they are gone
I listen to the birds' chatter
They are far now, they don't matter
I should now just carry on.
It is good to get a second chance
Life is short, we make mistakes
In choosing between true and fakes.
Find your music, then you dance.
The first steps are never easy
Some will watch and some will laugh
But you must play the second half
And dance, dance till you're dizzy.
"Where were you?" my friends come, ask,
Finding me became their task.

1.10

I greet, they laugh, their voices rise
The valley resounds with their laughter.
They ask me if I'd like some rice
At the restaurant that we'll go after
I now see the sun bleeding red.
The water looks a fiery bed
Lit by trembling fireflies.

The waves will meanwhile fall and rise.

They point at clouds and tell me, See!

A haunting landscape on canvas

Of Seurat's dots shaping a mass

Of water, rocks, sun, sky, and sea.

The wind turns icy, light fades soon.

Over the mountains, the rise of moon.

2.1

The trees sway gently, leaves shake and rustle

A thunderous squall; the green sea roars

I read the San Francisco Chronicle

Whose edit page is full of bores.

The state is divided—can two men

Marry each other? Or two women?

Is this how civilization will end?

Love needs help – who will defend?

Kim Tarvesh will back the petition

So adults can choose who they can marry

But Bible thumpers want the proposition

That rules Sally can only kiss Harry

Not Jack and Ennis nor Thelma and Louise

Priests say god says they're right. But in love, who is?

2.2

Ah, love: its secrets unknown
To mere mortals who suffer and pine,
As they drive through valleys, all alone,
They want some warmth, kisses, and wine,
Through windy roads and forests deep,
By Big Sur, with those valleys steep,
The city with a thousand lights
Promising discoveries every night.
But real life is not like that,
I know how hard it is to find
She who cares and he, who's kind,
And looks slightly funny in that hat.
And so you will go round and round
Until you end up homeward bound.

2.3

This city's streets rise high and low
Like a swinging stock markets chart
I travel many hours in BART
I don't care if it is so slow.
It lets me see the streets of this
City of winding roads that can
Make you giddy like a fan

But from the top, the view is bliss.
On that day when that old fog
Rolls in to come out and play
It is hide-and-seek near the Bay,
Slim women step out to jog
Wearing tight, day-glo leotards,
Pounding roads and waking guards.

2.4

That tower is thin like a pencil
Seen from the top of those twin peaks
Wait: this town is full of geeks:
Do they know what's a pencil?
A friend points out a chopper in the sky
"See? It belongs to Larry Ellison."
Not amused, I ask "Who's Ellison?"
He looks at me and rolls his eyes.
My friends are all bright engineers
They are among my country's best
Minds, India's gift to the West
But obsessed by choppers? That's unclear.
They are Ph.D.s, some more than one.
I know my place, for I have none.

2.5

The corner: Haight joins Ashbury
The clock is stuck at four-twenty
Coffee shops are cool and plenty
They also have organic curry.
The street smells of mocha Java
What? You want Marijuana?
The city's now clean. Hasta Manana!
The tea of the day is called kahwa.
It is from the Valley of Kashmir
That Indians and Pakistanis fight
Over who owns that lovely sight
At Haight, who cares? Have some beer.
There is now no need to shout.
Turn on, tune in, then drop out.

2.6

Psychedelic colours on the wall
Of homes and cafes and old shops
Don't worry, for there are two cops
To keep us safe as if in a mall.
Would Vikram Seth now recognize

If he came back to this pretty town
Does it live on its own past renown?
Or can it continue to surprise?
Vikram is so capable
He writes his novel, all in verse
With such ease that he might converse
In Mandarin, if you are able.
He's polite, and sometimes too coy
To tell you he wrote A Suitable Boy.

2.7

Orange, purple, green, yellow
The murals will look merry when
You see them tomorrow at ten
Whether from above or below.
Please be kind to this man's plight.
He now seeks your helping hand
He fought two wars for this free land.
He wants some money for tonight.
He will get stoned, he knows you know.
He still must get his massive kick
That keeps him going so make it quick
Or you will miss that evening's show.
You give him some, he gets his load
It was like that in On the Road.

2.8

There is a place where you will find
The spirit of your altered state
Not on a wide wine estate
But at a shop that feeds the mind.
Citylights is what it's called
Where people come and look around
For books and other volumes bound
Of greatest stories ever told.
The stacks are tall, some books dusty
The words sparkle when lights get dim
All along the Pacific Rim
The shop shines, feels no longer musty.
This shop won't go out of fashion.
It is the Beat Generation.

3.1

The next night I want wasabi
We haven't reached and my friends wait
They sit, nursing their Asahi
I say I'm sorry for being late.
A safe starter for me: tempura
Washed down with chilled Sakura
Vishal wants a roll called Avatar:

A new invention at sushi bar.
The food is fresh, you chew the nice
And crispy meat of today's shrimp:
The waitress pops up, like an imp
With hot sauce, certain we'd love to spice.
The salmon delicate, fine and pink
And Jiten says he will not drink.

3.2

His companion on the curvy road
From San Jose to Diamond Bar
Is All Things Considered, NPR;
Shreeya has Chipmunks on iPod.
Tomorrow Alicia will want some pho
Which isn't mild like warm miso
Nor spicy like chilled gazpacho -
The soup to have, if you're macho.
The fields are full of many crops,
Of garlic, oranges and wine,
Such a joy with friends to dine,
Glasses clink till music stops.
Dawn brings fog and Golden Gate disappears.
By noon it lifts; the icon reappears.

3.3

I think back to that distant time
At Half-Moon Bay, another sunset:
The pale sky gleams, yellow as lime,
My friends have just seen Jab We Met.
The serene beach glows in twilight
Udayan walks far, to the edge
Ameya follows to the rocky ledge
That silhouette: a divine sight.
That evening, I find leaving hard
Others walk. I wait and stare.
Waves crush and crumble, I despair,
Over words unsaid, and memories' shards.
The foam all white, the rocks are dark
I pine for what is not: skylark.

3.4

I'll return to this pristine shore
To look again at lifting mist
Look within to find my core
Discard worries, unclench my fist
Relax, let these tiny drops
Of water from this mighty ocean
Clean away the clinging props

Of past that clog my emotions

Free my self from chains of past

At the end of this continent

Unfurl my flag from the mast

Without the pained sentiment

And find the essence, the real meaning:

That after each end, there's a beginning.

SELECT
BIBLIOGRAPHY

Achebe, Chinua	*The Trouble with Nigeria* (1983)
Agosin, Marjorie	*Ashes of Revolt* (2002)
Andric, Ivo	*The Bridge Over the Drina* (1945)
Aung San Suu Kyi	*Freedom From Fear* (1995)
Blixen, Karen	*Out of Africa* (1937)
Bradbury, Ray	*Fahrenheit 451* (1953)
Buruma, Ian	*Murder in Amsterdam* (2006)
Calvino, Italo	*Invisible Cities* (1972)
Chandler, David	*A History of Cambodia* (1983)
	Voices from S-21 (1999)
Dalrymple, William	*The Last Mughal* (2006)
Dharker, Imtiaz	*Purdah and Other Poems* (1989)
Dickinson, Emily	*Complete Poems* (1976)
Drabble, Margaret	*Gates of Ivory* (1991)
Duer Miller, Alice	*White Cliffs of Dover* (1940)

Dyer, Geoff	*Jeff in Venice, Death in Varanasi* (2007)
Eliot, T.S.	*The Waste Land* (1922)
Enright, D.J.	*Memoirs of a Mendicant Professor* (1968)
Ezekiel, Nissim	*Collected Poems* (1989)
Fenton, James	*Out of Danger* (1993)
Frost, Robert	*The Collected, Complete and Unabridged Poems* (1990)
García Márquez, Gabriel	*News of a Kidnapping* (1997) *Living to Tell a Tale* (2002) *One Hundred Years of Solitude* (1967) *Leaf Storm* (1972)
Ghosh, Amitav	*Dancing in Cambodia, At Large in Burma* (1995)
Heine, Heinriche	*Almansor* (1821)
Hemingway, Ernest	*A Moveable Feast* (1964) *The Sun Also Rises* (1926) *For Whom the Bell Tolls* (1940) *The Snows of Kilimanjaro* (1936) *True at First Light* (1999)
Hemon, Aleksandar	*Nowhere Man* (2002)
Ignatieff, Michael	*Empire Light* (2003)
Iyer, Pico	*Video Night in Kathmandu* (1989)
Kazantzakis, Nikos	*Travels in China and Japan* (1964)
Kipling, Rudyard	*From Sea to Sea* (1887)

Kolatkar, Arun	*Collected Poems in English* (2001)
Kundera, Milan	*The Unbearable Lightness of Being* (1984)
Larkin, Emma	*Finding George Orwell in Burma* (2005)
Larkin, Philip	*Collected Poems* (2003)
Lewis, Norman	*Golden Earth* (1952)
Maguire, Peter and Ritter, Mike	*Thai Stick* (2014)
Mahfouz, Naguib	*Palace Walk* (1956)
	The Journey of Ibn Fattouma (1983)
Mak, Geert	*Amsterdam: A Brief Life of a City* (2001)
McGough, Roger	*Summer with Monika* (1990)
Mehta, Suketu	*Maximum City* (2004)
Mishima, Yukio	*The Temple of the Golden Pavilion* (1956)
Nabokov, Vladimir	*Pale Fire* (1962)
Nagra, Daljit	*Look We Have Coming to Dover!* (2007)
Neruda, Pablo	*Extravagaria* (1958)
	Memoirs (1974)
	Passions and Impressions (1984)
	Selected Poems (2010)
Nin, Anais	*Paris Chapbook* (1972)
Ondaatje, Michael	*The English Patient* (1993)
Restrepo, Laura	*Delirium* (2004)

Rushdie, Salman	*Midnight's Children* (1981)
	Shame (1983)
	The Moor's Last Sigh (1995)
Ryoi, Asai	*Tales of the Floating World* (1661)
Salinger, J.D.	*The Catcher in the Rye* (1956)
Saro-Wiwa, Ken	*Sozaboy: A Novel in Rotten English* (1985)
	Last Testament (1995)
Shen, Yanbing	*Tagore in Juewu* (1924)
Soueif, Ahdaf	*Cairo: My City, Our Revolution* (2011)
Sparks, Allister	*The Mind of South Africa* (1990)
St Vincent Millay, Edna	*Collected Poems* (1981)
Sturluson, Snorri	*Edda* (2008)
Tagore, Rabindranath	*Collected Poems and Plays* (2002)
Thoreau, Henry David	*Walden Pond* (1854)
Tjitrawasita, Totilawati	*Jakarta* (1982)
Tranströmer, Tomas	*Selected Poems: 1954–1986* (2000)
Toer, Pramoedya Ananta	*Footsteps* (1985)
Whitman, George	*Paris Testament* (2004)